The Favourite

The Favourite

Mathew Lyons

Constable • London

Constable & Robinson Ltd
3 The Lanchesters
162 Fulham Palace Road
London W6 9ER
www.constablerobinson.com

First published in the UK by Constable,
an imprint of Constable & Robinson Ltd, 2011

A copy of the British Library Cataloguing in
Publication Data is available from the British Library

ISBN: 978-1-84529-679-7

Typeset by TW Typesetting, Plymouth, Devon

Printed and bound in the EU

1 3 5 7 9 10 8 6 4 2

PEFC
PEFC/16-33-111
CATG-PEFC-052
www.pefc.org

For my father, John, and to the memory of my mother,
Molly, with gratitude and love

CONTENTS

Acknowledgements   ix

Introduction   1

Chapter I: A Decayed Estate   11

Chapter II: Leagues of Smoke   28

Chapter III: In a Country Strange   49

Chapter IV: The Deceits of Fortune   58

Chapter V: The World's Eye   75

Chapter VI: The Virgin Queen   88

Chapter VII: The Wind of Faction   108

Chapter VIII: The Fort of Fame   122

Chapter IX: Excess of Duty   136

Chapter X: The Right-flourishing Man   155

Chapter XI: The Sacred Anchor   187

Chapter XII: A Durable Fire   212

Chapter XIII: Hollow Servants   239

Chapter XIV: *Amore et Virtute*   251

Chapter XV: The Less Afraid   279

End notes   314

Bibliography   337

ACKNOWLEDGEMENTS

Two people above all have helped make this book what it is. Leo Hollis at Constable & Robinson has been everything a writer could wish for in an editor: patient and supportive, incisive and insightful, encouraging, rigorous and enthusiastic. My agent, Sarah Such, has nurtured this project to completion from the first tentative and unshaped conversations, always wise in her judgement and acute in her analysis and infallible in her advice.

On a personal level, first among all things to praise and give thanks for are my wife Helen – who has carried too much of the burden of this book's writing and to whose love and faith I owe more than she can know – and our children Isaac and Evie, who illuminate and warm all things in our lives with their boundless love, quizzical intelligence and quiet sarcasm.

I would also like to say a public thank-you to Alice Burden, Mike Dee, Julia Posen, Sue Sands, and Karl and Jane Woolley, for their great kindness, generosity and support for our family during 2010. I am grateful too to Sarah Elvins and Jane Housham, Catriona Jardine, and Richard Siddle for helping sustain my career during the writing of this book, and to David

Barraclough and Jenny Boyce, Kes Fielding and Jane Hodgson, and George Osborne and Lois Rogers for their hospitality and friendship.

The staff at the British Library, as always, have been unfailingly and unflappably helpful; I am immensely grateful to them. I would also like to thank Nicola Jeanes and Emily Burns at Constable & Robinson, together with my copy-editor Sophie Hutton-Squire, for their work on my behalf.

Note: Although I rather like the vigour, invention and variety of 16th-century spelling, I felt that on balance clarity was a greater virtue and I have therefore modernized spelling where required. There is no better illustration of the need for such standardization than the fact that William Stebbing, Ralegh's best Victorian biographer, logged 74 variant spellings of his surname. Although I have retained one or two other spellings in source material as a nod to such profusion, elsewhere I have standardized on that preferred by Ralegh himself.

But when I found my self to you was true
I lov'd my self, because my self lov'd you.
Sir Walter Ralegh

Minions are not so happy as vulgar judgements think them,
being frequently commanded to uncomely,
and sometimes unnatural employments.
Sir Walter Ralegh

INTRODUCTION

It was a cool spring morning and Elizabeth was at Greenwich Palace. She had been born here, like her father before her; it was her favourite place. The palace was built on the south side of the river just where the Thames loops down into Kent before returning to its eastward path to the sea; behind the turrets and gables of its brick river front lay courtyards and towers, gardens and park. When the court sat here, which was often, the great and lesser ships leaving London's quaysides for the Americas and the other unknown limits of the world were known to salute their passing with the smoke and roar of their guns, drawing courtiers and councillors alike to the palace windows. River traffic to and from the city to the west was brisk.

This particular morning Elizabeth was enjoying the small and precious liberty of a walk in the palace park. The wide silver-grey river was rough and unsettled; curlews flecked the shore. Green fields could be seen to the south through a gate in the park wall, pastures rising quickly out of the valley, studded with poplars; to the east, the palace meadow gave way to green marshland. As she walked, Elizabeth perhaps talked with the small coterie of men and women gathered about her.

1

She was no doubt lightly guarded, if at all, since she viewed such securities as an unnecessary evil – or rather, as a malignant affront to her freedom, no matter their necessity. But she walked quickly, nonetheless.

And then she stopped, and the illusion of free movement, of liberty, faded. In front of her the path gave way to thick wet mud. She looked around at her courtiers, imperious and expectant. They did not move and the moment filled with uncertainty and silence. Then a tall young man stepped forward. She must have known him a little: through his family, his reputation at court, through talk of his exploits elsewhere. He was Ralegh, a West Country man, a seaman and a soldier. She perhaps noted he was richly dressed, far beyond his status or his means. But then he swept off that sumptuous cape of his and, bowing low, laid it over the cold, wet mud at her feet. He had, surely, something graceful and witty to say to mark this small gift. She walked on over the cape, and looked at him again and wondered . . .

This book is about that moment: Ralegh stepping forward from the obscurity of his youth, stepping out into history's glare, and Elizabeth's wonder at him, his promise, his gifts. But while the story of the cloak itself is mostly a confection – whatever truth it holds, it has little to say about Ralegh's claims on his queen – the true story of their coming together is quite different and altogether more compelling, fraught with dangers for both of them. *The Favourite* does what has not been done before and traces Ralegh's rise to favour over several perilous years from which he was fortunate to emerge both alive and free. It examines anew the personal and political compulsions that drew them together, and then tracks the careful steps of their dance as Elizabeth negotiated, Ralegh at her side, the darkest years of her reign, overshadowed by the fear of conspiracy, assassination and war.

It is here that Ralegh's cloak, casually thrown down to stop Elizabeth soiling her shoes in the dirt, becomes a problem. After all, if you know one thing about Ralegh and Elizabeth, it is this story, or a version of it. It has seeped out from its place in anecdotal Tudor history into the popular consciousness, becoming an iconic image that seems wholly to articulate the strange and elaborate rituals of deference and favour that existed between a queen and her courtier, a parable of ambition, subjugation and power.

In the process, the personalities of Ralegh and Elizabeth, no less than the physical and emotional drama and drive of their relationship, have blurred. We recognize the shape of their poses, and think no further. The very ubiquity of the story contrives to give their relationship a sense of inevitability, so that we do not stop to examine either it or them on their own terms: how their individual trajectories brought them together and what it was about their own experiences and understanding of the world that made each attractive to the other.

We do not even stop to ask what kind of attraction it was that they felt. We feel glibly assured that money, sex and power were present in some measure, but we do not consider how difficult it might have been to establish and sustain a meaningful relationship with such potent and conflicting motives ever-present, nor really what such a relationship might mean in the context of a queen regnant and a minor courtier in a late Tudor court. How could any private bond form in such a relentlessly public forum? What reality could the intense, passionate and playful rhetoric of love – which both employed – actually describe? Where was the human truth in the complex negotiations with power that court life inevitably imposed on them?

These questions are at the heart of *The Favourite*. If it is a book about Ralegh and his extraordinary rise to power, then it is also about Elizabeth's struggle for personal liberty against the immense constraints of her position. Above all, in writing this book, I wanted to acknowledge, even celebrate, the ordinary contradictions of these two exceptional people, to rescue them from their own myths, restore to them some of the freedom for which they both so desperately and differently yearned.

To do this, I felt it was important to suspend the judgements of history, to follow them through the private crises and public struggles of their early lives to explore how they might have understood both themselves and each other at the point at which they met. I wanted to see their actions in the context of the moment, far from inevitable, and contingent on factors which may have otherwise been lost. The two portraits that emerged from this process are, perhaps, more flawed than we are used to, both damaged by their experiences, but more revealingly and credibly human.

For the same reason, I have chosen to focus exclusively on the early part of Ralegh's career – his rise to greatness. *The Favourite* is about what brought these two people together and what, at the very height of their relationship, they asked from and gave to each other. It is a book about the making of Sir Walter Ralegh, both the man who won Elizabeth's favour and the myth of the favourite forever casting his cloak at her feet, exploring those aspects of their stories which have never really been adequately explained. In the years of Ralegh's greatness these two people forged a myth that has survived for 400 years.

It may seem counter-intuitive that two such written-about figures from English history should remain with their relationship unexamined. Nevertheless, it is true. Ralegh customarily merits little more than a line or two in studies of Elizabeth, as if her choice of him reveals nothing about her beyond a mere attraction to men. In Ralegh's biographies, by way of contrast, Elizabeth acts as a kind of *deus ex machina*, appearing periodically to dispense or withhold favour but essentially, humanly absent from the wild narrative of his life.

In fact, Ralegh himself still hides behind the myth he created for himself in the long third act of his life as a self-styled political prisoner under – and ultimately martyr to – the arbitrary government of James I. Every full biography of Ralegh is written in the shadow of that great and tragic figure, mesmerized by Ralegh's mythopoeic gifts. The complexities of the man whom Elizabeth first favoured – the young Ralegh, a tangled contradictory mass of insecurity and ambition, of intellect, awkwardness, vanity and doubt – are lost.

One consequence of this is that an essential truth about Ralegh and his rise to power has never adequately been addressed: almost all of those who came across him at court loathed and distrusted him. Elizabeth was the shining exception – and yet her contemporary reputation as a brilliant judge of men and their uses rightly survives to this day.

Ralegh was, a contemporary later reflected, a man 'who had offended many and was maligned of most'. His greatness is apparent to us because we know what came after. It was not apparent at all to many of those who knew him. Many of his peers were jealous, both of his success and, no doubt, his gifts: jealous and not a little frightened. Even William Cecil, Lord Burghley, Elizabeth's longest-serving, most loyal and most trusted adviser, guardedly warned a friend that Ralegh's closeness to the queen meant he could do more damage to someone in an hour than he, Burghley, could do good in a year. But there has to be more to it than that.

The Ralegh of the 1580s – the man who seemed to seduce Elizabeth – was deliberately abrasive, manipulative and deceitful. It was, in a way, part of his charm – his outspokenness, his unwillingness to be cowed – and it was certainly integral to his identity. Moreover, Ralegh had a genius for self-advertising, although the idea, which the story of the cloak seems to perpetuate, that it was expressed through humility or deference, is to miss the man entirely. A more accommodating and deferent Ralegh would neither have risen so high nor left such a mark on the history of his own and later times. To understand him we need to suspend judgement, to note the unique and troubling circumstances of late sixteenth-century England and how they impacted on a young man with no meaningful prospects in life like Ralegh.

Yet if Ralegh the courtier was very much a self-conscious creation it is worthwhile pausing to consider what magnitude of will and intellect it might have taken to create and sustain that persona in the crucible of Elizabeth's court. Or, to put it another way, how great the emotional toll must have been: for all the bluster, there is a fragility to Ralegh that is easy to overlook, a desperate diffidence and insecurity. He wanted to be at the apex of the nation's power, but he also wanted to escape from it: that tension between his ambition and his self-doubt is one of the many things that is fascinating about him, but it also casts a different shadow on his relationship with Elizabeth, how he wanted and needed her – however one likes to quantify such needs – and how he wanted to be elsewhere too. This, the push and pull of their relationship – the almost narcotic pattern of indulgence and withdrawal – breaks the traditional frame through which we see them; ultimately Ralegh needed from Elizabeth something other than the wealth and status with which she famously favoured him. But what?

Equally, we may think of Ralegh as the archetypal courtier, using flattery and extravagant gestures to win pecuniary and other favours from his queen, but were those really the qualities for which she rewarded him? There were many such aspects of court life in which he, unlike many of his peers, played no part. There is no evidence, for instance, that Ralegh was ever involved in a key part of the later Elizabethan court calendar, the ritual displays of tilting – especially the Accession Day tilts – when those who aspired to preferment could present an idealized version of themselves to the court. This is perhaps particularly surprising given his reputation for ostentation: they were above all opportunities to dazzle, to draw attention to one's magnificence. More surprising still is the absence of any New Year gifts from Ralegh to his queen, unlike almost every other leading figure at court. This was another key ritual, another significant means of giving thanks and attracting favour. Elizabeth, everyone knew, was exceptionally fond of receiving expensive presents, particularly in the form of jewellery.

The truth, as always, is more intriguing. These lacunae point to a profound sense of aloneness that always hung over Ralegh, which may sometimes have been hauteur but which also spoke to a more complex sense of reticence and privacy than is generally acknowledged, an aloofness expressing both an extraordinary self-confidence and a deep-seated insecurity – a weakness wrapped up in a strength. He liked to do things differently, and he liked to do different things. When he sought Elizabeth's favour, it would be on his own terms – and that was not easy.

As for Elizabeth, while she certainly enjoyed such exhibitions of loyalty and affection, she did not need to reward courtiers as she rewarded Ralegh to earn them. If there is a temptation to assume that Elizabeth rewarded Ralegh with favour for being merely handsome and witty, then it must be resisted; neither of them merits such condescension. After her death, Ralegh was heard to complain bitterly about just such popular misconceptions, how he had to work hard for every favour he received and do many things – uncomely and sometimes unnatural employments, he called them – which he found morally questionable.[1] Far from being kind and generous to him, he said, she was in fact unjust and tyrannous.[2]

What, then, did she ask of him – and did he give it freely?

In fact, Elizabeth's attitude to Ralegh – and indeed other favourites – is more complex than the caricature might usually allow. One reason for that is the power of her mythology. 'Elizabeth I' and 'the Virgin Queen' seem to us to be synonyms, interchangeable and irrevocably linked. But the truth is that the Virgin Queen – imperious, unyielding, inviolate – is something Elizabeth became over time through a mixture of state propaganda, projection and, some would have said, a good deal of wishful thinking. The phrase itself was not actually addressed to her until the summer of 1578, and the myth itself only began to put down its deep roots once the prospect of marriage was finally off the horizon in the early to mid-1580s. For the greater part of her reign, to those who knew her, and to the many of her subjects whose conversations and dreams she inhabited, she was a more sensual and provocative figure, possessed of an ambivalently powerful sexuality, at once seductive and disruptive.

If Elizabeth's court still seems to us after 400 years to be a place of unusually heightened drama then one reason for it must be Elizabeth's refusal to marry. Elizabeth was fond of commenting on the bond between her and her subjects; she had no need for a husband, she said, because she was wedded to her people. It would be truer to say that she was wedded first of all to herself, since the strength of will it required to resist the pressure to marry suggests more a ruthlessly single-minded solipsism – albeit blessed with an acute political sense – than anything more altruistic. If the Elizabeth of the 1560s and 70s thought the safety of the realm was best ensured by her continued independence, she was alone in that view – and it was an opinion she never dared express openly.

After all, Elizabeth's preference for singularity meant that political power – perhaps particularly the soft power of grace and favour – was uniquely concentrated in her hands. There were to be no rival power bases to speak of at Elizabeth's court, no other royal household but her own, no factions that looked to anyone but her for their reward. The only other person with a significant claim on anyone's loyalty to the crown was Elizabeth's cousin, Mary Stuart, and she spent the last seventeen years of her life in Elizabeth's control, imprisoned in a sequence of more-or-less remote households about England.

Elizabeth's choice of an unmarried life also put all those around her at considerable risk: with no close family and no children there could be no clear succession, and that was widely and rightly understood to mean that a power struggle, and perhaps civil war, would follow her death. The security of the nation therefore relied absolutely on the continuing life of the queen: England in general, and Elizabeth's leading courtiers in particular, were one well-aimed bullet, one blow of a dagger away from personal ruin and public anarchy.

But then, why have favourites at all? Men whose claim on her sentiment seemed to disrupt and subvert the order Elizabeth sought to assert? And why, in particular, Ralegh, and why at that particular moment? Ralegh was, after all, the first post-marriage favourite: that is, the first man to whom she turned once she was at last liberated from the pressure to find a husband and procreate that had dominated the first twenty-five years of her reign. He was also the first favourite to rise after the marriage of the man widely considered by contemporaries to be the love of her life, Robert Dudley, Earl of Leicester, who was also, coincidentally or not, Ralegh's sometime patron. Who was using whom – and to what end?

To return to the iconic moment with which we began – Ralegh's cloak in the dirt, Elizabeth's feet upon it. It is an anecdote that has come down to us from one source only, and that not published until 1662, written by a man who was born some thirty years after the events he purports to describe. That does not make it untrue. Irrespective of its uncertain factual status, the story has survived because it appears to express a truth, or family of truths – about self-advertising deference and glamour and extravagance, about the arbitrary and superficial nature of royal favour.

But those truths are no more stable than the anecdote itself: to find the real truth about their relationship, we need to see them first as clearly as their friends – and enemies – did.

I: A DECAYED ESTATE

*I will not lose mine opportunity for any man, for time lost
is not recovered.*

EARL OF OXFORD TO HENRY HOWARD, LENT 1580

It was 27 December 1584 and Leopold von Wedel, the much-travelled younger son of a German noble family, boarded a boat from one of the many river stairs along the Thames in London and was rowed downstream, past the Tower, the city's great citadel, and the ship-heavy quaysides of Ratcliffe and Limehouse, to the royal palace at Greenwich, where the court was staying for the Christmas season.[1]

Elizabeth was formally still in mourning for the deaths, months earlier, of her last marriage suitor, the Catholic Duke of Alençon, and her leading Protestant ally in Europe, the Prince of Orange. In grief, at least, she was ecumenical. But the sobriety of mourning neither diminished the power for which she dressed nor disguised her vanity, which needed no excuse. In private her clothing was said to be simple, almost austere, but her public self was scrupulously luxuriant. Von Wedel noted how well her sombre black velvet robe displayed the silver and pearls she wore – pearls her favourite jewels – and how the silver lacework which fell loose over the velvet was so finely woven it seemed at times almost transparent, artfully catching and holding the eyes of the crowd who stood lining the room, watching her.

Elizabeth habitually ate little and drank less and preferred doing neither in public, only submitting to doing so on feast days such as this. Now, after service in the gilded pomp of the royal chapel, she consented to dine alone as the busy festive court looked on, sat at a long canopied table set with gold plate in a great room, the walls of which were hung with tapestries worked in gold and silk, its doors leading back to the deceptive sanctuary of her privy chambers.

Forty silver dishes were laid before her and two youths stood by, ready to serve. The first, dressed in black, helped her to such food as she chose; the other, in green, held her cup while she ate, kneeling when she took it from him to drink. Von Wedel doesn't say so, but the two must have been handsome: it was the only absolute criteria for appointment in her household.

To the right of her table stood a small group of elite courtiers, fine old gentlemen Von Wedel calls them, who included William Cecil, Lord Burghley, the lord treasurer, and by some distance the queen's longest serving and most trusted adviser, and two of her favourites: Robert Dudley, Earl of Leicester, the master of the queen's horse, and Sir Christopher Hatton, the captain of her guard. Von Wedel had been in England some months, long enough to pick up the local gossip, and he paused to note that 'the queen for a long time had illicit intercourse' with Leicester, although he was now married, and that Hatton was her lover thereafter.

From time to time as she sat eating, Elizabeth would call one of these men over, and he would kneel before her and the two would talk. When she dismissed him, he bowed deeply, and would do so again when he reached the middle of the room in his retreat from her.

Both the essential isolation of her office and the singularity of the choices she had made were apparent in the scene as Von Wedel described it. This was already her twenty-fifth year on the throne and she had recently turned fifty-one. She knew by now that she would be the last Tudor on the English throne; somewhere at the back of her mind she must have known it since the moment in November 1558 when her sister Mary died and the crown passed to her. She had spent her whole life resisting the pressure – social and political, national and international – to wed, and there is little doubt that she relished the public responsibility such resistance brought, no less than the private freedom.

Yet however much loneliness became her, it did not define her.

The first set of dishes were replaced with others but Elizabeth did not linger to taste them. She rose and three noblemen brought her a silver-gilt basin of water in which to wash her hands. Among them was Philip Howard, Earl of Arundel, whose father, Thomas Howard, Duke of Norfolk had been executed for treason a dozen years before, and whose recent conversion to Catholicism was still a secret from the queen and her inquisitors.

Then the dancing began. The senior figures at court had precedence, but soon the young gentlemen and ladies, discarding swords and mantles alike, took to the floor. Von Wedel marked how beautiful the women were, and how in the course of the dance everyone changed partners, bowing courteously, and passing on.

Elizabeth herself now sat on a cushion on the floor beside a bow window and summoned whom she pleased among the courtiers to talk with her. With dinner over she could uncoil a little and be friendly with all of them, joking and laughing familiarly. But Von Wedel saw that with one of them, the familiarity extended to an extraordinary tenderness and intimacy in so public a place. He knew the man's name, but had misheard it: it was, he thought, Ral. There was no distance, no formality, no barrier at all between the two of them: she pointed to a spot of dirt on his face and moved to wipe it away with her handkerchief; he shrugged away her fussing and stopped her hand, the queen's hand, removing the blemish himself.

> It was said, [Von Wedel writes,] that she loved this gentleman now in preference to all others; and that may be well believed, for two years ago he was scarcely able to keep a single servant, and now she has bestowed so much upon him that he is able to keep five hundred servants.

Von Wedel himself seems to savour these splinters of insight into a closed exclusive world, and the scent of intrigue and scandal they carried, but the envy and resentment of his sources at court are apparent in the contempt of the hearsay he recorded. The speed of Ralegh's rise from provincial oblivion, no less than its trajectory, seemed to many to be unnatural, an affront to the order of things.

Henry Yelverton, the government counsel, would say of Ralegh at his trial in 1618 that 'he hath been as a star at which the world has gazed'.[2] The line is often quoted, and its usage is startlingly modern: there *was* something of the celebrity about Ralegh, a man whose personal qualities – his charisma, his charm, the addictive eloquence of his wit – seemed to outshine his public talents.

Yelverton's sequel is less well known: 'stars may fall, nay they must fall, when they trouble the sphere in which they abide'.

At the peak of his favour, Ralegh had no office at court, no place in the firmament: he was unfixed, fluid, protean, unstable. Trouble personified. For Ralegh's enemies, his eclipse was only a matter of time.

But between Ralegh and his enemies stood the queen. And, for the moment, he had her heart. The question Ralegh's contemporaries asked themselves was: how could such a thing have happened?

Ralegh's family had centuries-old roots in Devon and some cachet, as village names such as Colaton Raleigh and Combe Raleigh still attest, but the status of his actual parents is more ambivalent. One Jacobean observer described him as starting out 'a bare gentleman . . . well descended, and of good alliance, but poor in his beginnings', another as 'of an ancient family but decayed in estate'.[3] Like many things in Ralegh's life, this was superficially true – but appearances were deceptive.

Walter Ralegh's date of birth is unknown, but was most likely some time in the late summer or early autumn of 1554. He was born in Devon, at a modest farmhouse named Powreshayes, near East Budleigh, between Exeter and Sidmouth, which Ralegh's father, also called Walter, had been leasing since the 1520s from the Dukes, a mercantile family from Exeter. The house, which was altered and extended in the seventeenth century, still stands today. It bordered on Woodbury Common, where local families grazed their livestock. The Raleghs' lease, however, encompassed 'lands, meadows and [. . .] pastures from the premises unto the towns of Woodbury and Lympston and with the pasture of the wood called Haywood'.[4] Beyond here, the dense trees known today as Hayes Wood, was the sea, a mere couple of miles to the south.

Ralegh was fond of the house, sentimental even, and felt a deep and primal rootedness to the area. We might adduce the force of his attachment from the fact that the first property we know him to have owned was at Colaton Raleigh, a few miles away. Ralegh would also habitually describe himself as 'of Colaton Ralegh' in official documents – for instance as late as 1597 in his will, written at his then home, Sherborne Castle – despite apparently never having lived there.[5]

That Ralegh's family did not own the house in which they lived does not seem to imply great prosperity, but that is a misleading impression. Ralegh's father had inherited several properties which he leased out and no doubt accrued other rights and interests over the years. The younger Walter Ralegh was witness to several such transactions, the first when he was no more than five.[6] But property was not the family's only – nor even its principal – source of income.

Ralegh's father had two sons by his first marriage to Joan Drake: George and John, both born in the 1520s and therefore long become men by the time Ralegh himself was born. Neither, from what records we have, appear to have been particularly reputable individuals, but those records do give some insight into the family's financial status. In particular, there was an incident in 1557, while Walter Ralegh was deputy vice admiral of the south west, which brings the character of the family into clearer focus.

The two elder sons, on their father's ship the *Katherine Ralegh*, named for his third wife and Walter's mother, boarded a Portuguese merchant ship, the *Concepcion of Vienna* and despoiled it. In so doing, they threatened to drown the terrified Portuguese crew aboard. Arrested for the piracy on their return to England, George and John posted a bond of 500 marks – a substantial sum – against their appearance at the quarter sessions on 13 December. Neither appeared, thus forfeiting their bonds – an interesting fact, in itself suggesting that the family had money to lose – and the exasperated and increasingly desperate merchants petitioned the Privy Council for redress:

> John and George Rawleigh have been and are by the means of their father Walter Rawleigh so conveyed from place to place and from time to time kept so secretly that your said orators, though they have most diligently caused them to be sought, yet they could not hitherto nor yet cannot have them found and arrested . . . thus your said orators . . . are not able by the ordinary course of the law to recover the same, being themselves but strangers and poor men without friendship and the said Walter Rawleigh being a man of worship of great power and friendship in this country . . .[7]

The sense of easy complaisance with conspiracy against the law – or at the very least indifference to legal process where it abutted personal interest – illuminates the record: the thrill of secrets well-kept, the power of family and its associations to dumbfound searches and enquiries, the sly pleasures of sleight-of-hand. It was an unusual environment for an impressionable young boy.

Yet if Ralegh's family had earned a national reputation in the 1570s when Ralegh himself emerged on the capital's crowded streets, it was associated with Christian piety.

In late 1558 in the dog days of Mary's reign, the church authorities in Bristol brought before them on a charge of heresy an old, poor and perhaps itinerant woman named Agnes Prest, who had abandoned her husband and children to bear witness to her faith in a reformed church. She refused to equivocate: challenged on the nature of the sacrament she told them they should be ashamed to say that a piece of bread, that might also be eaten by mice or consumed by mould, could become the body of Christ. 'Let it be your God,' she said. 'It shall not be mine.'[8]

In prison, Prest received several visitors, among them a 'certain worthy gentlewoman, the wife of one Walter Rauley, a woman of noble wit and of a good and Godly opinion'. With her was an older sister, Joan, wife of Sir Anthony Denny. It was undoubtedly a courageous act on the part of Katherine Ralegh, but it was Prest who offered succour and spiritual strength at the meeting. When Katherine returned home she told her family that she had never heard any woman, and certainly not one of such lowly status 'talk so godly, so perfectly, so sincerely, and so earnestly: insomuch that if God were not with her, she could not speak such things: to the which I am not able to answer her . . . who can read, and she cannot.'

This is the only moment in which Katherine Ralegh, Walter's mother, appears in the record, the only snatch of her speech we have. What does it tell us? She is clearly educated, self-consciously so, at a time when even for a gentlewoman it was by no means a given, and it is not difficult to discern a sense of social pride, of sensitivity to status, in what she says. But there are also more complex currents running through her words – an uncertainty about that very status, a self-doubt, an anxiety – that are instructive in light of Ralegh's own corrosive insecurities, his instinct to doubt.

None of which helped Agnes Prest. She was burned at the stake outside the walls of Exeter, a woodcut for ever capturing her martyrdom in the pages of Foxe's *Book of Martyrs*.

Katherine's private epiphany was public currency, appearing in the second 1570 edition of Foxe's book. It seems more than likely that the Raleghs actively disseminated the story themselves: one possible conduit is the Exeter antiquarian John Hooker, later close to Ralegh himself and always close to his family, particularly on Katherine's side.[9] It can certainly have done the Raleghs' moral status in the reborn Protestant England of Elizabeth no harm: they would always be well served by what passed for the Elizabethan media.

The truth of that observation is also apparent in the way Ralegh's father is portrayed in the second edition of Holinshed's *Chronicles*, revised in 1587 by Hooker, when Ralegh was at the apex of his influence and authority. The same year Ralegh rewarded Hooker with a sinecure, the stewardship of the Devon town of Bradninch, now subsumed into the city of Exeter. It is a story that also illuminates other, troubling aspects of Ralegh's familial inheritance.

In May 1549, sometime in Whitsun week, amid growing unrest in the West Country at the aggressively Protestant church regime then newly instituted under Edward VI and recently enforced through the use of the first *Book of Common Prayer*, Walter Ralegh had been riding the handful of miles from Hayes Barton to Exeter. The road runs through the village of Clyst St Mary. He overtook there an old lady on foot clutching her rosary beads and chastised her for clinging to such superstitions.[10]

Tensions were already simmering after Sir Peter Carew, a cousin of Katherine's and a military man with a militant contempt for those resistant to the new order, had tried to smoke out rebels at Crediton by firing the barns in which they were hiding. In the circumstances, the woman took Ralegh's admonition to be a direct threat. She reached the church, already packed for service, and declared that Ralegh had threatened to burn them all out of their houses if they did not repudiate their faith and the immemorial comfort of its rituals.

The parishioners, incensed by what they had heard, spilled angrily out of the church, some fanning out into nearby villages to raise the county, others felling trees to block the roads, and placing cannon on the bridge over the river Clyst. A group of them overtook Ralegh on his return from Exeter. Their blood was up and they would have probably dragged him from his horse and killed him on the spot if he hadn't slipped from them into the sanctuary of a nearby church, aided by a group of Exmouth seamen. Ralegh would escape from there, only to be recaptured and held prisoner in St Sidwell's church just beyond the walls of Exeter. He must have been held for weeks, if not months, and lived under constant – that is, oft-repeated – threat of death.

Exeter itself was laid siege to. Its gates were broken, its walls undermined; water supplies were cut and markets stopped; hay carts were set on fire and rolled into its densely packed streets. It was guerrilla warfare. Eventually, however, on 4 August the uprising was smashed. Clyst St Mary, raised by Ralegh's high-handed contempt, was given cause to rue its reaction. 'The fight was very fierce and cruel, and bloody was that day,' reports Hooker, a likely eyewitness. 'Some were slain with the sword, some burned in the houses, some shifting for themselves were taken prisoners, and many thinking to escape over the water were drowned, so that there were dead that day one with another about a thousand men.' Shortly after the battle, those taken prisoner were summarily executed.

Clyst St Mary is just eight miles from Ralegh's home at East Budleigh. There must have been many families in the area who had good cause to hate the inhabitants of Hayes Barton. We can only speculate on the impact of such animosity on young minds, but certainly our Walter Ralegh would prove thick-skinned, apparently so inured to insult there was a relish in its rejection. 'If any man accuseth me to my face, I will answer him with my mouth,' he said. 'But my tail is good enough to return an answer to such who traduceth me behind my back.'[11] The ability to seem at ease in a climate of contempt would prove a valuable asset throughout his life: it was a lesson he had been forced to learn early.

As for Ralegh's father, when he was finally freed from St Sidwell in Exeter, he sought compensation for his ordeal by relieving a parishioner, one Alice Rogers, of some of the church's valuables, including a silver cross, a silver spoon, a censer, an incense boat, a chalice, and church vestments, among which was a cope of fine cloth, the best the parish had, valued at the not inconsiderable sum of twenty marks. Later challenged in Exeter Cathedral to return the cope, Ralegh replied with terse disdain: 'if it were not cut already for the sparwer [canopy] of a bed they should have it'.[12]

Having ecclesiastical vestments recut for domestic use was more than expedience, an eye for the main chance; it was in itself a religious, if not political statement. Protestant authorities were not merely concerned to remove images, icons and other Catholic artefacts from church: what was not destroyed was to be explicitly de-sacralized, put to profane use, insult and ideology merging in a single brutal gesture of contemptuous utility.[13]

The episode underscores what would seem to have been some of Walter Ralegh senior's defining characteristics: a sense of self-righteousness and moral superiority that elided into a kind of entitlement. Opportunism and expedience were dressed up as – or perhaps merely expressed through the language of – personal integrity and pious faith.

A man is more than the sum of his parents' failings, but taken together with what we know of Katherine Ralegh, the first suggestions of a fatal undertow to Ralegh's own personality are here apparent. In constructing his public persona, Ralegh would take after his father and his name would be a byword for self-aggrandizement, for ambition, vanity and pride; but he would privately experience his successes with a churning visceral sense of worthlessness and doubt, fear and self-loathing. It was his parents' gift to him: he grew up to be a man divided against himself.

There is no reason to suppose that Ralegh disapproved of his father's *modus operandi*: it was, in many respects, characteristic of post-Henrician England. But nevertheless, it was to his mother's side of the family that Ralegh cleaved, even from a young age. Closest in every sense were his step-brothers the Gilberts – John, Adrian and, in particular, Humphrey – Katherine's three sons from her first marriage.

Born in 1537 and schooled at Eton, Humphrey would, like Ralegh later, attend both Oxford and the Inns of Court. Before Ralegh had learned to walk, Gilbert had been introduced to the household of the princess Elizabeth. He spent the next two decades alternately promoting voyages in search of the North West Passage, which many hoped would provide a westerly route, free from Spanish dominion, over the top of the Americas to the riches of the East, and leading military campaigns with varying degrees of success.

In Ireland, inspired by the example of his cousin Sir Peter Carew, and with just 500 men at his command, Gilbert's methods were notoriously cruel. The soldier-poet Thomas Churchyard, also close to Ralegh, described in a defence of Gilbert how he would kill every man, woman and child he came upon in enemy country, burning and laying waste to anything of worth. When he camped he had the head of every enemy cut from its body and laid either side of the way to his tent. '[It did] bring great terror to the people,' wrote Churchyard, 'when they saw the heads of their dead fathers, brothers, children, kinsfolk and friends, lie on the ground before their faces, as they came to speak with the said colonel.'[14]

Ralegh himself was proud, boastful even, of Gilbert's methods: 'I never heard nor read of any man more feared than he is among the Irish nation', he wrote in 1581 to an apparently unimpressed Walsingham. But re-posted to the Netherlands after his Irish triumphs, Gilbert's ambition had collided with his character flaws, most notably poor leadership skills and an inability to negotiate his way through the ebb and flow of complex political loyalties, and he returned with his reputation shaken.

Gilbert almost certainly owed his early introduction to Elizabeth to Katherine Astley. Long referred to by Ralegh biographers as his great aunt, she was, in fact, an aunt, the eldest sister of their mother. Ralegh himself referred to her as such in a letter of 1601. Astley, or Champernown, as she then was, had entered Elizabeth's household around 1537, rising to the pre-eminent position of governess ten years later. She would become chief gentlewoman of the privy chamber on the princess's accession, and her sway was considerable: Astley 'had such influence with the queen that she seemed, as it were, patroness of all England', one hostile observer wrote.[15]

Her character comes through clearly from the record: passionate, kind, quick-witted, warm, incautious and ferociously loyal, although that loyalty – commingled it must be said, with a talent for misjudgement – would land her with spells in prison on more than one occasion. In some respects, she was not all that dissimilar to her nephew. Elizabeth, who returned the loyalty with a revealingly uncharacteristic resolution and lack of hesitancy, called her Kat and adored her:

She hath been with me a long time and many years, and hath taken great labour and pain in bringing me up in learning and honesty . . . we are more bound to them that bringeth us up well than to our parents, for our parents do that which is natural for them – that is, bringeth us into the world – but our bringers-up are a cause to make us live well in it.[16]

She was, in short, a much-needed mother figure.

Elizabeth's dependence on Kat should not surprise us: Elizabeth's early life was dominated by fear and instability, her identity and character endlessly compromised by factors outside her control. Kat was anything but consistent, but her constancy in care of her mistress was immoderate and absolute. It was one of the very few things of which Elizabeth could be certain.

Elizabeth was the third of Henry VIII's children to survive to adulthood. Before her came Mary, born in 1516 and the only one of the six children conceived by Henry and his first wife, Katherine of Aragon to live; and Henry Fitzroy, born in 1519, the result of her father's short-lived affair with his nineteen-year old mistress, Elizabeth Blount.

Fitzroy died in July 1536. It may be unfair to make him alone carry the stain of illegitimacy; bastardy was a condition most of Henry's children passed through at different times. Henry's marriage to Elizabeth's mother, Anne Boleyn, in January 1533, illegitimized the then sixteen-year-old Mary; Elizabeth herself would be bastardized by act of Parliament in June 1536 following the execution of her mother. During her sister's reign she was considered by many, not least among them Mary, as no better than 'the illegitimate child of a criminal who was punished as a public strumpet'.[17]

Born at Greenwich on 7 September 1533, Elizabeth was not yet three when Henry had Anne beheaded on manifestly false treason charges, at the heart of which were alleged adulteries with five men, including her brother George. Henry would go so far as to admit the truth about her to his next wife, Jane

Seymour, saying that Anne 'had died in consequence of meddling too much in state affairs'.

Elizabeth can have had few, if any, memories of her mother. But shortly after her accession, Alexander Ales, a Scottish theologian in exile on the continent, wrote to her with congratulations on her coronation, and praise for her as an upholder of the reformed faith. Such professions were not uncommon, dry encomia to Elizabeth's providence and virtue; to many, her arrival on the throne seemed to offer a deliverance they had not dared to look for. Yet Ales' letter was more than that.

At its heart was a moving account of her mother's suffering – martyrdom, even – at the behest of her father. Indeed, it is Ales who gives us the only surviving testimony of the infant Elizabeth with her mother. The date would have been 30 April 1536. 'Never shall I forget the sorrow which I felt when I saw the most serene queen, your most religious mother, carrying you, still a little baby, in her arms and entreating the most serene king, your father, in Greenwich Palace, from the open window of which he was looking into the courtyard, when she brought you to him,' Ales wrote.

Henry, Ales says, was angered at the sight of her, but hid his feelings well. He was, in fact, at that moment in conference with the Privy Council planning her fall.

Crossing the Thames later in the day, Ales heard the thunder of cannon from the Tower of London to announce Anne's imprisonment. There was a show trial at the Tower on 15 May; she maintained her innocence with dignity and courage. Four days later Anne was beheaded on Tower Green; Henry did, however, allow her one mercy: death by sword rather than axe.

Ales had dreamed of her execution that morning, he said, uncomfortably confiding in Elizabeth his recollection of 'the queen's neck, after her head had been cut off, and this so plainly that I could count the nerves, the veins, and the arteries.'[18]

Less than six months later, Kat Champernown joined Elizabeth's household. The former heir to the throne, now illegitimate, had just turned three.

That Elizabeth and Ralegh were raised by sisters transforms our perception of their relationship: it gives them a hinterland. It was, too, a unique bond, subtle and profound as the shared experiences of childhood are, rooted deep in memory and patterns of thought, yet for precisely that reason unarticulated and unacknowledged too.

And for Elizabeth, it may have had a particular significance. Her court would always have the vertiginous emotional dynamics of an extended family, bound together in a raw tangle of loyalty, love and mutual loathing, but Elizabeth herself had no close family left. She had come to the throne aged twenty-five with little experience of any long-term relationships beyond her household, which thereby took on a familial as well as a functional role, and Kat Astley was at the heart of it. When she died in July 1565, Elizabeth's grief was visible to all.

But it is a bond that disturbs some assumptions about Ralegh, too. For all that he would be an outsider at court, a man of indeterminate but certainly not significant social status, Ralegh also had an entrée to Elizabeth that was imbued with intimacy and which spoke to Elizabeth's private, pre-accession world. Indeed, aside from her profound ties to Kat, Elizabeth also lived for some months in 1548 at the house of Ralegh's uncle, Sir Anthony Denny at Cheshunt in Hertfordshire. Denny had been a privy councillor under Henry VIII and, by the end, one of the king's few intimates: it was Denny who advised him to prepare himself for God's grace when death approached.

It is no wonder Elizabeth liked the way Ralegh thought, too, the heft and bounce of his intellect. The Champernown sisters were women to whom education was sacrosanct, self-defining. Biographers have long wondered at Ralegh's prodigious learning and, more than that, his riotous appetite for knowledge. It may well have been a habit of mind learned at home. Katherine Ralegh's sense of self-distinction in her education is evident, and with her sister's example it becomes clear why.

Champernown herself taught the young Elizabeth such subjects as mathematics, astronomy, architecture and history, and gave her a grounding in several languages, among them French, Italian and Flemish; at age six, under Champernown's care, Elizabeth so impressed a visiting courtier that he wrote to her father that she spoke 'with as grave a gravity as she had been forty years old. If she be no worse educated than she now appeareth . . . she will prove of no less honour to womanhood than shall beseem her father's daughter'.[19]

So for all that we might characterize the rural Devon of Ralegh's childhood as remote from the centre of power, which clearly it was, the complex network of family bonds in Tudor England – together with the centrifugal force of court politics – also served to collapse that distance, bringing proximity to power and influence to the furthest reaches of the kingdom – and certainly to Hayes Barton.

The queen may have been distant, but she was a real presence in the life of the young Walter Ralegh. They were already connected.

II: LEAGUES OF SMOKE

[A]void her Majesty's suspicion that you doubt Monsieur's love to her . . . though I promise I think she has little enough herself to it. Yet what she would have others think and do, you have cause to know.

EARL OF LEICESTER TO SIR FRANCIS WALSINGHAM

There was more than a little of Anne Boleyn in her daughter. Henry's bitter repudiation of his second wife, and the subsequent reign of Mary, who had her own sorrows to avenge, have erased much of Anne's life from the record. Her stay as queen was brief, too. But between the official silences and the officious slanders there are glimpses to be had of a vivacious young woman, cultured, educated, self-assured – not exactly beautiful but compelling nonetheless – a woman who loved the spontaneity and freedom of music and dancing in her bedchambers, was physically affectionate with her friends, charged with nervous energy: bold, intelligent, unafraid.

When she became queen herself, Elizabeth showed no particular inclination to rehabilitate the memory of her mother – publicly at least. Here, as in most things, she was politically circumspect, unwilling to do anything but that which was absolutely necessary to maintain power.

There were, however, quieter restitutions to be made: she adopted Anne's badge of a crowned white falcon coming to rest on a barren tree which bursts forth in roses, and, more private yet, she wore a jewelled locket ring on one of her exquisite, much admired hands which opened to reveal facing cameos of herself and her mother.[1]

But that is not to say that her feelings towards Anne were mere calculus, tempered and untroubled. There is evidence, in fact, that she experienced her maternal inheritance as a tangle of powerful, competing, primal emotions that she struggled to suppress. A prayer Elizabeth wrote in the late 1560s, for example, attempted to tame some of this raw, incoherent matter, to place it in a controlling narrative of gratitude for her delivery into her kingdom:

> [F]ormerly, when I was in my mother's womb, a fall into sin stained me, on account of which ... I was most worthy of miscarriage; yet Thy fatherly hand led me out from thence and allowed me to be born into the light ... And yet (unhappy me) my youth – indeed my cradle – breathed forth nothing but the dung of that prior life, whence yet again I have had to await your coming as a Judge angry with me. But Thou through Thy infinite goodness hast called me, most unworthy from courtly pleasures to the delights of Thy kingdom.[2]

There is a curious self-loathing here, but its moral disgust has no focus. The past in which its squalor is located is indeterminate: the courtly pleasures Elizabeth has been saved from – which may or may not be her own – seem to occupy the same time-frame as her cradle days, which themselves fold back into her unborn life in Anne's womb, deserving miscarriage. Deserving, perhaps, to be the child that Anne miscarried in January 1536, changing places with that wished-for boy, Elizabeth's nominal younger brother, whose birth would have been Anne's redemption, the price of her life.

Yet Elizabeth let her mother's mutilated body remain where it was, unredeemed, in the chapel of St Peter ad Vincula in the Tower beside the green where her blood was spilled. It was not a decision taken lightly. Elizabeth had time enough to dwell on her mother and what of hers she shared – and on the nature of liberty, of captivity and its shadow, death – when she too was sent to the Tower by her sister Mary in 1554, like Anne expecting execution. It was the defining crisis of her young life.

Something of the sort was probably inevitable: Mary came to the throne in the summer of 1553 intent on unpicking Henry VIII's rejection of papal authority and her brother Edward VI's subsequent embrace of reformation thinking, and the stakes for all concerned became too high. Under Henry's Act of Succession, until such a time as Mary had a child, Elizabeth was the heir to the throne. Elizabeth's continued liberty – physical as much as of conscience – was therefore a constant threat to the regime.

Mary's government wasn't alone in recognizing the fact. Throughout the reign, ill-fated Protestant plots and rebellions rose and fell around Elizabeth, who – as the obvious and only beneficiary – was not unreasonably suspected of complicity.

The most promising of these conspiracies occurred early in 1554, seizing on news of Mary's plans to marry Philip of Spain to inflame nationalist sentiment against the regime. Among the ringleaders were Ralegh's kinsman Sir Peter Carew, who vowed to raise the West Country, and Nicholas Throckmorton, the father of Ralegh's future wife, although it has been marked down in history to its Kentish figurehead, Sir Thomas Wyatt.

After some successes in Kent, Wyatt failed to find support in London and he and the last of his followers surrendered at the Temple Bar on Fleet Street on 7 February. Three days later Elizabeth was summoned to London for questioning about the attempted coup. The government sent three knights backed by 250 men to bring Elizabeth to court from her house at Ashridge in Hertfordshire. They came around ten in the evening, alarmingly late, suggesting an urgency of purpose that could only bode ill for her. One of her ladies asked that they return in the morning, but the knights followed her up into Elizabeth's privy chamber and forced their way in.

Her health, as often with those who seem to exist on nerves, was married to her mental and emotional condition, and she lay weak and bedridden. But public composure was an article of faith for her, and she rose to the terror of the occasion.

'Is the haste such,' she asked them, 'that it might not have pleased you to come to morrow in the morning?'

'Our commission is such,' they replied, 'that we must needs bring you with us, either quick or dead.'

She left with them the next day by nine in the morning, carried in the queen's litter to expedite her progress. It is thirty miles or so from Ashridge to Westminster, but Elizabeth's journey took five slow days, and she passed in and out of consciousness several times. Mary's men guarded her at night and she slept little.

By the time she arrived in London, riding down Highgate Hill and into the wet spring streets of the city, she was so bloated with fear – 'swollen and disfigured' the French ambassador said – that some thought she would die before answering her accusers.[3] There were gibbets and hanged men everywhere you looked, the bruised and broken fruit of the government's fearful vengeance against Wyatt's attempted coup.[4]

Weak and ill as she was, Elizabeth made the effort to pull herself upright and had the litter's curtains opened to reveal herself, dressed in the pure white robe she had chosen that morning, to the growing crowd of citizens who followed her. Renard, the imperial ambassador and architect of the impending Anglo-Spanish alliance, reported that 'her pale face kept a proud, haughty expression in order to mask her vexation', but a less hostile witness might have said she was determined not to show how afraid she was.[5]

Elizabeth understood as well as anyone, and certainly better than Renard, the drama of the royal presence, the rhetoric of style, of magnificence, of physical grace, and the necessary eloquence of gesture to translate image into symbol into icon. The people saw in her instead a dignity under pressure, mastering her illness and fear to demonstrate to the world the authority of innocence.

Elizabeth was interrogated, implausibly claiming ignorance of what the rebels had done in her name and otherwise finding new skilful ways to say nothing with any purchase. Asked on more than one occasion to submit to the queen's mercy, she refused, pointing out that, no crime having been proved against her, she had no need for forgiveness: courage, stubbornness and pride were interdependent qualities for her. Later, she idly scratched on the glass of a window pane the phrase: 'Much suspected by me/nothing can be proved': it was a bold claim, but it was hardly a ringing declaration of innocence.[6]

On Saturday 17 March, the Earl of Sussex and William Paulet, the Marquis of Winchester, came finally to escort her to the Tower, a prospect that held a special dread for Elizabeth. Another – albeit unwilling – rival to the throne, Lady Jane Grey, had been beheaded there just the month before. She asked if she could write to the queen, protesting that the Tower was 'more wonted for a false traitor than a true subject'; but as much as anything the aim was procrastination, deferral, delay, Elizabeth hoping as she always would that time might remedy what her limited capacity for action could not.[7] She missed the tide.

Nevertheless, Elizabeth was ordered to the Tower the next day, Palm Sunday, at nine in the morning. Her retinue had been stripped from her, and she was left with just an usher, two grooms and three gentlewomen to accompany her. The record is silent on their identities, but if Elizabeth had been allowed a choice, Kat Astley would surely have been among them.

It was raining as her barge was rowed downriver and the boatmen were reluctant to attempt to shoot the bridge, that is, to take their craft through the narrow spans of London Bridge, a dangerous and unpredictable manoeuvre as the force of the water caused sometimes deadly currents and countertides as it broke against the arches. Most travellers disembarked to cross on foot, but Elizabeth's keepers would not countenance such a thing with so few men to support them.

The rivermen pulled against the tide to keep the boat upstream, hovering uncertainly above the bridge. They were right to be afraid: when they finally made the attempt, the turbulent waters yawned beneath the barge and fell away as the men fought to steer it to safety, and its stern ground on the mud and gravel of the river bed beneath the bridge, for a brief while unable to move.

When they reached the Tower and drew up at Traitor's Gate, Elizabeth refused at first to leave the barge. The two lords had disembarked ahead of her, and Paulet turned back and told her curtly that she had no choice; he offered her his cloak against the rain, but she dashed away his hand.

Elizabeth had a lucky talent for inspiring care in others without having to plead for it. The spring river was swollen and as she finally stepped out its waters lapped over her shoe. Sir

John Bridges, the lieutenant of the Tower, came forward kindly and said to her, 'Madam, you were best to come out of the rain', but when the doors were locked and bolted behind her she was visibly shaken. She did not expect to leave alive.

Once inside she was confined with her gentlewomen to a small three-windowed chamber on the first floor of the Bell Tower at the south-east corner of the fortress. Renard, for one, was sure of her guilt: '[S]he has been accused by Wyatt, mentioned by name in the French ambassador's letters, suspected by her own counsellors, and it is certain that the enterprise was undertaken for her sake,' he reported to Mary's future father-in-law, Emperor Charles V.[8] To remain safe, he added, Mary must seize the opportunity to execute her sister.

Desperate for the slightest breath of liberty she asked for somewhere outside to walk. She would be ill if she could not, she said. The request was denied. Thinking perhaps of her mother's last hysterical, heartbroken days, she asked if she could at least be free to walk in the queen's chambers where Anne Boleyn had been held captive, and even that request had to be referred to the Privy Council.

Elizabeth received the news with glum surprise. 'Well,' she said, 'if the matter be so hard that they must be sued unto for so small a thing . . . God comfort me.'

The request was allowed – but only on the understanding that she could not walk without the company of her gaolers, and only if the windows were closed and she made no attempt to look out. Here Elizabeth paced in the airless rooms, no less certain than her enemies of what was likely to follow; she thought of writing to Mary to beg for the same mercy as her mother received, the sword before the axe.[9]

Despite its profound suspicions, however, the government was unable to find evidence of her treachery, and Elizabeth was released on 19 May to house arrest at Woodstock. When her gaoler, Sir Henry Bedingfield first arrived at the Tower with his hundred-strong blue-coated escort, she grew agitated, fearing the worst, and asked those about her if Lady Jane's scaffold was still standing.

Her state of mind did not improve. On the first night of the journey to her new captivity, they stopped at Richmond and Elizabeth, dismayed at being attended in her chamber by Bedingfield's men, asked her usher to pray for her, since she was certain to be murdered that night.[10]

In Elizabeth's later prayer of thanks for her delivery from 'prison, custody [and] the maws of lions' the hot physicality of her terror is almost palpable, but she ultimately owed her freedom to her own obduracy, her self-control and intelligence. Mary's authority was weak and her government divided and Elizabeth had faced it down.[11]

There was a strength to be drawn from her resilience under pressure, from her ability to endure existence on a fatal precipice and then slowly find her way back to solid ground. But the experience of a narrow and precarious confinement also confirmed for her the value of her liberty, and the price she set on it was high.

Liberty became a kind of addiction, going beyond reasoned principle and resentment of control to an almost physical craving, a psychological need. Henceforth she would respond to constraints on her personal freedom with something between revulsion and offence. Years later, as attempts on her life became more frequent, Elizabeth's advisers counselled her to refrain from her habitual garden walks alone or otherwise undefended. 'I had rather be dead than put in custody,' she replied.[12]

Elizabeth largely spent the remaining years of Mary's reign abjectly abandoned, in a kind of internal exile, mostly at Woodstock, where she was guarded by sixty men during the day and ninety at night. Bedingfield was instructed to ensure that she had no unauthorized conversation that he did not overhear, and no correspondence that he did not read. Five or six bolted doors and gates separated her rooms from the garden, the only outside space she was allowed, and they were locked behind her whenever she moved between them.

It was a confinement Astley shared, and she, too, was under continual observation, suspected no less than her mistress. As a result, Kat had two further spells of imprisonment in 1555 and again in 1556, when Elizabeth also lost three other ladies to the Tower. 'They would fetch all away at the end,' was Elizabeth's despondent reaction.[13] On Kat's release, the government dismissed her from her duties and forbade her from attempting even to approach her former pupil.[14] It would take Elizabeth's accession for the two to be reunited.

The loneliness of office is a modern cliché, but Elizabeth experienced it to an extreme, being alone possessed of an intrinsic power and status it would be fatal to exercise. Outside the dwindling circle of intimates in her household Elizabeth could trust no one, and it was here more than anywhere that the formidable persona she adopted as queen, at once dynamic and intransigent, wary and unyielding, was forged.

She had always seemed extraordinarily self-possessed, of course: within a few weeks of arriving in England in the summer of 1553, Renard was noting warily that 'The Lady Elizabeth is greatly to be feared, for she has a spirit of enchantment.'[15] Now there was something else: her singularity and apartness became marks of honour for her, integral to her identity, and a vital source of her natural authority and control. That she lived to take the throne, observed the Venetian Michael Surian, was 'owing to her courage and to her great power of mind, being similar to that of the King her father'. She had declined to rely upon anyone save herself, he said, and had found she lacked for nothing.[16]

But if Elizabeth's craving for liberty was at its most intense in the personal crises of her sister's reign, it was at its most consistent in her life-long attitude to marriage. Indeed, Elizabeth did not need Ales to remind her of what surrender to Henry's will had cost her mother: marriage and the need to resist it had been part of her life as long as she could remember.

As early as April 1537, less than a year after the death of her mother, Henry's Privy Council had begun discussing her marriage prospects.[17] Legitimate or not, Elizabeth was a useful political tool in shoring up both English national security and the stability of the Tudor settlement; hereafter, the subject was rarely off the table. Six years later, Henry was offering her to the young son of the Earl of Arran to buy the favour of Arran himself, then regent for Mary Stuart, who had succeeded to the Scottish throne the previous December, less than one week old. In October 1545, not long after her twelfth birthday, Henry was hoping she might marry Philip of Spain.[18]

And so it went on through her teenage years. In July 1551, Jehan Scheyfve, the imperial ambassador, was reporting 'more rumours about a project to marry the Lady Elizabeth, sister to the King, to M. d'Aumale, brother to M. de Guise; though other people still speak of the King of Denmark's eldest son . . . and some still believe it may come to pass.'[19] A few months later, the details had changed, but the gossip remained the same: 'They say that the Earl of Pembroke, who is a widower, is trying to obtain her in marriage.'

There was one new sliver of information, however, that assumes greater significance in retrospect: 'she refuses her consent'.[20]

It seems counter-intuitive, given that the first two decades of her reign were dominated by the subject, but Elizabeth did not want to marry. She said so, repeatedly and often, to almost everyone who would listen. 'If I could to-day appoint such a successor to the Crown as would please me and the country I would not marry,' she told de Silva, the most amiable of a string of Spanish ambassadors to her court, in 1565. 'It is a thing for which I have never had any inclination. My subjects, however, press me so that I cannot help myself, but must marry or take the other course, which is a very difficult one. There is a strong idea in the world that a woman cannot live unless she is married, or at all events that if she refrains from marriage she does so for some bad reason.'[21]

In fact, Elizabeth decided young that she did not want to marry. Robert Dudley, by then the Earl of Leicester, discussed his own hopes of marriage to her with the French ambassador in December 1565. 'I have known her since she was eight years of age, better than any man in the world. From that time she has always invariably declared that she would remain unmarried.'[22] It is testament to the force of Elizabeth's personality – and flirtatious genius – that he, and many others, still continued to hope that she would relent, but marriage and its threats had defined her life from childhood and she sought to define herself against – or perhaps despite – it. It was a sign of her difference.

Under Mary, the government's objective in marrying Elizabeth became explicitly coercive, with the express intent of using it to repress and control her. As one observer noted drily: '[I]t was imperative to give her a husband who was a Catholic, or who might have authority over her'.[23] In November 1553, the suggestion that she might be wed to Philip II's eight-year-old son, Don Carlos, was under serious consideration; a year later, one of Mary's advisers was casting around elsewhere in Europe for someone suitable: 'she might be married off to some poor German prince; for that would be the safest way to dispose of her'.[24] The disinterested contempt is still audible. No less tangible, in hindsight, is the underestimation of Elizabeth, her calculation, courage and strength. She continued to resist.

Of course, none of these proposals were unusual and royal children, however doubtful their legitimacy, were political and dynastic commodities before they were feeling human beings. Personal considerations might be part of the equation but were rarely allowed to dominate; Henry VIII's troubled series of consorts were evidence, if it were needed, of what problems could arise when private passions corroded the decision-making process.

When she came to the throne in November 1558, marriage was widely, perhaps universally, perceived as a necessity. One of the more obvious lessons to be drawn from the long crisis of Henry VIII's progeny, which had poisoned England for some thirty years prior to Elizabeth's accession, was the high premium a nation should place on a stable succession. A disposition towards virginity was the only credible argument which bought Elizabeth both personal and political space from the unrelenting pressure to wed and provide the nation with an heir.

What was unusual – incomprehensible, even, to those about her, whose lives no less than their livelihoods might ultimately depend on the wisdom of her judgement – was Elizabeth's cautious, but increasingly articulate, resistance to marriage. The originality of the idea ought to shock us; it was radical, unprecedented, uncharted territory. Moreover, given that her hand in marriage was a key piece in the geopolitics of Europe – and more than that, in the struggle for religious hegemony across the continent – she was in a sense resisting the pressure of the entire Christian world when she hedged, hesitated and demurred. It was an extraordinary act of will.

Yet the political capital inherent in her eligibility could not be ignored and her marketability brought influence for England across Europe.[25] Elizabeth was pragmatist enough to recognize that necessity might force her hand, or even that her heart might soften, and she was in any case temperamentally opposed to the idea of opportunities or options closing for ever: not yet the virgin queen, she was for the moment merely unwed – there is a difference.

Moreover, marriage was also one of the few levers of state that was inarguably and exclusively hers. Paradoxically, then, the very fact of her availability bought her control, room for manoeuvre, a breathing space for England even as it promised constraint for Elizabeth herself.

When Elizabeth came in great pomp to the Tower of London for the first time as queen, on 28 November 1558, she was heard to say: 'Some have fallen from being princes of this land to be prisoners in this place. I am raised from being a prisoner in this place to be the prince of the land'. Once inside she took time to revisit her prison in the Bell Tower and reflect on the strange workings of fortune and revel – here more than anywhere – in the absoluteness of her liberty.[26]

She was right to dwell on the almost miraculous nature of her redemption, her resurrection. But she was quickly to find, if she did not know already, that her own freedom from coercion did not correlate with that of her nation from instability and fear; indeed, it seemed likely that she would have to sacrifice the former to ensure the latter. Whereas in captivity, Elizabeth's security had been synonymous with her liberty, now to most people they appeared antithetical to one another. It would be two decades or more before the nation would again accept that the two were inextricably linked.

The England Elizabeth inherited was a nation unwound, uncertain, exposed: thirty years of political, religious and dynastic discord had rotted the institutions of government and ravaged the governing social elites. 'It is also a fact, incredible though true,' noted one shocked continental observer in 1559, 'that during the last twenty years three princes of the blood, four dukes, forty earls, and more than three thousand other persons have died by violent death.'[27] Many others had experienced imprisonment, poverty and years in exile.

The numbers may not be precise, but the point still stands: England was broken. It was utterly divided, with no clear majority loyal to either Protestantism or Catholicism; it was at war with its two nearest neighbours, France and Scotland, whose offensive alliance found physical form in the person of Mary Stuart. Its currency was devalued, its exchequer bare. It had just lost the last of its lands in continental Europe, an inheritance that stretched back several hundred years. 'I never saw, nor I think if I should have lived this five hundred years heretofore past, I should not have seen at any time England weaker in strength, men, money, and riches,' wrote the scholar and diplomat Sir Thomas Smith.[28]

But England's safety as a Protestant outlier off the coast of mainland Europe depended on ensuring that its principal Catholic enemies, France and Spain, remained deep in mutual loathing and did not find common cause in England's destruction. No one was under much illusion as to the scale of the challenge: in the words of Ralegh's friend Ralph Lane, England was caught between 'the mistrust that all men have in generally of the ambition of France' and 'the fear of the noted malice of Spain of long time against her majesty conceived'.[29]

To the west, Ireland, Catholic and rebellious, needed to be suppressed. The northern threat from Scotland, which could not be suppressed as long as it had an ally in France, had to be neutered. East across what is now the North Sea lay the Spanish Netherlands, an enemy dominion tolerable as long as Spain was weak there, but on no account to fall under French influence.

It was a complicated play, and England had one card only as the game began: Elizabeth. The possibility of her marriage, of England's strategic alliance with a rival power was something neither France nor Spain were happy to countenance.[30]

But the prize of England, Elizabeth's hand, was to prove an infinitely deferred hope, a tease, something whose power resided in the implied possibility of claiming it; whereas for the English to let it be captured would be to court defeat. England itself would be subject to a foreign power, be it Hapsburg or Valois, and allying with one through marriage would be to seal the animosity of the other, something England, quite literally, could not afford at the beginning of the 1560s. Other offers from elsewhere in Europe were viewed through the same prism: would the resulting alliance help shore up English national security?

Yet behind the mask of national interest lay more personal discomforts and enmities, too. Philip was of course Elizabeth's brother-in-law, as the husband of her late sister Mary, and Philip believed, not without reason, that Elizabeth and England had much to be grateful to him for. His failure to convert his efforts and expense into a more durable and effective dominion was, he felt, a personal humiliation as well as a political threat and an insult to the Catholic church.[31]

As for France, it was at war with England at the close of Mary's reign, something Elizabeth sought to rectify almost immediately. But Elizabeth was incensed by the arrogance of Mary Stuart in claiming the English throne to be rightfully hers. Then sixteen years old, with ten of them lived in France, her maternal homeland, Mary had recently married the dauphin, François, and she made her ambitions quite clear by proudly quartering the English coat of arms with her own when she learned of Mary Tudor's death.

As the granddaughter of Henry VIII's sister Margaret, Mary had a strong claim to the throne; indeed, for those who regarded Elizabeth's dubious legitimacy as the child of Anne

Boleyn sufficient to bar her from the succession, it was stronger than Elizabeth's.[32] A later report has her joining a group discussing a portrait of Elizabeth. Was it a good likeness of the queen of England? 'Nay, it is not like her, for I am the queen of England,' Mary replied.[33]

De Feria, the Spanish ambassador, goaded Elizabeth on the subject: 'We then touched upon the pretensions of the queen of Scots which the French have put forward at which she is much offended, and she began to rave against them and said what she would do if it were not for other reasons.' Philip's ambassador purred with delight at finding a topic which so riled her.[34]

Mary would continue to be Elizabeth's most potent rival for the throne, but not on behalf of France, where she quickly became marginalized after the death of François in December 1560. But if there was hope that relations between the two countries would be more placid thereafter, it was misplaced: within a few years France would be fractured by a series of civil wars, disguised as wars of religion, that would almost outlast the century and the old tensions and mistrusts re-emerged in new and complex forms.

National diplomacy would of course be conducted with the Catholic French royal family, but the English government's sympathy and self-interest – and perhaps as importantly those of its governing class – lay largely with the Protestant Huguenot faction. It was an intricate dilemma.

There is little to be gained from a full accounting of all the foreign suitors who expressed an interest in winning Elizabeth in her first decade as queen. She herself rattled off a by no means complete list to date to de Silva in 1565, not without a certain pride: 'Marriage was suggested to me with the King my brother-in-law; the king of France has proposed as well as the kings of Sweden and Denmark, and I understand the Archduke Charles also,' she told him, enquiring playfully why Philip's son had not been offered too.[35]

Each suitor sent ambassadors to the English court, extravagant equally of gifts and hopes and praise – the Swedish ambassador spent more than forty thousand crowns to expedite his mission – and each returned home disappointed.[36] But they all served a purpose, even if it wasn't apparent to anyone but Elizabeth: to buy England time while its finances were rebuilt and its cautious religious settlement took root; to keep its enemies guessing, uncertain, off-balance, poised awkwardly between interest and alarm at the latest news.

But towards the end of the 1560s, as Philip II became confident that Elizabeth did not want to marry, and no less impatient for the overthrow of a kingdom he half thought of as his own already, the tenor of the discussions changed, and Elizabeth's attention became focused on possible French suitors – to dally with if not to actually marry – to underwrite English security.

A match with the Duke of Anjou, troublesome son of the formidable Catherine de Medici and brother of the French king, was first suggested, with some trepidation, by Sir Henry Norris, Elizabeth's ambassador to France, in the summer of 1568. It had been discussed at the French court as a means of detaching Anjou from the influence of the Guise faction, and the Huguenots were much in favour.[37]

The extent to which Elizabeth's affections, no less than her body, were understood to be a political commodity is apparent, not only from the calculations being made at the French court, but also from the fact that, when Norris' letter came to England, she does not seem to have even been consulted about its contents. Cecil replied on behalf of himself, Leicester and Pembroke, saying that they did not mislike the overture and doubted that it would get very far, but suggested that Norris should proceed as though it might.[38] For the moment, their instincts were correct: the idea melted away.

Two years later, however, by which time Catherine and her pliant son, Charles IX – himself once floated as a possible suitor for Elizabeth – were increasingly anxious to see Anjou safely out of France, the English were receptive. The political landscape in England had changed irrevocably: the marriage negotiations took place in the aftermath of the Northern Rebellion in the autumn of 1569, led by the Catholic earls of Northumberland and Westmorland, and against the background of the unfolding Ridolfi plot, which had sought to depose Elizabeth in favour of Mary Stuart, who, it was planned, would then marry Thomas Howard, Duke of Norfolk. The Spanish ambassador, de Spes, had played a leading role in planning these attempts against Elizabeth, and Spanish military support was integral to both.

Indeed, opposition to the Anjou marriage was explicitly a part of the conspirators' agenda: in a letter Ridolfi – a Florentine banker resident in London – drafted on Norfolk's behalf, Norfolk is made to say that 'if the queen of England and her ministers should be allowed to carry out their designed match with the Duke of Anjou, and unite this crown with that of France; for the prevention whereof, if his majesty will aid me, I, with my friends in this kingdom, offer to oppose them by force and defeat them'.[39]

Moreover, on 1 May 1570, the Bishop of London had woken to find a document pinned to the door of his house by St Paul's. It was a copy of Pope Pius V's bull of excommunication against 'that servant of all iniquity, Elizabeth, pretended queen of England', which Ridolfi had smuggled into England. The bull not only absolved Catholics of any oaths of loyalty towards her, but forced on them a choice: it was no longer acceptable to passively accept or tolerate the Elizabethan settlement.

[We] declare that the aforesaid Elizabeth is a heretic and a favourer of heretics, and that her adherents in the matters aforesaid have incurred the sentence of malediction, and are utterly separated from the unity of the body of Christ; and that she is wholly deprived of her pretended right to the aforesaid kingdom, and likewise of all and every dominion, dignity, and privilege ... And we command and interdict all and every one of her barons, subjects, people, and others, that they shall not dare to obey either her, or her laws and commandments; and he who shall act otherwise, shall incur the same sentence of malediction.[40]

Henceforward, to be a Catholic in England was, explicitly, to be a traitor. 'There can be no room for any excuse or defence,' the Pope had said.

Given that Spain had unmistakeably revealed its hand as an enemy of England, it is hardly surprising that England was attentive to the French proposals. And yet the papal bull, as it was designed to do, made religion an even sharper thorn in Elizabeth's crown: there was no longer any middle ground. Elizabeth herself recognized it, personally instructing her then ambassador to the Valois court, Francis Walsingham, that 'of necessity it must be especially prejudged that Monsieur shall not have authority to exercise the form of religion in England that is prohibited by the laws of our realm.'[41] Burghley, who tended to look sympathetically on candidates for marriage as long as they weren't Dudley, quietly hoped that Anjou, with a kingdom in his grasp, might find it in his conscience to renounce his faith, but his suggestion that Anjou 'may prove a noble conqueror of all popery in Christendom' proved wishful thinking – a hint of how desperate Burghley believed England's situation.[42]

Anjou stubbornly refused to compromise. Catherine de Medici told Elizabeth's ambassadors early the following year that he must be free to exercise his religion openly; he was currently fasting for Lent so devoutly, she said with evident distaste, that he had become lean and evil-coloured. Catherine was no particular fan of religious enthusiasm; her devotions were political and dynastic. Nevertheless, Anjou must be allowed to celebrate high mass in public with all due ceremonies and songs, in a chapel reserved for his use. One of the English diplomats exploded: 'Why, Madame, then he may require also the four orders of friars, monks, canons, pilgrimages, pardons, oil and cream, relics and all such trumperies.'[43] It was, as everyone knew, a dealbreaker.

Almost immediately, there was a half-hearted suggestion that Charles IX's youngest brother, the Duke of Alençon, might be a suitable candidate, being 'not so obstinate, papistical, and restive like a mule as his brother is'. The French also assured a slightly bemused English diplomat that Alençon was 'more apt ... for getting of children' than his brother.[44] Walsingham, who had been more sceptical than Burghley about the Anjou marriage, seemed willing to be persuaded this time, but there were obstacles which demonstrate that personal sentiment weighed at least as much with Elizabeth as matters of state.[45]

Alençon had suffered from smallpox as a child and Elizabeth raised the extent of his disfigurement with the French royal family. 'The pock-holes are many and thick rather than great or much apparent, saving in the bluntness of the nose, which might rather be expressed by pencil than with pen,' came the game reply from an English diplomat.[46] It was not encouraging.

Alençon was also unusually short. Elizabeth questioned Burghley on the point, and he told her that he was around his own height. 'Say rather the height of your grandson,' Elizabeth snapped.[47] Then there was the matter of his age. He was just eighteen in 1572 – the same age as Ralegh in fact – and Elizabeth baulked at marrying someone who was twenty-one years younger. To put it another way, she feared being made to look – or perhaps simply being – ridiculous.[48]

Looking on, the Spanish were particularly sceptical. 'There is a league of smoke between the queen of England and the king of France, it is said with the object of marrying the queen to the youngest brother of the king,' reported a London agent to the ambassador in August 1572. 'But everybody knows that the queen will never marry, so that our friends think the league will not last long.'[49]

They were right to be cynical. What enthusiasm there had been ebbed away and the foreign marriage project seemed to be finished for good. Elizabeth was finally alone. But at what cost?

III: IN A COUNTRY STRANGE

It is more profitable to steal a safe retreat, than to abide the uncertain event of battle.[1]

SIR WALTER RALEGH

The fine webs of international politics, of diplomacy and war, were weighted with issues of faith, nationalism and identity, and their tremors could be felt even in obscure and far-flung backwaters. In Devon, the young Ralegh was not absent from the great dramas of state: they defined his life too, offering opportunities for advancement, and threats to be resisted. It was all personal, and men of less ambition than Ralegh found it impossible to remain passive; he too hungered for the freedom to act.

However parochial the Tudor west may seem, however local the concerns of the property-owning classes to which Ralegh belonged, there were also wide horizons within reach. There was, of course, always the sea. But if Ralegh sought familial role models, as he seems to have done, among the network of cousins, close and distant, on his mother's side, the multitudinous Champernowns and Carews, the geopolitics of continental Europe offered the most exciting prospects – especially France.

Among the older generation, there was Sir Peter Carew. A wild youth – one childhood anecdote has him led home on a leash through the streets of Exeter by his father after one outrage too many – he was more or less abandoned by his parents to a life of servitude at the French court, from which he was fortunate to be rescued. Over the next few decades, as part of a restless career that mingled extensive continental soldiering with growing status in Henry VIII's retinue, his travels would take him down the length of Italy, from Venice to Naples, to the siege of Buda and ultimately to the court of Suleiman the Magnificent in Constantinople.

When Mary came to power, the Protestant Carew played a leading role in Wyatt's doomed rebellion, attempting to raise the west against the Spanish marriage. Recognizing the cause was lost, he stole away to Caen on 23 January 1554, over a week before Wyatt arrived in London, on one of Walter Ralegh's ships. His actions at Clyst St Mary and elsewhere a few years previously had lost him whatever hope he might have had of raising the county in his wake.

One of Ralegh's uncles, John Champernown, had died fighting the Ottoman Turks at Vienna in 1561. Another, Arthur Champernown, already had a number of ships operating in the Channel under the banner of the Huguenot Admiral de Coligny, engaged in the highly lucrative and ethically satisfying activity of preying on Spanish shipping, especially that which ferried funds to Spanish troops in the Netherlands.

The young Ralegh, however, fell under the spell of John's son and heir, Henry Champernown. In 1566, aged thirty-one or so, Henry had led a group of like-minded gentlemen to enlist in the imperial army in its fights against the infidel in Hungary. The struggle was short-lived, and Champernown was on his way back to England the following year when he delayed to join the French Huguenot forces fighting their Catholic compatriots outside Paris at the battle of St Denis.

The Huguenots were defeated at St Denis, but Champernown returned home inspired and undeterred. Throughout the spring and summer of 1568 support for the Protestant French, largely organized by John Hawkins, flowed incessantly from Plymouth to the Huguenot stronghold of La Rochelle in the form of cannon, powder, munitions and money, as the French ambassador bitterly complained to Cecil. England could not afford, economically or politically, to support Protestant fellow-travellers overtly on the continent, but its genius for the covert and disingenuous was flourishing. Private enterprise was encouraged to accomplish policy aims that Elizabeth dare not avow.[2]

On the ships' return journeys to Plymouth, their holds were packed with the rewards of the Huguenots' predatory shipping: fine cloth from the Low Countries, sack from Andalusia, wine from the south west, salt, bells and plate from despoiled Catholic churches. The quaysides were stacked with merchandise, ill-gotten or otherwise.[3]

It was to La Rochelle that Ralegh, aged perhaps fourteen, sailed in November with Henry Champernown and a small cavalry troop; we have Gilbert's friend Churchyard to thank for the information. From La Rochelle – which the desperate townspeople fortified day and night despite the prosperous activity in the port – the cohort made its way inland, joining the army of the Comte de Montgommery in time to see action at Jazeneuil on the seventeenth of the month.

Jazeneuil, situated on the road from La Rochelle to Poitiers, was little more than a skirmish, but it ended in defeat. The army marched north towards Saumur on the Loire but had to retreat as the forces of the Duke of Anjou threatened to cut off their rear. It was one reason why the English were keen to use the promise of marriage to detach him from the Catholic faction.

The two armies faced off for three days before submitting to the terrors of winter. 'It was the severest . . . for twenty years,' wrote François de la Noue, governor of La Rochelle. 'Not only did it freeze hard, but the frost was so terrible that even the foot could not march without falling, much less the horse.' The appalling conditions compounded the misery of civil war, perfectly caught by an Englishman writing back to London:

> Having consumed the store of the last year and wasting that on the ground which should serve for the year to come, so as a present desperation and a piteous mourning doth invade every sort, as though their calamities should have none end, but with the end of their lives together. And that withal the dreadfulest cruelties at once of the world, plague, hunger and the sword, which god of his goodness cease in them, and preserve from us; and to this is joined an incredible obstinacy of either side, even hardening their hearts with malice and fury to the utter extermination one of another.[4]

Ralegh and his few fellow English gentlemen had to sit out the bitter winter before campaigning began again in spring. The wait took its toll. 'Have lost many footmen this winter', Champernown reported back matter-of-factly to Cecil on 6 February from Niort.[5] It was a bleak introduction to contemporary warfare for a teenage boy.

The new season, however, brought further disaster. Champernown's men joined the Huguenot army at Jarnac on 13 March 1569, which was split between the leadership of Admiral Coligny and Louis Prince de Condé. The Huguenots, outmanoeuvred by the superior cavalry of the Catholics and trapped with the river Charente at their backs, were routed. Condé himself surrendered, only to be cut down. Some said he was shot in the eye. The significance of his death to the Catholic forces can be inferred from the number of men who laid claim to the deed. Condé's body was strapped to an ass and paraded through the town, the triumphant army crowing in its wake.

Looking back in later life on these campaigns, Ralegh displays a pragmatism that might be thought cynical if one had illusions about the battlefield being a place for idealistic enthusiasm. Musing on the loss of Condé, he wrote:

I remember it well, that when the prince of Condé was slain after the battle of Jarnac ... the Protestants did greatly bewail the loss of the said prince, in respect of his religion, person and birth; yet, comforting themselves, they thought it rather an advancement than an hindrance to their affairs; for so much did the valour of the one outreach the advisedness of the other, as whatsoever the admiral intended to win by attending the advantage, the prince adventured to lose by being overconfident in his own courage.[6]

It is the pronouncement of the professional soldier: practical, contemptuous of ideology. It is also that of a man, by temperament and inclination, disdainful of aristocratic glories; to Ralegh, nobility and rank were tools of leadership, not character traits.

Ralegh was back in Devon with Champernown the following month, presumably having hastily retreated to La Rochelle with the surviving Huguenot forces. But Champernown spent the summer raising a larger force and returned to La Rochelle – again with Ralegh behind him – on 20 September. It was a difficult crossing, hugging the Brittany peninsula and coasting around the northern rim of the Bay of Biscay, and Ralegh – ironically, despite his reputation, never a good sailor – would have taken some consolation in the following week spent enjoying all the good entertainment the port could offer: warfare was not the only education the campaign could offer a teenager.

On the 28th the summons came to join the main army. The hundred-strong company rode out under a black flag and the motto, *Finem det mihi virtus*: Let virtue be my end. But they were already too late. The Huguenot forces, under Coligny, had been ravaged, all but destroyed, at the Battle of Moncontour on 3 October. The remnants of the army were regrouping at Niort two days later when Champernown and his horsemen rode in, trumpets braying and standard flying. Their timing could hardly have been worse.

For Ralegh, there was a brutal lesson to learn. Over the coming days the men would owe their lives to brilliant but inglorious leadership – the antithesis, perhaps, of Champernown – and many more of their fallen comrades would have been alive still if such judgement had been exercised before the battle:

> A sure rule it is, that there is less dishonour to dislodge in the dark, than to be beaten in the light ... that worthy gentleman Count Lodovick of Nassau, brother to the late famous Prince of Orange, [made] the retreat at Moncontour with so great resolution as he saved one half of the Protestant army, then broken and disbanded; of which myself was an eye-witness, and was one of them that had cause to thank him for it.[7]

The virtue of retreat from an indefensible position was a lesson worth learning.

From Niort, Coligny took the men south, beside him the young Henri, Prince of Navarre, later Henri IV. Over the next month, ragged, almost without hope, they picked their way slowly down to the Huguenot stronghold of Montauban in south-west France, on the banks of the Tarn. 'They had not a horse who could put one foot before the other,' gloated the Catholic general Monluc.

Then from Montauban, the Huguenot army swept out to exact a kind of revenge, the wild and senseless violence of humiliation and defeat, rampaging through the countryside south of the Garonne burning the fields as they went, crossing into Languedoc and plunging down towards Toulouse with fire and slaughter in their train, and pressing on to Carcassonne, Montpellier and the sack of Nîmes.

There was some semblance of conventional military glory in all of this perhaps – the gluttonous rewards of rape and theft – but Ralegh's one recorded memory of the campaign – smoking Catholics out from a cave in the Languedoc where they had fled with their money and valuables – does little to suggest there was anything that tended more to virtue than terror. Such were the ways the politics of dynasty, marriage and faith played out in practice.

The campaign did, however, bring an end to the black-flagged cohort: most of Champernown's gentlemen died in France, Churchyard said. Their captain was among their number, dying an unglamorous illness-induced death in La Rochelle on 28 May.

Perhaps, in a sense, Ralegh outgrew the youthful idealism that led him to enlist in his cousin's company. Certainly such idealism as he may have had does not seem to have outlived the experience. Finding common cause with the Huguenots was, among other things, a noble gesture. In what sounds like a memory of soldiering through the winter of 1568–9, Ralegh would later write of how Alexander the Great was praised by his men for getting down from his horse and walking with them when they 'could not endure the extreme frost [or] make way but with extreme difficulty through the snow'.

Ralegh's own assessment is caustic:

> What can be more ridiculous than to bring other men into extremity thereby to show how well himself can endure it? . . . I shall rather commend that captain that makes careful provision for those that follow him, and that seeks wisely to prevent extreme necessity, than those witless arrogant fools, that make the vaunt of having endured equally with the common soldier, as if that were a matter of great glory and importance.[8]

Whatever Ralegh sought from his youthful experiences of war, its principal impact was to impress on him a profound understanding of the meaning and experience of defeat. He was still restlessly ambitious, but the nervous explosive energy that led him to war, the lust for limitless freedom of action, now also had to accommodate an acute awareness of failure and its shames, which in turn fuelled the anxiety, insecurities and doubt that came so fluently to him.

Ralegh's scant references to the war are downbeat, as well they might be. He gives every indication of thinking that life itself was generally preferable to the lively reputation of the grave, and that victory, howsoever won, always outweighed honourable defeat. It is hard to imagine him agreeing with the professional soldier Sir Roger Williams that, 'There can be no brave encounter without men slain on both sides . . . the more dies, the more honour to the fight.'[9]

Ralegh would not dispense with gesture; indeed, his

vocabulary of such rhetoric would be immense. But there was always an end in sight, a purpose, a reward. The French wars of religion were, by way of contrast, an obscene exercise in pointlessness, 'begun and carried on by some few great men of ambitious and turbulent spirits, deluding the people with the cloak and mask only of religion, to gain their assistance to what they did more especially aim at [... inflicting] barbarous murders, devastations and other calamities'.

If Ralegh ever believed in great causes for their own sake again, he kept it very well hidden. On this, he and Elizabeth were of a like mind.

IV: THE DECEITS OF FORTUNE

I have misgoverned my youth, I confess it: what shall I do then? Shall I yield to misery as a just plague appointed for my portion?

GEORGE GASCOIGNE

Some time in London in the autumn of 1577, Gabriel Harvey, a self-consciously brilliant young Cambridge academic, opened up his copy of *The Steele Glas*, a satirical poem by George Gascoigne, published the previous year. He flicked past the portrait of Gascoigne and his warm, almost affectionate letter of dedication to Lord Gray of Wilton, and alighted on one of the volume's three commendatory poems. It was signed: 'Walter Rawely of the Middle Temple'. A compulsive – indeed, obsessive – annotator of other men's work, Harvey paused to note down a rebus he had heard based on the poet's name:

The enemy to the stomach, and the word of disgrace
Is the gentleman's name, that bears the good face.[1]

Beside this, in the margin, Harvey wrote by way of explanation: 'Rawley'.

The poem for his friend Gascoigne was Ralegh's first step on the public stage. But, as Harvey's scrap of gossip shows, Ralegh was already enjoying a kind of celebrity in London's close-knit world. In 1577 Ralegh was still young: twenty-three or so. At six foot, he was exceptionally tall for the age, literally head and shoulders above most of his peers. His face was lean, sporting a neatly trimmed beard; his eyes – 'sour lidded', it was said – were blue, piercing and watchful beneath dark eyelashes and thick, dark unruly hair. There is laughter behind them, but it may be at our expense.

Later versions of the rebus – it would make numerous appearances in commonplace books over the decades – replace the word 'good' with 'bold', 'effeminate' or 'brazen', reflecting changing attitudes to Ralegh's meteoric rise at court and widespread distaste for his arrogance, a meme that attached to him early.[2] By and large, the more people saw of him, the less they liked, and the contempt was mutual.

But for now, that is all ahead. In the autumn of 1577 Ralegh has, to all intents and purposes, arrived.

After his return from France at the end of the previous decade Ralegh retreated from the record, and when he resurfaced in 1574 he seems a less confident figure: indecisive, half-hearted, adrift. Like many aspiring gentlemen, Ralegh attended one of the two great universities – in his case, Oriel College, Oxford – but he failed to persevere with his studies and apparently did not matriculate. The slow arduous route to influence and power through formal education was not for him; patience, it would seem, was not one of his virtues.

From Oxford, Ralegh made his way to London. It was an obvious choice as a stepping stone to preferment, but there is one point to make about Ralegh's decision that is easily overlooked, and that is what he has not chosen: the sea.

Privateering and other, more licit kinds of trade could have certainly made him wealthy, but he clearly wanted something more than that, or something else. Perhaps he didn't yet know what himself.

In fact, the first documentary evidence for Ralegh's arrival in the capital is as one of a small flurry of West Country students switching from Lyon's Inn, an old Inn of Chancery just off the Strand, and already in decline by the early 1570s, to one of the Inns of Court, the more powerful Middle Temple, in the first two months of 1575.[3] The first to go, Peter Carew on 29 January, was a kinsman of Ralegh's, albeit distantly so even by an Elizabethan's generous understanding of the term. Another Devon student, George Eveleigh, remained close enough to Ralegh for the latter to petition Sir Walter Mildmay, Chancellor of the Exchequer, on his behalf in 1586 with regard to unpaid tax liabilities.[4] The third was Hugh Michell, of Trelow in Cornwall.

Switches of Inn were relatively rare, so it is more than likely that there was an element of herd instinct in the move, cleaving to the comfort of the local and known; after all, Carew and Eveleigh lived no more than twenty miles from Ralegh's childhood home. Moreover, they were all Oxford alumni: Carew and Eveleigh were fresh down from Exeter College.[5] They were joined before the year was out by Richard Champernown, the son of Ralegh's late cousin and captain, Henry Champernown. The details reinforce the sense of this being a Ralegh with whom we are unfamiliar, for while he has rejected his father's ships as the basis for a career – Ralegh was always a man who wanted to be somewhere else, doing something different – he is nevertheless diffident about the alternatives, seeming socially insecure, staying close to the familiar and known, nervously finding his feet in the capital. He could not decide between the two worlds – private and public, parochial and national – that called him; indeed, in some senses his whole career was an attempt to reconcile the two, a fact that Elizabeth alone seems to have acknowledged.

Ralegh, 'gent., son of Walter R., of Budleighe, Devon, esq', was the last of the group, joining as a bencher on 27 February.[6] As with the move to London, the choice of Middle Temple was an expression of ambition, even as Ralegh's diffidence led him to cling to the security of kinsmen and other kindred spirits. Lyon's Inn was technically affiliated to the rival Inner Temple, and its students had been able to transfer to it freely for nearly twenty years, so Middle Temple must have had something specific to offer him. One factor may have been size: the Middle Temple was a bigger stage for an aspiring young man and with some 200 members sharing 138 chambers it was more than twice the size of Lyon's Inn.[7]

Moreover, Middle Temple was very much on the rise. Its magnificent new hall had been completed only a couple of years previously. The hall still stands today, much as Ralegh would have seen it: its deep hammerbeam roof suspended improbably over the oak benches; its great carved screen, writhing with vines and wild, rude figures. Ralegh's own coat of arms, which now features in one of the windows, is a more recent addition.

But Middle Temple also had close associations with both the West Country and with England's seamen. Drake, although not a bencher, was a regular visitor, and one of the architects of Elizabethan maritime expansionism, Richard Hakluyt the elder, was still a barrister here when Ralegh arrived in 1575, books on cosmography and maps strewn about his chambers.

Hakluyt's advice and learning was highly valued among the nation's merchants and adventurers, and Ralegh's half-brother, Sir Humphrey Gilbert, sought him out when planning his 1578 voyage to the New World, in which Ralegh would play a leading role. It was Hakluyt's namesake, cousin and ward who would write *The principal navigations, voiages, traffiques and discoveries of the English nation*, better known as Hakluyt's *Voyages and Discoveries*. He and Ralegh had probably already met at Oxford and the two would become close friends, sharing a vision of England's imperial transatlantic destiny that was both providential and highly personal. But while belief in America made national greatness and vast private reward almost indistinguishable, it also had many of the attributes of a cult. Enthusiasm was limited to a few adherents, who had access to and control over the secret knowledge that fed their faith; setbacks, when they came, only fuelled their zeal for vindication.

The Temple itself was towards the western edge of the city, the limits of which were marked by the Temple Bar on Fleet Street a few yards to the north, where Wyatt and his men had finally surrendered. The phrase 'from the Tower to the Temple' was commonly used to encompass the great sweep of the city. Beyond the Bar was the Strand, lined on its riverside with great medieval episcopal mansions – now occupied by noblemen and courtiers, among them the earls of Leicester, Bedford and Arundel – the road running west to Charing Cross, where it followed the curve of the river to the south and the court in the gaggle of buildings that comprised the palace of Whitehall, and then on to Westminster.

To the east was the city, up Fleet Street and through Ludgate. Northwards were open fields to Holborn: Lincoln's Inn and St Giles were still pasture. The Bermudas, an ancient liberty and safe haven for cut-throats, pimps and thieves, lay a stone's throw to the west. But the heart of the Temple was its church, like all Templar churches based on the Dome of the Rock in Jerusalem and the only church in London to be circular rather than cruciform. It was, like St Paul's, much more than a place of worship: it was one of the principal meeting places in the city – to wait here was to 'walk the round' – and its pillars hung with the petitions of the poor. The narrow lanes outside likewise thronged with supplicant clients in search of redress, with merchants on business, with pleasure-seekers, cutpurses, prostitutes.

The study of law itself was just one of the reasons that drew young men to the Inns of Court. Proximity to power; networking; a London base: motives varied. Certainly for Ralegh, the law was no draw at all: he later admitted that 'If I ever read a word of the law or statutes before I was prisoner in the Tower, God confound me.'[8]

Drawing in a socially diverse range of young men, from noblemen to threadbare country gentlemen – Shakespeare's Justice Shallow, sequestered in rural Gloucestershire, was an Inns of Court man – the Inns were a meeting place for the sometimes dissonant streams of contemporary thought. The intellectual, cultural, political and religious currents of the day flowed through them, often finding voluble, sometimes vicious expression in the ambitions and activities of the students. John Hawkins, another Devon seafarer with Middle Temple connections, was stabbed as he rode near Temple Bar one October morning in 1573; Hawkins was lucky to live. His attacker was a fanatical Puritan Middle Temple man – unhinged, in fact – who mistook Hawkins for Sir Christopher Hatton, whom he considered friendly to recusancy.[9] Hatton's real crime, however, was to be the queen's current favourite.

We might usefully think of the Inns as a kind of club, a place to be seen and associated with, as much as somewhere to pore over precedents or attend interminable legal moots. Those who attended the Inns had earned themselves an unattractive reputation in London which had little enough to do with scholarship: they were louche young men, drunken, violent, libidinal, vain.

Indeed, Ralegh and Gilbert's friend Thomas Churchyard has left us an acidly ambivalent portrait of Ralegh and his peers in a little-regarded poem written the following autumn. They are gallants from the glittering court, parading through the streets in their gorgeous clothes, swaggering proudly – 'jetting' is Churchyard's word – through St Paul's, vainglorious, 'making love/To every painted post', but thirsting for experience, lost in wanton revels all year round, greedily sniffing out every feast, dancing, running to cockfights and worse, palming cards and cheating at dice, roisting, wild of tongue.[10]

This cannot be taken wholly at face value of course: the callow self-mythologizing of many young men is evident behind Churchyard's description, and we know from another member of Ralegh's circle that, for all the braggadocio, some were in fact notoriously bad gamblers. The poet and polemicist George Whetstone, another Inns of Court man, writing of his fellow students, noted that like many of those new to London they were easy marks for professional thieves: 'Expert shifters ... dally with young novices as a cat doeth with a mouse; yet before bedtime they will make their purses as empty of money as the cat the mouses head of brains'.[11] Ralegh is not so certainly in this group, however: he later won heavily from the young Earl of Northumberland at cards.

But, it must be said, Ralegh's time at Middle Temple seems to have been notable less for his studies – which reveal no more commitment than his time at Oxford – than for his extensive exploration of all such vices, together no doubt with others that have gone unremarked. He has shed his insecurities, or learned how to hide them behind a more brazen persona. Stephen Powle, a lifelong friend of Ralegh's, had joined Middle Temple in 1574; some fifteen years later, he would affectionately recall 'my bedfellow at the Inns of Court and many years' companion, riotous, lascivious and incontinent Rawlegh'.[12]

Ralegh and Powle roomed in the old medieval Templars Hall, which had been converted into chambers a year or two before, and which stood off Middle Temple Lane to the east, near the Temple Church. The vivid image Powle conjures of his friend is entirely of a piece with one of the seventeenth-century antiquarian John Aubrey's more salacious anecdotes:

> He loved a wench well; and one time getting up one of the maids of honour up against a tree in a wood ('twas his first Lady) who seemed at first boarding to be something fearful of her honour, and modest, she cried, 'Sweet Sir Walter, what do you me ask? Will you undo me? Nay, sweet Sir Walter! Sweet Sir Walter! Sir Walter!' At last, as the danger and the pleasure at the same time grew higher, she cried in the ecstasy, 'Swisser Swatter Swisser Swatter'.

Aubrey's facts are often wrong and his gossip by its nature unverifiable, but there is undoubtedly truth in his reflection of the public *personae* of his subjects, the image they projected intentionally or otherwise, to their peers. Whether Ralegh was more sexually predatory than his contemporaries is unknowable, that he was considered so seems unassailable. He seems to us to have been compulsively seductive, the libidinal drive part of a wider need for intellectual and social dominion: '[Ralegh] desired to seem to be able to sway all men's fancies, all men's courses', observed his gambling friend, Northumberland.

And, of course, it was a reputation energized, its frisson enhanced, by Ralegh's later proximity to Elizabeth. There seems an inevitability to the attraction of these apparently exclusive, competing iconic forces; and, drawn together as they were, the charge generated by their collision crackled with possibilities.

The documentary record for Ralegh's early years in London is thin, but what evidence there is points to a lack of focus, indiscipline, an unwillingness – or inability – to exert any self-control. It is of a piece with his apparent aimlessness and drift, and it infected those around him too. Von Wedel joked that England's absurd inheritance laws meant that eldest sons received everything and that younger sons, like Ralegh, either entered some kind of office or pursued highway robbery.[13] At this point Ralegh could go either way.

It was a problem that had been magnified by Henry's dissolution of the monasteries, which had erased a great swathe of career opportunities, the church hierarchy having been a rich source of employment for younger sons and scions alike. Ironically, this happened at precisely the same time that progressive Reformation ideology was driving an expansion in education – biblical exegesis required supple minds, after all – equipping many bright and not so bright young men with a tool for which there were insufficient uses in society. In one stroke, that exemplary Elizabethan figure, the malcontent, was born: intelligent, educated, disaffected, mostly unemployed.

A month or two after Harvey made a note of his name, Ralegh emerged onto the record again, in unpromising circumstances. It was 17 December 1577 and he stood before a Middlesex justice of the peace named Jasper Fisher, a man whose own name – ironically given Ralegh's future reputation – was a byword in London for vanity and ambition. In fact, they may well have been standing in Fisher's vast new-built Bishopsgate mansion, a lavish attempt to buy social status on borrowed money, known across the city as Fisher's Folly.[14] Two men stood with Ralegh, one of them his servant, William Pansfurthe.[15]

We know a little of what had occurred: the stuff of low drama. Pansfurthe and his brother Richard, both servants of Ralegh's, together with eight others, had been out after curfew the previous evening, and had been challenged by the night watch. 'Disturbing the peace' was the official charge. They were passing a place called Wenloxbarne, a former predendary manor for St Paul's; the road between the City wall at Aldersgate and Ralegh's out-of-town lodgings in Islington cut through its fields.

On being challenged the men drew swords, one of them shouting out to the watch in the winter dark: 'Rascals and drunken slaves come and ye dare and we will be your deaths'. Whatever the state of the watch, Ralegh's men had themselves been drinking. They then fled. The night watch came after, intent on arrest. The accused turned, swords at the ready, and attacked the watchmen with such brutality that the constable of Wenloxbarne, Antony Howson, was expected to lose his life. The gang then made away to the nearby house of an acquaintance.[16]

The back story to this is lost. It may in any case be trivial, a drunken nothing, we cannot tell: the violent, beer-sodden servant is hardly a new character in literature, or history. But neither is the servant as proxy for master. Indeed, the record is littered with them, and, as we shall see, some of Ralegh's men will have an untold story to tell about his rise to favour.

The Pansfurthe brothers may have been out on Ralegh's business; they may simply have been drinking for too long. Either way, the Pansfurthes do Ralegh no credit: their behaviour is too close to what we know of his own from these years.

Although the man Ralegh whom Fisher saw may be indistinct to us, Fisher saw enough to size him up, no doubt on the basis of Ralegh's fastidiously expensive clothing, as a man with money to spare. Ralegh would always dress for effect, but now – perhaps more than at any time in his career – it was a kind of artifice, an illusion. 'It was a long time before he could brag of more than he carried at his back,' a friend said, but that was missing the point a little: as the antiquarian Thomas Fuller recorded, he spent most of his money on clothes.[17] Appearances were deceptive, as they were intended to be, 'there being nothing wherein nature so much triumpheth, as in dissimilitude', Ralegh said.[18]

The sureties Fisher required for William Pansfurthe were high: he demanded £200, £150 of which would be from Ralegh's purse. These were, by any measure, significant sums of money – particularly for an offence like breach of the peace. Looking through the Middlesex Session Rolls, £40 seems more the going rate, although the individual justice had wide discretion. By way of further comparison, in September 1589 when Kit Marlowe's friend Thomas Watson killed a man in self-defence in Hog Lane, across the way from Fisher's Folly, his bail, too, was set at just £40.[19]

Two days later, it was Richard Pansfurthe's turn to appear in front of Fisher. This time, the sums demanded were £80 plus 100 marks – perhaps £140 in total – and Ralegh ran out of money. He could only afford to contribute the 100 marks; two friends stood for the outstanding money.

It may be no coincidence then that whereas on 17 December, Ralegh was noted as merely a gentleman of Islington, two days later he was emphatically 'de curia' – of the court – applying a little none-too-discreet leverage on the justice, who had greeds of his own to feed.

This then is how, almost in silence, history marks the introduction of Ralegh at court to his queen. We do not know when or where or through whose offices it was effected. All that can be said is that Elizabeth's favour did not come quickly or easily to him, that whatever the strength of the bond they shared through the Champernown sisters, it was not enough to buy access or reward. To exploit its intimacy, he would first have to get close to her. With Elizabeth, everything had to be earned.

As for Ralegh, however obscurely, he was in the queen's service now and the challenge for him was to gain her attention, to prove that he was worthy of her interest, of her affection and love. But how much was he prepared to give?

Contemporary political theory taught that the monarch had two bodies: like their subjects, princes had a human, mortal body – the body natural – with all its weaknesses and flaws, but they also had a second notional body – the body politic – occupying the same corporeal space as the first, which was a vessel for the divinity that sanctioned kingship.[20] Ralegh's friend, the poet Edmund Spenser, used the theory to explain, in a 1589 letter to Ralegh, his treatment of Elizabeth in *The Faerie Queene*. In the eponymous queen herself, he wrote:

I conceive the most excellent and glorious person of our sovereign the queen . . . And yet in some places else, I do otherwise shadow her. For considering she beareth two persons, the one of a most royal queen or empress, the other of a most virtuous and beautiful lady, this latter part in some places I do express in Belphoebe.

Spenser goes on to acknowledge that he had drawn on Ralegh's own characterization of Elizabeth for his portrait of Belphoebe, the intimate and human aspect of the queen.

When Ralegh knelt before her for the first time, no such distinction was possible: he had to address both aspects of Elizabeth simultaneously, and his was an act of reverence and submission to the authority of the monarchy before it was a display of human courtesy: he would have seen her as at once an unmarried woman of, by Tudor standards, more than middle age and a quasi-divine figure, a literal embodiment of the nation's greatness and safety. Unfortunately for Ralegh, in this instance both were notoriously difficult to please.

In December 1577, Elizabeth was forty-four; Ralegh had been just four years old when she ascended the throne. Her physical beauty was beside the point: her presence was compelling enough – she was the queen after all – but she was certainly striking. Her face was long, oval, with thin lips and a strong profile that echoed her father's; red-gold hair, its brilliance softened by age, fell in ringlets over bone-white skin; and fair eyebrows arched over intense, autumnal eyes – bright, lively, penetrating, inquisitive, knowing, insightful – that seemed black to some in the torchlit, shadowed spaces of the court.

People noticed her hands too – as she wanted them to – long, elegant fingers of which Elizabeth was evidently proud; it may be no coincidence that she chose as a remembrance of her mother something she wore on her hand. Opinions were divided on her height; perhaps not everyone knew she wore heels.

The hands are revealing: like her, they were always busy. Her energy levels – physical, nervous, intellectual – were exhausting, and as a result her health was resilient but unstable, if not exceptionally so given the pace she set. The fashionable pallor that otherwise seemed pleasingly translucent, radiant even, in health, in illness resembled the bloodless flesh of a corpse.[21]

Averse to strong smells and perhaps to sensory overload in general, she rarely drank wine, disliking its disabling effect on her judgement, and when she did drink, it was always mixed with three parts water.[22] At mealtimes she confined herself to watered beer. She relaxed by translating Seneca, it was said. A woman who ate little and slept less, she talked late into the night with those who could stay with her. It was particularly onerous for Cecil, who was usually working by six a.m.[23]

Elizabeth's mornings were slower – she didn't like them, in fact – but she was fond of brisk winter walks through the frost in her gardens to make her feel awake again, alive. Indeed, brisk was her preferred pace for life: she habitually threw herself into the most vigorous dances at court and loved to hunt, too, riding ferociously hard late into the afternoon, outpacing even her master of the horse.

These traits reveal how she coped with her fear of imprisonment and constraint: they were visceral reactions against a sense of confinement that seems to have haunted her since her incarceration under Mary. Her own court, for all the liberty it afforded her, was suffocatingly claustrophobic and impossible to escape from entirely. After her death people remembered her fondness for pacing in her galleries or out in her gardens buried in conversation with her closest friends, harried by time, by events and their pressures; but also how she used to rest in the afternoons, drained by the insistence of such things, lying on a richly embroidered Indian couch in her privy chambers, still talking, the windows open for breezes that came through the gardens, savouring the few transitory breaths of reprieve.[24]

Talk was her element, however. Dazzling in her wit – by turns self-deprecating, affectionate, sarcastic, acid-sharp – Elizabeth was intoxicatingly verbal. When required, she had a bravura disdain for honesty that only someone in complete command of their tongue could aspire to. It is no wonder men failed to penetrate her intentions.[25] Yet with her facility for language came a certain bitterness at its limitations: as she told the French ambassador, 'words are no better than leaves'.[26]

Action began, she sometimes seemed to think, where talk ended; talk itself only offered another subtle kind of prison.

Always attentive, she was an acute listener, solicitous of confidence no less than kindness, with the rare ability to make all those who talked with her feel as if they alone were favoured with her ear.[27] But there was a darker side to this skill, and she worked to catch interlocutors out with indiscretions and inconsistencies, lulling such natural caution as they had with her kindness and charm and then pouncing with almost vicious pleasure when they said too much. Councillors were summoned one by one to discuss matters of state late into the night, only to be challenged the following morning on their contradictions, disagreements and dishonesties.[28] Hatton put it well: 'The queen did fish for men's souls and had so sweet a bait that no one could escape her network.'[29] The analogy drips with the queasy insight of one who had been snared.

She had too an easy, disarming informality that could turn in an instant into a towering royal disdain, haughty, implacable, terrifying.[30] As the daughter of Henry VIII, there was a viciously imperious side to her that left no doubt as to her strength and power: she inherited all of her father's natural authority and was unafraid to wield it. 'She seems to me incomparably more feared than her sister and gives her orders and has her way as absolutely as her father did,' noted De Feria, the first Spanish ambassador to her court, warily.[31] Even her longest-standing and most loyal minister, William Cecil, later Lord Burghley, who had been part of her household since 1550, could be reduced to tears at the mere thought of what she would say to him when things went awry.[32]

Those who lived and worked alongside her were never sure what to expect of her, nor confident in their predictions of her wants. This was, at least in part, policy on her part: throughout her reign she managed those around her with a judicious use of uncertainty and deferred gratification, and deftly played off those insecurities and hopes against one another. It was bound up in her caution, another legacy of the Marian exile, the ingrained security she found in her own comfortable deceits: 'the art of dissembling with others had stamped such a deep impression upon the queen's own nature and passions, as she fixed upon nothing with precipitation,' observed one contemporary. 'The distrust she had of all sides obliging her to the justice of equal hearings.'[33]

To a man, her government bemoaned this, regarding it as indecision pure and simple, an inscrutable feminine disease – even Leicester, who had known her since childhood.[34] They experienced it as debilitating and atrophic, a peculiarly enervating kind of torture best articulated by Sir Thomas Smith, Burghley's successor as secretary, writing to his predecessor in a series of letters in early March 1575:

> This irresolution doth weary and kill her ministers, destroy her actions and overcome all good designs and counsels . . . I wait whilst I neither have eyes to see or legs to stand upon. And yet these delays grieve me more and will not let me sleep in the night . . . It maketh me weary of my life . . . the time passing almost irrecuperable, the advantage lost, the charges continuing, nothing resolved, and therefore, such number of things unanswered, whereupon her Majesty's ministers lie still in suspense . . . I can neither get the other letters signed, nor the letter already signed . . . permitted to be sent away, but day by day, and hour by hour, deferred till anon, soon and tomorrow. . .[35]

They failed to recognize this for what it was: a discreet but unyielding form of control. After all, Elizabeth had no trouble reaching quick and firm – even brutal – decisions when the moment required it. When she took power she quickly acted to people the court with those dependent on her, bravely asserting a discontinuity with the treacherous politics of the Henrician era which had dominated much of the century. It was Elizabeth who demanded that Norfolk's secretaries be threatened with torture when news of his treason broke: if they persisted in being uncooperative, she wrote to the interrogators, 'then you shall cause them to be put to the rack and to find the taste thereof till they shall deal more plainly or until you see fit'.[36]

This then was the Elizabeth whose favour Ralegh sought, but the disparities in their relative statures reveals the apparent absurdity of such an aspiration. She was a prince with almost two decades of experience negotiating the byzantine complexities of politics and religion, international, national and intensely personal. He was a young man experienced in military defeat but little else, living a kind of extended childhood, unable to stick at anything long, hedonistic, headstrong, uncertain of his ambitions and uncommitted to anything except himself – and with apparently little enough enthusiasm even for that.

It is no surprise he has failed to attract her attention, then: he is a blur of his own making. It will take a crisis of his own for Ralegh to come to his senses.

V: THE WORLD'S EYE

My life is in the open, and I have so so many witnesses that I cannot understand how so bad a judgment can have been formed of me

ELIZABETH TO GUZMAN DE SILVA, SPANISH AMBASSADOR

In the centralized state that England was becoming the court would be a single place, a building; indeed, Elizabeth's court spent most of her reign at the royal palace of Whitehall, particularly over the winter months. But neither Whitehall, nor Greenwich, nor Hampton Court nor any other royal palace defined the Elizabethan court. In most meaningful senses, the court was wherever the queen happened to be; it was why she could never escape it.

The court was not a building, nor even necessarily a system, although it was also that; it was a social organism, a household, a hive. But perhaps 'hive' is too easy, too stable; the court was rather a swarm, an ecosystem, rigidly structured, stultifying and oppressive in its intensity, yet permeable and indeterminate, too, endlessly ordering itself, gorging on the favour of its sun.

For Ralegh, at the margins, the centre where Elizabeth presided was immeasurably distant: his many peers at court were not merely an intimidating barrier by virtue of their number, they were inevitably largely hostile, since for Ralegh to succeed, they must fail. The rewards, the favours and gifts were finite: one man's gain was another man's loss.

Two bodies of men protected the queen's person: the gentlemen pensioners, an elite ceremonial bodyguard some fifty strong – although they usually worked in teams of twelve – who wore elaborate gold chains and carried gilded halberds, and whose status meant that they were permitted to accompany the queen in the presence chamber. More numerous were the yeoman of the guard, of whom there were 130 or so under their captain Sir Christopher Hatton, who stood guard outside the chamber.

The court was still modelled on – still was – a household teeming with countless minor servants: grooms of the chamber; yeoman waiters; officers of the spicery; porters; sergeants at arms; messengers; yeomen of the Mall; a yeoman of the flagons; the marshall; footmen; musicians; the surveyor of the ways; officers of the buttery; the cooks and boilers; officers of the cellar; the heralds at arms; and so on.[1] But they – like the ushers and pages, the clerks of the counting house, and maids of the wardrobe – were merely the footsoldiers, as it were. More significant household servants, who also had their own staff in attendance, included Lord Chamberlain Thomas Radcliffe, the Earl of Sussex; Sir Francis Knollys, the treasurer of the household; Sir Thomas Heneage, the treasurer of the chamber; Sir John Fortescue, master of the great wardrobe; Sir James Crofts, comptroller and Richard Warde, cofferer of the household.

Some of these figures also held positions in the emerging parallel structures of the state – Sussex, Knollys and Heneage, for example, were privy councillors – but it would be a mistake to read too much into the distinction between the two worlds: they were one and the same. The authority of such men was personal, in essence derived from the favour of the queen, and their influence spread as far as their discretion allowed.

Indeed, the Privy Council was by no means the only, or even consistently the most important, arena for discussion of matters of state. Elizabeth acted, both formally and informally, to restrict its power and ensure that it did not presume too much on her right to govern. On the second day of her reign she dismissed as many as twenty of Mary's privy councillors and appointed only five new councillors of her own in their place. She would always guard the gift of membership closely: Heneage had to wait nearly thirty years for his elevation to it; Ralegh never made it at all, much to his chagrin.

Yet while this smaller Privy Council was certainly a more effective deliberative body, Elizabeth customarily undermined her council's authority by seeking advice from outside it, both in ad hoc discussion with privileged individual councillors – in particular Leicester, Sussex, Cecil, and, later, Walsingham – and also in conversation and soundings with trusted ministers, diplomats, courtiers and merchants such as Nicholas Throckmorton, Heneage and Sir Thomas Gresham, although there were many others besides.

In this way, Elizabeth could both indulge her favourite activity – conversation – and also gain access to a much wider and more sensitive range of sources than she could ever hope to access formally. Quite apart from the numerous webs of familial loyalties and affections, of patronage and duty that were interwoven across the polity, many of those at Elizabeth's court had significant contact networks across Europe from their years of Marian exile; Gresham's commercial operations, meanwhile, stretched from Sweden to Tripoli. Much has been written about the effectiveness of Walsingham's intelligence network, but the reality is that it was just one among many. Elizabeth plugged into them all.[2]

Alongside these exclusively male societies were the equally unofficial channels of intelligence and patronage inherent in Elizabeth's privy chambers, a distinct economy exclusive of the wider household, and the only networks which also empowered women with political muscle. By their very nature these were yet more ad hoc, conversational, not exactly informal by virtue of their function, but certainly social, unrecorded, and there is no doubting their influence on both judgements and events at Elizabeth's court: 'Learn before your access her majesty's disposition by some in the privy chamber, with whom you must keep credit,' recommended Sir Robert Beale, clerk to the Privy Council. 'That will stand you in much stead.'[3] This had been Kat Astley's realm, confirmed by Elizabeth when she had been queen for little more than twenty-four hours.

There were of course also plenty at court who had no formal position at all, and for whom attendance was simply the physical manifestation of their last best hopes. It is into this category that the young Ralegh uneasily falls; unfortunately for his prospects, there were many others just like him. He had already made clear through his indolence at both Oxford and the Inns of Court a disinterest in formal and vocational education as the basis for a career, but how then was he to earn his favour? The possibilities as evidenced by his circles of friends offered many lessons but little in the way of certainty.

Harvey doesn't say so, but the rebus on Ralegh which he noted in the margins of *The Steele Glas* was spoken by Henry Noel, a young Leicestershire gentleman. Noel was an integral part of Ralegh's circle in these early years and they had much in common: both men were younger sons in an age in which almost all wealth and privilege accrued to the eldest son. Theirs was a world of conspicuous extravagance and artful self-mythologizing necessarily built out of personal debt and a hand-to-mouth desperation, an existential need to be useful.

It wasn't simply that these men needed employment; they needed a stage, an arena in which to both demonstrate and amplify their talents and worth. 'Where many younger sons, of younger brothers, have neither lands nor means to uphold themselves . . . there can it not be avoided but the whole body of the state (howsoever otherwise healthfully disposed) should suffer anguish by the grievance of these ill-affected members,' Ralegh would later write, somewhat sententiously.[4]

Noel was a few years Ralegh's senior; he had left Cambridge without a degree and was trying to attract preferment at court. He was responding to Ralegh's own rebus on his own name:

The word of denial, and the letter of fifty
Makes the gentleman's name that will never be thrifty.

Ralegh's is the crueller, more candid judgement, but he was right in his assessment: Noel was notoriously extravagant, and as a consequence endlessly in debt. Sir Francis Bacon, looking back from 1625 remembered one of Noel's mordant, self-deprecating witticisms: 'Henry Noel would say that the courtiers were like the fasting days; they were next the holy days, but in themselves were the most meagre days of the week.'[5]

Noel was the epitome of that curious species, the courtier as adornment. A skilled dancer and musician, his primary fame at court would come from his status as a lead participant in one of the most self-consciously extravagant spectacles in the court calendar, the Accession Day tilts.

Aside from the social and therefore political cachet of participation, the tilts were an opportunity to create or reposition your image at court, to display, in Ralegh's phrase 'the false beauty of our apparent actions'.[6] Each year, tilters spent months developing symbolic disguises or personae, which would then inform the designs on their armour, their horse's furniture, the liveries of the serving men, and the chariots on which the tilters made their entry to the tiltyard – often drawn by exotic animals, among them lions or camels. The device would be explicated to the queen and the wider audience – the tilts drew thousands of spectators each year – by one of the tilter's servants in a speech, often humorous but always pointed, and in an impresa, or painted shield, gifted to the queen on the tilter's behalf.

It was not wholly unreasonable to seek preferment this way – Christopher Hatton for one had caught the queen's eye when dancing the galliard, and he ended his career as lord chancellor – but the risks of the strategy were obvious: the effort of maintaining the fiction was considerable, competition was great and the expense even greater. Debt, perhaps the most pervasive reality in the life of aspiring courtiers, intensified the challenge yet further; for some, at least, it became too much.

Another close friend of Ralegh's, the soldier-poet George Gascoigne, author of *The Steele Glas*, was one such gentleman. Some twenty years Ralegh's senior, George Gascoigne was the elder son of a prosperous and successful Bedford landowner. He too had a spell at the Inns of Court, in his case at Gray's Inn, before seeking favour at court, seduced by the fantasy of wealth and pleasure it seemed to offer.

> The stately pomp of princes and their peers,
> Did seem to swim in floods of beaten gold,
> The wanton world of young delightful years,
> Was not unlike a heaven for to behold.

Gascoigne spent prodigiously, as Noel would after him, to pretend a status, a lifestyle, an attitude, he could not in fact sustain.

By his own account, this was not only unsuccessful as a strategy, but also brought him close to ruin. This failure was a scab Gascoigne returned to pick more than once in his work, not least because it was a highly public shame: fifteen years after Gascoigne's death, the caustic pamphleteer Thomas Nashe could still joke about 'having sung George Gascoigne's Counter-tenor' as a euphemism for debt, the Counter being one of Tudor London's debtors' prisons.[7]

Gascoigne's life seems to offer Ralegh a wide selection of such cautionary tales. He was not the first to seek both refuge from his creditors and possible personal fortune on the battlefield, nor would he be the last to discover the impossibility of such hopes. Gascoigne's first campaign was Sir Humphrey Gilbert's ill-fated Flanders expedition in the summer and autumn of 1572, and his friendship with Gilbert seems to have been the sum of Gascoigne's rewards. He was later widely suspected by the Dutch of having sold the Flemish town of Leiden to the Spanish in return for safe passage for his men in February 1574, adding betrayal to the already long list of his perceived faults, which by now also included atheism, espionage and manslaughter.[8]

It is presumably through Gilbert that Ralegh met Gascoigne, although he also knew Ralegh's cousin Edward Denny well. Other mutual friends included the poets Churchyard and Whetstone.

Having failed at soldiering, Gascoigne then tried to refashion himself again, this time turning to literature as a way of earning patronage. Indeed, his reputation as it has come down to us is as a literary innovator: to him we award the first English prose comedy; one of the first English tragedies; the first non-dramatic satire, which is also the first blank verse poem; one of the first English novels; one of the first English masques; the first piece of English literary criticism; and so on.

All those firsts are significant, not least because there were no seconds: Gascoigne rarely followed anything up or repeated himself, thus failing to build a consistent reputation for anything except, perhaps, inconstancy, a not particularly saleable commodity. The superficiality of the man, but also something of his charm, is apparent in his swaggering admission that he wrote, as much as anything, for the pleasure of celebrity: 'A fancy fed me once, to write in verse and rhyme . . ./To hear it said there goeth the man that writes so well.'[9]

By the time of *The Steele Glas*, however, even those hopes were dissipating. When Gabriel Harvey opened his copy of that book, the first thing he would have seen was a portrait of the author on the verso. George Gascoigne looks out at the reader, books over his left shoulder, an arquebus and other weapons over his right. Beneath the portrait is Gascoigne's motto: *tam marti quam mercurio* – made for war as much as wisdom.

But it is not in fact the motto, or the ephemeral signifiers behind Gascoigne that draw the eye. It is the face: worn, desperate, old and, as it turned out, a year from death. It is the face of a man cornered, an implication that is enhanced by the books and weapons: they frame him; but they also confine him. He is trapped between them – and the narrow choices they offer – and his eyes seem to say that he knows it.

It says a lot about Ralegh that he revered Gascoigne: after his friend's death in the autumn of 1577, around the time Harvey was scratching his notes in *The Steele Glas*, Ralegh adopted Gascoigne's last motto as his own. A man of action and a man of judgement: that was the pitch, and like today's corporate slogans, it was notionally accurate, but also wishful. It said much more about how Ralegh wanted to be seen than how he actually was.

But then Ralegh and his peers were comfortable making and remaking themselves: 'We labour hard to publish our abilities and conceal our infirmities,' he wrote, 'and our inquiry into ourselves is so slight and partial that few men are really what they appear to themselves to be.'[10] The acknowledgement of self-delusion, developed from an observation about the necessary deceptions of public life, is pure Ralegh: perceptive and self-critical, intellectually honest yet also a cynical affirmation of amoral values. This self-awareness is a key reason why Ralegh did not face the same challenges met by many of his peers when the perfected idea of themselves, transposed out of the controlled environment of the court, collided with more stubborn unpliable realities in the world beyond. He may have traded in illusions, but he held precious few himself beyond the great promise of America.

Nevertheless there was much for Ralegh to think about in Gascoigne's fate with regard to his own nascent career, and the eventual decision to adopt his friend's motto suggests that he wanted to redeem him, to vindicate an idea that Gascoigne, defeated by poverty and debt, articulated but could not embody. The Gascoigne Ralegh knew was a failure – at best, a serial under-achiever. Harvey's ultimate assessment of his sometime friend is damning but judicious:

> Want of resolution and constancy, marred his wit and undid himself ... Many other have maintained themselves gallantly upon the sum of his qualities ... It is not marvel, though he had cold success in his actions, that in his studies and loves, thought upon the wars; in the wars, mused upon his studies and loves.[11]

It was a lesson Ralegh would take to heart. But not yet.

Ralegh may have learned most, however, from perhaps the least reputable of his friends: Thomas Cobham, one of those who stood bond for Ralegh's servants in front of Jasper Fisher.

Cobham was a well-known London figure, to be sure – in some ways a figure on the national stage – but for all the wrong reasons. He stalks the pages of the state papers for two decades, a mischievous and malevolent shadow the regime seemed incapable of dispelling. Yet his life has the archetypal arc of a certain kind of courtier, great youthful hopes trending always down, horizons shrinking, options closing.

Cobham was born in 1533, a younger son in the most powerful family in Kent, that of George Brooke, ninth Baron Cobham. Along with several family members, he was active in Wyatt's Kentish rebellion of 1554; indeed Holinshed identifies him as one of the ringleaders despite being just twenty years old. He was sentenced to a traitor's death, but Mary commuted his sentence after his father begged her forgiveness, much to the disgust of the imperial ambassador.[12]

He was, however, confined to the Tower for several years; his deep-etched graffiti, 'Thomas Cobham, 1555', can still be seen carved into a window frame overlooking Tower Green. Two of his books still survive in the library of Magdalen College, Oxford – bequeathed by Ralegh's future brother-in-law Arthur Throckmorton. Both volumes carry Cobham's own scratched verses bemoaning the actions of fortune; pitying himself, his sorrows; hoping for 'the happy day' ahead.[13]

Released in early 1557, Cobham nevertheless quickly showed how little he was capable of mastering himself: compulsive, careless, changeable, a sail for every wind. By the end of the summer he was back in the Tower, having stabbed a Catholic in a fight in Fleet Street and, on another occasion, having led a gang of thieves into the house of an uncle in Blackfriars and stolen 200 marks.[14]

In March 1564 he was arrested for an act of piracy against Spanish shipping in the Bay of Biscay, which had descended into a vicious and prolonged gunfight, leaving more than forty

English dead. Refusing to offer a plea in court, he was sentenced to death a second time. He escaped by claiming benefit of clergy, an already anachronistic medieval right that enabled clerics to escape civil justice if they could prove their literacy by reading psalm 51, the *miserere*, commonly known as the 'neck verse', irrespective of any actual affiliation to the church. Cheating death again, it would hardly be surprising if Cobham believed himself to have a charmed life, floating free from the ordinary restraints of justice.

Cobham disappears from view after 1565. When he resurfaces in October 1569 he is a prisoner in the Tower again. Here he met the Duke of Norfolk, imprisoned for suspected involvement in the rebellion of the northern earls. Cobham quickly became involved on Norfolk's behalf, devising various means to smuggle information in and out of the Tower, be it in empty bottles stuffed with cotton or in whispered exchanges between two privys. In this way he found his way into the camp of Mary Stuart, and eventually into what became known as the Ridolfi plot.

He was returned to the Tower for a fourth time in October 1571 for his role in suppressing incriminating letters and documents from Ridolfi to his hapless English correspondents. There he stayed until April 1574, around the time that Ralegh must have arrived in London. The offences with which he is associated become increasingly small beer thereafter; the only one of any significance was his rumoured collusion with Hawkins, Frobisher, and two other unnamed captains, to lead five warships out from the Thames to attack Spanish shipping on behalf of the Huguenots.[15] For all that Cobham's maritime activities spilled over into outright piracy they are still on a continuum with those of his more reputable peers, different in quality perhaps but not in kind. He belongs more clearly to the hazardous morality of the aspiring courtiers, putting the creation of personal wealth above all else. In this sense, his kinship with Ralegh – as with Gascoigne, Noel, et al – is clear.

Morality for these men was conditional: a mask to be worn in service of self-advancement, not an end in itself. They regarded personal success and the accrual of wealth as their highest moral calling. 'Poverty is oftentimes sent as a curse of God; it is a shame amongst men, an imprisonment of the mind, a vexation of every worthy spirit [. . . it] provokes a man to do infamous and detested deeds,' Ralegh wrote. His early years in London gave him ample opportunity to observe the truth of the insight.

Yet what Cobham had that Ralegh did not was a safety net: his family was among the most important in England, not least because of its pivotal role in the defence of Dover and the Cinque Ports. He had influence, and used it shamelessly. When report of Cobham's death in Flanders came to Burghley on 22 October 1578 there seems to be a sense of eagerness and relief in his brief note of it.[16]

If these men exemplified the choices presented to Ralegh, it was part of his genius that he would assume all of them on his own terms: the value of fashionable extravagance and conspicuous consumption, the need for self-promotion as a vital adjunct to military prowess, the power of literary expression as a kind of positional social politics, and so on. But perhaps the best lesson was one he learned from Cobham: a well-connected man could thrive as a law unto himself. After all, if we know anything about the young Ralegh it is that he does not want to be one among many: he had left the university and the inns of law behind him, and he remained aloof from the tournament lists and other means of making oneself known. He craved a sense of difference, something that was his own.

Vanity is a lonely vocation, however, and as yet, in 1577, Ralegh had no appetite for the struggle. He had arrived in London but was searching for a way in, an entrée, to the inner circles at court; all his choices seemed hard and unappealing. Perhaps he wasn't yet sure enough of his success, or desperate enough to risk failure; in any event, he sought easier pickings elsewhere, still enjoying his recklessly extended childhood of drinking, gaming and wild, extravagant talk. In a self-effacing, cautious move Ralegh sought the patronage and support of a nobleman; it was his misfortune, or his carelessness, that, towards the end of 1577, he chose the Earl of Oxford.

VI: THE VIRGIN QUEEN

We did all love her, for she said she loved us.

SIR JOHN HARINGTON

The year 1578 would prove to be a watershed for Elizabeth. By the autumn, she would receive her final offer of marriage; she would lose her principal favourite Robert Dudley, Earl of Leicester, to Lettice Knollys, widow of the Earl of Essex; and she would hear herself addressed for the first time as 'the Virgin Queen', the epithet which has grown to subsume her personality entirely.

We can date this last event precisely, in fact, to the evening of Thursday 21 August. In the queen's privy chamber within the Bishop's Palace at Norwich, during her progress through Norfolk and Suffolk, Elizabeth was watching a masque in which figures from classical mythology, dressed in purple taffeta and white silk, passed across the stage, delivering speeches to her and presenting her with gifts. Just two lines, written by one of Leicester's acolytes – a little-known actor and poet named Harry Goldingham – and given to Diana, goddess of the moon, to speak, served to frame perceptions of Elizabeth for the next 430 years: 'Who ever found on Earth a constant friend,/That may compare with this my Virgin Queen?'

If there is a temptation to dismiss this as a happily neutral descriptive phrase, it should be resisted. Earlier in the summer, the Duke of Alençon – the pox-scarred younger brother of her former suitor Anjou – had sent two envoys, Bacqueville and De Quissy, to England to confirm his interest in seeking Elizabeth's hand in marriage. They had arrived at Dover on 25 July and made their way via London to the court at Long Melford on 30 July, discussing the proposal in private conversations with the queen on 3 August. They stayed attached to the progress, and were joined by an ambassador from the French king Henri III in Norwich on 19 August. The French can hardly have been alone in recognizing that paeans to the perpetual virtues of chastity were clearly, at this precise moment, somewhat less than abstract moral philosophy. It was certainly not the sort of thing to slip Elizabeth's notice. On a different occasion, some years earlier, she had watched a comedy at court in the company of the Spanish ambassador. 'The plot was founded on the question of marriage, discussed between Juno and Diana, Juno advocating marriage and Diana chastity,' de Silva recorded. The play came down decisively in favour of marriage. The queen turned to him. 'This is all against me,' she confided.[1]

Of course, Elizabeth had been conscious of virginity as a political tool since the earliest days of her reign. In her first speech to Parliament, on 10 February 1559, less than a month after her coronation, and in response to a petition from the House of Commons that she should quickly seek to marry, Elizabeth held out the hope that 'whomsoever my chance shall be to light upon, I trust he shall be ... as careful for preservation of the realm and you as myself', but she also articulated a vision that 'in the end this shall be for me sufficient: that a marble stone shall declare that a queen, having reigned such a time, lived and died a virgin'.[2]

The creation of the virgin queen may well have been intended by Leicester as a means of constraining Elizabeth's choices, of limiting her freedom to choose Alençon.[3] Instead, it became a kind of liberation, freeing her decisively from the tyranny of expectation for the first time in her life. She used it to invert the accepted paradigm of a female monarch – that strength and security lay in her marriage and procreation. By fashioning a new identity in this way, Elizabeth manufactured a positive choice for herself out of the Alençon courtship, which many thought ridiculous in any case. Should she step back again from marriage, she wouldn't simply remain unwed, abandoned and alone, she would be asserting instead that chaste Amazonian independence could both literally and metaphorically represent the best hope of an inviolate sovereign state. As she had told de Silva long before, the English people were inclined to suspect the motives and morals of a woman who declined to marry. Here at last was her rebuttal.

The truth is, it had been a long time coming. Since the very beginning of the reign, there had been a school of thought that Elizabeth should marry an Englishman, but that very quickly elided into concern about the absence of suitable candidates, and alarm at Elizabeth's behaviour with those she seemed to favour. In lieu of obviously appropriate bridegrooms, gossip flooded the space. '[N]early every day some new cry is raised about a husband,' a disdainful de Feria reported just a month into the reign.[4] '[T]his nation cannot be treated in the usual way, for inside their heads is a perpetuum mobile,' said another foreign visitor.[5] Talk was impossible to contain.

The preferred candidate in the first few months of her reign, particularly among the people of London, was a now obscure English courtier named Sir William Pickering.[6] Handsome, athletic, vain, Pickering was another Wyatt alumni, and had fled to Caen with Sir Peter Carew when the rising failed; perhaps there was a certain symmetry in the idea of a veteran of that campaign receiving the ultimate reward.[7] He certainly had Elizabeth's ear, and there was talk of secret visits to his rooms. Pickering swaggered around town on the strength of such rumours, challenging the Earl of Bedford to a duel for speaking ill of him, and publicly reprimanding the Earl of Arundel as 'an impudent discourteous knave' for suggesting that he was getting ideas above his station.

But people tired of talking him up and his star faded quickly.[8] In the meantime, identifying suitors for Elizabeth had become a national pastime; bets were being laid on the possible starters and Pickering's price was quoted in London at 4 to 1 on.[9]

The other Englishman who had quickly emerged as a candidate for the queen's hand in the early months of 1559 was Sir Robert Dudley, generally referred to as Mylord Robert – *Milort Roberto* in the Spanish correspondence – until Elizabeth raised him to the Earl of Leicester in 1564. He was a younger son of John Dudley, briefly Duke of Northumberland, who had tried unsuccessfully to anoint Lady Jane Grey – his daughter-in-law – as queen in Mary's place. Robert Dudley, active in his family's treason, was lucky to have his death sentence lifted. Nevertheless, he had been a prisoner in the Tower alongside Elizabeth, in the Beauchamp Tower.

She appointed him master of the horse the day after her accession but their relationship predated that. Dudley claimed to have known her since she was eight, and it was said that during Mary's reign he had sold property to support Elizabeth financially.[10]

Dudley was taken seriously from the first. Despite the uncomfortable and inauspicious fact that his elder brother, father and grandfather had all been executed for treason, and his lack of social status as the younger brother of a family that had lost its land through attainder, it seemed apparent to most observers that if Elizabeth married for love – if she chose what Sussex called 'the man at sight of whom all her senses are aroused by desire'[11] – then Dudley was the man.

Athletic in his youth, superb on horseback and in the lists, a fine dancer, Dudley was physically charismatic, possessed of a muscular grace and elegance that underlined his essential gravity of purpose. He was, in fact, a serious-minded man prone to intense silences which some found unsettling, threatening even, in their profundity. Numerous portraits of him survive; they suggest a long face, the sharpness of its features masked a little by a luxuriant moustache and goatee, auburn where his hair was dark. The mouth is small and full, the eyes revealing little but a cold and cautious hauteur.

Despite his prodigious patronage of the arts, his private interests tended more towards the comforting clarity of mathematics and the cool judgements of history; many suspected he actually found his own greatness the fittest and most fruitful subject for serious contemplation. But he undoubtedly had considerable personal charm, although it is not apparent in the portraits and it was not sufficient, in the end, to persuade Elizabeth to submit to him. Whatever she said to Dudley in private, when Elizabeth referred to the matter in public, her support for him was always studiously conditional: 'She had told me also with an oath that if she had to marry an Englishman it should only be Robert,' reported de Quadra to Philip.[12]

Absent an actual decision from Elizabeth, Dudley relentlessly talked up his own prospects to anyone who would listen and endeavoured, with varying degrees of clumsiness, to make it a *fait accompli*. 'My lord of Leicester sings his old song unto his friends, that is, that he had the queen in very good tune,' a friend wrote wearily to Cecil in 1570.[13] It was part of his vanity to believe he could push Elizabeth beyond the hypothetical and make a reality of their marriage.

Dudley's many detractors credited him with Machiavellian cunning and demonic subtlety, as if Dudley had a monopoly on deceit at court. Much of the evidence suggests quite the opposite about him. Dudley was equally likely to be ponderous, needily pressing down on events to make them bear the weight of his aspirations. Cecil, of all people, reported that Dudley once cornered him in his rooms and pompously informed him: 'I know that you desire to marry the queen to a foreigner; I will now tell you plainly that I aspire to the hand of the queen; and it seems to me that she is not so well disposed to any one as to myself, and therefore request you to give up all other plans.'[14]

The Dudley marriage certainly existed as a real prospect in his mind – 'the sails of his expectation somewhat swelled therewith', one courtier elegantly noted – and it certainly had a vivid life as a more or less lurid fantasy in the fertile swamps of court, city and country gossip.[15] Whether Elizabeth seriously entertained the possibility, as opposed to allowing Dudley and others to think that she did, is more difficult to assess. For a woman who wished to avoid marriage, there was a certain art to her flirtation with such a union: how else to explain the coincidence that the one person whom she appeared most disposed to marry was also the one candidate everyone in England, the clamour for an ordered succession notwithstanding, was united in thinking unsuitable? Was England so poor, it was said, that no one could be found to stab him?[16]

Yet Dudley could be forgiven the faint air of desperation that taints his attempts to conjure a genuine marriage from Elizabeth's insinuations. His first wife Amy, never suffered to appear at Elizabeth's court, had died in 1560 in circumstances that hinted strongly but inconclusively at foul play: neglected by her husband, she had been found dead at the bottom of the stairs, her neck broken. Mary Stuart's observation on the tragedy – 'The queen is going to marry the master of her horses, who has killed his wife to make room for her' – gleefully articulates what many contemporaries privately thought.[17]

But as the years passed and that prospect dimmed to extinction, the contradictions in his position sharpened into poignancy. Whatever licence his favoured status allowed him, it also came with brutal constraints. His public freedom was almost without horizon; his private horizons were severely limited. As he wrote to his mistress, Lady Sheffield, in the early 1570s, 'is there nothing in the world next [the queen's] favour that I would not give to be in hope of leaving some children behind me, being now the last of our house.'[18]

Beneath the bombast, there was something quite forlorn about Dudley's dependence on Elizabeth.

Although Dudley's precedence in the queen's affections went without question, Elizabeth nurtured a series of other occasional favourites through the 1560s and 70s, most notably Christopher Hatton, a young Inner Temple man who enemies said caught her eye as a dancer at an Inns of Court New Year masque for the queen in January 1562. By the summer of 1564 he was a gentleman pensioner, active in the lists and elsewhere, and in July 1572 he was appointed a gentleman of the privy chamber and captain of the queen's guard. Later he became a privy councillor and, eventually, lord chancellor.[19]

Hatton was another younger son from an exceptionally modest background, his family being minor Northamptonshire gentry. Perhaps that explains his almost pathological humility towards Elizabeth: his letters to her are oleaginously self-abasing. An illness-enforced absence of two days from his queen, for example, drew this forth from him:

no death, no, not hell, not fear of death shall ever win of me my consent so far to wrong myself again as to be absent from you [for] one day . . . Would God I were with you but for one hour. My wits are overwrought with thoughts. I find myself amazed. Bear with me, my most dear sweet Lady. Passion overcometh me. I can write no more. Love me; for I love you . . . Shall I utter this familiar term (farewell)? Yea, ten thousand thousand farewells . . .[20]

The hysterical undertone to Hatton's devotion speaks to a dizzying insecurity, both heightened and highlighted by his decision not to marry – which Mary Stuart claimed had been forced on him by Elizabeth – and which manifested itself in rages of jealousy and possessiveness that were impossible to assuage. But, paradoxically, it also lays bare the sense of incapacity, of helplessness, that to one degree or another all of Elizabeth's favourites had to contend with, the fear of being discarded.

None of her favourites liked to dwell on their subjugation beneath her – a kind of impotence – but it was a servility they had no choice but to accept. As Hatton's friend Edward Dyer, wrote to him bluntly in a period of disfavour during which Hatton became overwrought at the temporary rise of another favourite, 'though in the beginning when her Majesty sought you (after her good manner), she did bear with rugged dealing of yours, until she had what she fancied, yet now, after satiety and fulness, it will rather hurt than help you'.[21] Elizabeth would no longer tolerate the outbursts of jealousy and doubt that she had hitherto allowed him; he was on notice.

It is in part the emotive, highly charged rhetoric of love and abandonment that Hatton employed that has led Elizabeth's relationship with her favourites to be cast in purely sexual terms – explicitly or otherwise. But that perspective merely continues a tone of salacious prurience that predated her accession to the throne, and was, in fact, particularly personal to Elizabeth: indeed, one strand of it had begun to grow years before out of the malignant hostility to Anne Boleyn. Elizabeth 'has lived loosely like her mother and is now with child,' gossiped Renard maliciously to Philip of Spain in 1554.[22]

Another strand found roots in Elizabeth's own behaviour. She may, as she claimed, have remained chaste throughout her life; but there was a tension between her self-imposed standards of queenly decorum and how she behaved during her sometimes less than decorous infatuations. The rules were as tractable as she wanted them to be at any given time: as she told Kat Astley, 'If I had ever had the will or had found pleasure in such a dishonourable life . . . I do not know of anyone who could forbid me'.[23] Echoing her fear of physical confinement, she would brook no constraints on her behaviour – hypothetical or otherwise – whatever the cost to her reputation. And this despite having discovered during her brother Edward VI's reign how deadly unconstrained passion could prove for her.

Thomas Seymour, the lord high admiral – probably forty in 1547 – was the younger brother of Edward Seymour, Duke of Somerset. The brothers had been propelled from their inherited status among the minor gentry by Henry's choice of their sister, Jane, to be his third wife, and they were, therefore, uncles to the new king. Edward had to all intents and purposes made himself lord protector and as a consequence was the most powerful man in Edwardian England – and, not uncoincidentally, probably the richest. Thomas was no less ambitious, but also slothful and greedy, envious and resentful of his elder brother's power and status, and a compulsive, if impetuous, conspirator.[24] Against the express wishes of both his brother and the Privy Council, Seymour had secretly married Henry's widow, Katherine Parr, four months after the death of the king, thus bringing himself into the orbit of Elizabeth, then fourteen, who lived in Katherine's household.

It transpired that he was as interested in Edward's younger sister, despite the twenty-five-year age difference, as he was in Henry's widow. Indeed, Seymour was collecting key figures around the throne, building a power base of his own to counterbalance his brother's influence over the king: not long after his marriage, Seymour also bought the wardship of the then ten-year-old Lady Jane Grey – next in line to the throne after Elizabeth – from her father. It seems he hoped to marry her to Edward.[25]

Reduced to bare, naked scraps of information like this, Seymour appears wholly charmless; but that would be misleading. By virtue of his energy, voluble wit and excellent connections, Seymour was considered a catch at Henry's court, and he certainly had charm enough for the young Elizabeth when he turned his attentions to her. She was seen to blush with something like pleasure at the sound of his name, and there seems little doubt, despite his behaviour, that she fell for him: he would be the first of many eloquent, ambitious, argumentative men whom she would favour.

But Seymour did more than charm. Kat Astley later told how he would often come into her bedchamber early in the morning, in his nightgown still and bare-legged.

> If [Elizabeth] were up he would bid her good morrow and ask how she did, or strike her upon the back or on the buttocks familiarly ... And if she were in her bed he would open the curtains and bid her good morrow, and make as though he would come at her. And she would go further in the bed, so that he could not come at her; And one morning he strove to have kissed her in her bed.[26]

Katherine Parr, by now pregnant, became aware of her new husband's behaviour as spring folded into summer, and attempted to appropriate, control and normalize it by participating herself. Kat Astley remembered how she joined Seymour on a morning visit to Elizabeth's bedchamber and the two tickled her as she lay in bed. But she could not wholly neutralize the hints of threat and menace that lay behind such childish games. On another occasion, Katherine held Elizabeth down in the garden while Seymour cut her black gown into a hundred pieces. By this time, Seymour had managed to appropriate the master-key for Elizabeth's chamber door.

It is hardly surprising that the turbulent undercurrents that ripple through these events should finally surface more explicitly, and matters came to a head when, one day in May, Katherine surprised the two of them together in a room, Elizabeth in Seymour's arms. Katherine acted: Elizabeth was removed from the household and sent to live with Kat Astley's brother-in-law, Sir Anthony Denny, at Cheshunt. Elizabeth would not see Katherine alive again; Henry's last wife gave birth to Seymour's daughter in August, but died of complications a week later.

Freed of his wife, Seymour continued to press for Elizabeth's hand, a suit that some in Elizabeth's own household unwisely supported, among them Kat. But it was Seymour's concurrent plan to kidnap Edward VI that would prove his undoing. With characteristic rashness and over-confidence, he had confided in one of Edward's grooms at St James' Palace one morning how easy it would be to kidnap the king. He had, he pointed out, brought with him more men than there were guarding the house. His arrest was followed by interrogations for Elizabeth and her household, as the Privy Council attempted to discover if he had indeed proposed to Elizabeth – and perhaps more importantly, if she had accepted. Their games quickly came to light. Elizabeth was not shamed by their discovery – while there was a degree of complicity, perhaps even willingness, it is not difficult to see her as little more than a victim of Seymour's lust and ambition – but she was nevertheless severely embarrassed.

Not long after, rumours started circulating that she was carrying Seymour's child – the first of many occasions when gossip would father offspring on her. Seymour himself was executed not long after. Elizabeth, commenting on his death, caught the man perfectly: 'this day dies a man with much wit and very little judgement'.[27] Yet Elizabeth's own judgement was not always particularly prudent when it came to men. She may or may not have been a virgin; but her behaviour was sometimes certainly somewhat less than chaste. Convinced of her own innocence, she often failed to see – or perhaps merely did not care – how more hostile elements might construe her behaviour.

In 1562, for instance, she came close to death from smallpox. For a few days, her life seemed in the balance, and Elizabeth's shock at the severity of her illness is audible in a prayer of thanks she wrote to mark her delivery from death. Her gratitude did not prevent her offering God a sharp rebuke for the risks He ran with her life: 'Thou hast strongly disregarded in my danger, and left my people stunned.'[28]

She herself stunned those around her in the midst of the crisis, by ordering that in the event of her death, Dudley was to be made lord protector, on an income of £20,000. But while vociferously denying that their relationship was anything but chaste, she seemed to immediately undermine her contention by ordering that 'a groom of the chamber, called Tamworth, who sleeps in Lord Robert's room, [was] to be granted an income of £500 a year' – an extraordinarily large sum, in the circumstances. The unmistakable suggestion that she was somehow buying Tamworth's silence hangs over the generosity of the gift.

Indeed, Elizabeth's relationship with Dudley was viewed as something between a source of bawdy humour and a national disgrace. Stories, rumours and jokes were in constant circulation, and slanders are scattered through the surviving legal records. As is the way with such things, they elaborated over time, rising from mere accusations that 'Lord Robert did swive the queen', through to claims that she had borne one of his children, then two and eventually five.[29] Even courtiers like Francis Osborne at the close of her reign heard rumours that they had an illegitimate son living in Venice.[30]

An extraordinarily obscene libel on Dudley, circulated after his death and describing his punishments in the afterlife, pictured him chained to 'a naked fiend in the form of a lady [. . . and forced to] charge with his lance of lust against the centre of her target . . . and run his ingredience up to the hard hilts into the unsearchable bottom of her gaping gulf . . . drown the member of his virility in the bottomless barrel of her virginity, through which runneth a field of unquenchable fire which at every joining together did so hiss his humanity'.[31] The identity of the virgin fiend is withheld, but not difficult to guess.

Hatton, like Leicester, was also suspected of illicit intercourse with her; the traitor Edmund Mather, for one, said that, 'Mr Hatton . . . had more recourse unto her Majesty in her privy chamber than reason would suffer if she were so virtuous'.[32] It was said by a fellow courtier that Hatton 'did swear voluntarily, deeply and with vehement asseveration, that he never had any carnal knowledge of [Elizabeth's] body', the violence of the denial undercutting the very assurance he was trying to give.[33]

In fact, it is hard to overstate the extent to which Elizabeth's body – her sexuality – was public property. The Spanish had a contact in her laundry to report on her menstrual cycle; the

French historian Brantome, who had visited the court in the late summer of 1561, had heard that her vaginal canal was too narrow for childbirth.[34] Long after her death, Ralegh's associate Ben Jonson was telling friends that she had a membrane over her vagina that, in Jonson's phrase, 'made her uncapable of man, though for her delight she tried many'.[35] Jonson's statement is no more than one might expect from a man with a taste for controversy and a filthy mind, but such talk was commonplace in the continental courts and palaces. Mary Stuart had heard it from Ralegh's friend the Countess of Shrewsbury – Thomas Cobham's erstwhile mother-in-law – and relished relating it back to Elizabeth.[36] The French king Henry IV – formerly a Huguenot ally as prince and then king of Navarre – would say that there were three things it was impossible to discover, one of which was whether Elizabeth was a virgin.[37]

So overpowering was Elizabeth's sexual identity, and the sense of her political authority as being somehow eroticized by her exercise of it, that awareness of it seeped into the unconscious. The London astrologer and physician Simon Forman was in the habit of recording his dreams in his casebook. Several about Elizabeth survive, of which that of 23 January 1597 is perhaps the most compelling:

I dreamt that I was with the queen, and that she was a little elderly woman in a coarse white petticoat all unready . . . She had a long white smock, very clean and fair, and it trailed in the dirt and her coat behind . . . And so we talked merrily and then she began to lean upon me, when we were past the dirt, and to be very familiar with me, and methought she began to love me. And when we were alone, out of sight, methought she would have kissed me.[38]

At the time of writing, Forman was forty-six, two years older than Ralegh. Elizabeth was sixty-three.

Others had no compunction about sharing their fantasies. A late Gascoigne poem for Elizabeth features a strikingly inappropriate passage in which he imagines how the queen lays 'her mighty mace aside/And strokes my head'.[39] The government's torturer, Richard Topcliffe, accompanied his inquisition of one Catholic priest with the brag that:

> he was so familiar with her Majesty that he many times putteth his hands between her breasts and paps and in her neck; that he hath not only seen her legs and knees but feeleth them with his hands above her knees; that he hath felt her belly and said unto her Majesty that she had the softest belly of any woman kind; that she said unto him, 'be not these arms, legs and body of King Henry?' to which he answered, 'yea'; that she gave him for a favour a white linen hose wrought with white silk.[40]

The congruence of sadism and lust here is of course particularly troubling, but it is worth noting that Topcliffe goes on to claim to his victim that he has his authority to torture direct 'from her Majesty', not from the Privy Council, as if that authority, that absolute power to break his fellow men in search of sedition and other guilts, were conveyed through – and were indivisible from – precisely the sexual dominance he claims over his sovereign.

Elizabeth's physical intimacy with those around her, her tactility, her flirtatiousness, encouraged such flights from reality. Some, perhaps many, merely found it unsettling. One of her gentlewomen of the privy chamber, Elizabeth Leighton, the queen's first cousin once removed, delicately recorded her discomfort in a letter to her husband: 'nothing you can wish to be added to your fortune shall want my consent, though it were for the favour of her Majesty, which is much for a wife to agree to'.[41]

As late as 1597, the same year that Forman noted down his fantasy, the French ambassador André Hurault, Sieur de Maisse reported how 'She kept the front of her dress open and one could see the whole of her bosom, and passing low, and often she would open the front of this robe with her hands as if she were too hot' and that 'when she raises her head, she has a trick of putting both her hands on her gown and opening it insomuch that all her belly can be seen'.[42] Of course, the revealing clothes Hurault describes were late fashions, but the provocative carelessness of her gestures was doubtless more durable.

We cannot know the truth about Elizabeth's relations with her favourites, but it would be foolish to deny the way Elizabeth allowed, perhaps encouraged and enjoyed, these relationships to be eroticized: in some ways it defined how she negotiated the more treacherous reaches of interpersonal politics. She was acutely aware of the power of physical intimacy, using it deftly – the playful caress, the affectionate kiss – to imply other more politic intimacies: favour, sympathy, concord, access. But there was usually also a practical point: emotional satisfactions could be achieved through the same means as political ends. They were her creatures, insecure, ambitious men with little in the way of status, land and power to fall back on should they fail her. And, being thus beholden to her, they could act as her proxies, or otherwise serve her purpose, to effect her will in ways that other, more established principals at court could or would not.

Hatton's uses included ensuring that Elizabeth's own voice and opinions were heard in the Houses of Parliament, for example, and he later proved an effective manager of several major treason trials, including that related to the Babington conspiracy. Leicester himself, the only favourite with whom marriage was ever mooted, served a range of political purposes beyond the private pleasures Elizabeth derived from his company. As already noted, the fact that he was so clearly Elizabeth's preferred candidate for a husband helped neuter much objection to her remaining unmarried. Loathed for his political power, his alleged influence over Elizabeth, his status as a parvenu, his newfound wealth, his apparent amorality – Dudley was her lightning rod, attracting discontent and other, stronger subversive tensions away from her and her government.

Although raised a Protestant, he positioned himself as the English Catholic candidate for marriage – almost certainly with Elizabeth's connivance – thus allowing her a degree of control over potential turbulence that she would not otherwise have. De Silva, for example, was led to believe that Dudley had an understanding with the Pope regarding the marriage project.[43] He had, the ambassador thought, the Catholics all on his side.[44]

As Elizabeth knew, the deferral of hope, the promise of redemption, was a powerful incentive to loyalty, stability and quiescence in the precarious early years of her reign. Dudley, as was his wont, evidently overplayed his hand and de Silva, for one, found his professions of loyalty to Spain – given a degree of credibility by Dudley having served in Philip's army during Mary's reign – tiresome, wearily referring more than once to Dudley's 'usual submissive protestations of his obligation to serve your Majesty, [made] at too great a length for me to repeat'.[45] But for some years the strategy worked.

Later, when the idea of an Elizabeth–Dudley marriage became impossible to sustain, Dudley realigned himself with his natural base among the more zealous Protestants and Puritans, which again gave Elizabeth a certain leverage over a fractious and troublesome section of her people. Indeed, Ralegh's cynical, astute observation that Condé had sided with the Huguenots 'to gain a party and be made thereby the stronger' could have been made with Leicester in mind. It is no wonder, given this *volte face*, that the Catholics despised him: Morgan's bitter, despondent comment to Mary Stuart that 'Leicester is not born to do good to God's people' is among their more charitable comments.[46]

The 1584 polemic *Leicester's Commonwealth*, a judicious and hugely popular invective largely written by Ralegh's friend Charles Arundell in exile in Paris, says of Dudley that, 'being himself of no religion, [he] feedeth notwithstanding upon our differences in religion, to the fatting of himself and ruin of the realm'.[47] Dudley's reputation has never really recovered. He received extraordinary rewards from Elizabeth, but she exacted a heavy price. As Dudley's letter to Lady Sheffield, quoted above, reveals, the personal cost had been weighing on his mind for some years.

Eventually, in the summer of 1578, he decided to act.

At the end of Elizabeth's progress through Norfolk and Suffolk, on Tuesday 23 September, she dined at the Earl of Leicester's house at Wanstead. Two days earlier, he had married Lettice Knollys. It is traditionally said that Elizabeth did not find out about Leicester's marriage until late the following year, despite it being 'exactly known to the whole court, with the very day, the place, the witnesses, and the minister that married them together – yet no man durst open his mouth to make her Majesty privy thereunto'.[48] While no explicit evidence survives that contradicts this version of events, it is nevertheless wildly implausible that Elizabeth could have been kept ignorant of such news for so long by so many people. After all, the court was hardly a byword for discretion at the best of times and it is difficult to credit that no one among the swollen ranks of those who loathed Dudley could have denied themselves the delight of breaking such news. Moreover the plausibility of the idea is in no way strengthened by tracing the story to its original source in *Leicester's Commonwealth*, Arundell's scabrous libel.

But there are different kinds of knowledge, and it may be that Elizabeth wished not to hear the details of the ceremony while nevertheless recognizing the reality that it enshrined. Certainly it is difficult to read this letter from Hatton to Dudley of June 1578, after the latter had excused himself from the court at Hampton prior to the East Anglian progress, without believing that Elizabeth knew very well what was going on, and sought an outlet for her emotions by displacing them, not for the first time, on Hatton:

> Since your lordship's departure the queen is found in continual and great melancholy: the cause thereof I can but guess at, notwithstanding that I bear and suffer the whole brunt of her mislike in generality. She dreameth of marriage that might seem injurious to her: making myself to be either the man or a pattern of the matter. I defend that no man can tie himself or be tied to such inconvenience as not to marry by law of God or man, except by mutual consents on both parts the man and woman vow to marry each to other, which I know she hath not done for any man, and therefore by any man's marriage she can receive no wrong, with many more arguments of the best weight I could gather. But, my Lord, I am not the man that should thus suddenly marry . . .[49]

We may not hear Elizabeth speak herself, but the sense of resentful melancholy, a wounded loneliness that cannot fully be articulated – words, rarely, having failed her – seems clear even in Hatton's cautious retelling. Whatever the precise nature of their relationship, and however compromised it was by political necessities, the strength of the bond between her and Dudley was not gainsaid by anyone. It might be said, in fact, that the fantasy of marriage with him had been the single greatest emotional commitment of her life, and she had lavished both political capital and popular goodwill on it.

Now it was over. While Dudley remained a close companion, politically and emotionally, until his death, he would also have other calls on his devotion to answer over which she had no command. Elizabeth, despite the crowds about her, was more alone than ever; and yet she had been rejected. For now, perhaps, there was the Alençon marriage proposal to relish, a last dish to linger over. But after that?

VII: THE WIND OF FACTION

Things are not at such liberty that men may choose their path
LORD HENRY HOWARD TO ELIZABETH, *CIRCA* 29 DECEMBER 1580

Edward de Vere, the seventeenth Earl of Oxford, was twenty-seven in 1577. His father had died when he was twelve and he had spent his teenage years as a royal ward in the household of Sir William Cecil. The two could hardly have been more different: one England's pre-eminent royal servant whose rise from the gentry was predicated on formidable self-discipline and a punishing capacity for work, the other the latest beneficiary of one of the oldest patrimonies in England, his title having been passed down in unbroken succession since the twelfth century. His inheritance was worth some £12,000 per annum, but Oxford sold almost all of it to fund his extravagant lifestyle.[1] While his career had moments of splendour – success at the tilts, enlightened patronage of literature and drama – the few glories only serve to emphasize the surrounding vacuities: it was the epitome of wasted promise.

The tone for it was set in 1567 when Oxford killed Thomas Brinknell, an undercook in Cecil's kitchen, in the rear courtyard of Cecil House on the Strand while practising a new move with his rapier. The technique, called foining, involved lunging forward with point unguarded to pierce the thigh, and had been introduced to England by Oxford's friend Rowland Yorke, who had served alongside Gascoigne on Gilbert's ill-judged Netherlands campaign of 1572.[2]

To avoid scandal, Cecil leaned on the coroner's jury to return a verdict of suicide: Brinknell, it was decided, had killed himself by running on to the point of Oxford's rapier. This wasn't simply a genuflection before Oxford's superior social rank: Cecil married his daughter Anne to Oxford in 1571, a union that cemented the Cecil family's rising status and gave Oxford access to some much needed capital and Cecil's boundless political patronage. It brought Anne, however, little other than misery and shame: Oxford, brooding in his father-in-law's shadow, effectively abandoned her for the best part of ten years, refusing to support her financially, and vigorously denied paternity of their first child.

Nevertheless Oxford was accomplished in what one might call the demonstrative arts – swordplay, tilting, dancing and so on – and Elizabeth's keen eye for such things alighted on him soon enough. 'My Lord of Oxford is lately grown into great credit,' wrote Gilbert Talbot from court to his father, the Earl of Shrewsbury in May 1573. 'The queen's majesty delighteth more in his personage and his dancing and valiantness than any other.'[3] But he lacked the will, discipline and motivation to succeed politically at court: hard graft was not his style and his promise would always be betrayed by a shallow impetuosity. Several sources suggest that he was close enough to the Duke of Norfolk, a first cousin, to be more than sympathetic to his treasons, and he may even have plotted to free Norfolk from the Tower and hustle him away to the continent. There were rumours, too, of him leading an English force to fight alongside the Spanish in the Netherlands.[4]

In any event, both Elizabeth and the demands of life at court bored and frustrated him, and he bridled at being reprimanded by the queen for his profligacy. He left England twice – in 1574 without the requisite royal approval and again in 1575 – much to the delight of the Catholic exiles in Antwerp and elsewhere. He spent a year in Italy, returning to England in April 1576 where his new-found Italianate fashions were the subject of both envy and ridicule. Some time that summer, under the influence of a priest named Richard Stephens recently returned to England from the English seminary at Douai, Oxford secretly reconciled with the Catholic church.[5] Elizabeth and her government were broadly tolerant of those English men and women who had been raised as Catholics; they were much less sanguine about those who converted: it was perceived as an aggressive act against the state, and – in the light of the 1571 papal bull – implicitly an act against Elizabeth herself. Oxford, fickle-headed as Talbot said, soon found himself in deeper waters.

On his return from the continent, he drew around him a clique of like-minded courtiers and noblemen, not coherent or organized enough to frame a conspiracy, despite occasional gestures in that direction, but full nonetheless of a sullen and venomous antipathy for the status quo. Key figures included several leading members of the Howard family, including Henry, younger brother to the executed Duke of Norfolk, and his nephew Thomas, and Lord Charles Howard of Effingham, another branch of the family. Also often present were Lord Edward Windsor, Lord Henry Compton, prominent Catholics such as Sir William Cornwallis and minor courtiers such as Henry Noel, Henry Burgh, Charles Arundell, Francis South-well, William Tresham, George Gifford, and Arthur Gorges, the last a cousin of both Arundell and Ralegh, who like Arundell claimed kinship with the Howards. Gifford, Gorges and

Tresham either were already, or would soon become gentlemen pensioners. Other more peripheral members, not least because they were only intermittently at court, included Edward Stafford, the future ambassador to France; the earls of Northumberland, Ormonde, and Southampton; Thomas Lord Paget; and Philip Howard, Norfolk's son, later the Earl of Arundel.

And then there was Ralegh.

The most obvious bond Oxford's group shared was Catholicism. Howard of Effingham, Windsor, Northumberland, Paget, Southampton and Tresham had been born into the faith; others – among them Oxford himself and his closest friends Henry Howard, Charles Arundell and Francis Southwell – had been recently reconciled. Philip Howard, for one, would revert to the old faith over the coming years. Of the rest, most can be shown to have strong Catholic connections, familial or otherwise. Gifford was nominally Protestant but his family were strongly Catholic and his brother William, later an active propagandist against Elizabeth, had left England in 1573 and would eventually become archbishop of Rheims. Noel's record is similarly ambivalent: an active patron of several Catholic writers and musicians, he later kept a French monk in his household who spied for the French ambassador at court, and was one of those who had a copy of Arundell's vicious satire *Leicester's Commonwealth*, which the government tried very hard to suppress.[6]

But the group's Catholicism distracts from the more general reactionary nostalgia of its worldview. The animus that Oxford and the Howard set felt against the new establishment wasn't purely, or even principally, religious. It was fed by resentment of the rising gentry families, of which Cecil was the most egregious and of course most powerful example; by a sense of sour entitlement, the humiliation of proud men excluded from positions of influence that their ancestors had held; by a faintly misogynist distaste for the way Elizabeth managed the court, and in particular favourites such as Leicester; and by the emotional security and comfort they identified in older, more ritualized social and religious practices, in which they found a sense of timeless order and stability. They felt that their vision of England and its polity was truer, more deeply rooted than that offered by the centralized Elizabethan settlement.

Ralegh's biographers customarily dismiss his association with Oxford as a brief flirtation lasting a few months in 1580. Keen to clear Ralegh of the taint of Catholicism and conspiracy that defined Oxford's circle, it is surmised that he must have been there as a spy for Walsingham or Leicester. There is in fact no evidence for such an assumption, whereas there is evidence that he was already a significant member of the group by the end of 1577, since his presence was noted at Oxford's table alongside Harry Burgh, grandson of the Earl of Lincoln, who was killed in a duel in January 1578.[7] It may be the case that Ralegh merely drifted into the group with little actual volition rather than making an active choice, drawn in perhaps by friends and kinsmen such as Noel and Gorges, or through mutual acquaintances of Gascoigne or Cobham. But even so, the fact that he stayed in Oxford's circle for several years tells us much about his attitude to faith and politics and reveals more complex and ambivalent approaches to both than his mythos traditionally allows.

His presence was, in some senses, the first flowering of that radical indifference to religious categories that he developed during his time in France: he didn't care much what other people believed, it was the politics of their actions that concerned him. He had evolved a minimalist approach to morality and dogma: almost everything reduced to questions of power and advancement; he was careless of credal and political faultlines except insofar as they offered personal advantage.

Ralegh, in common with many of his friends, would be accused more than once of atheism: it was a charge levelled at early companions such as Gascoigne and Oxford, and later ones such as the mathematician Thomas Harriot and the poet Christopher Marlowe. He himself would be investigated by a diocesan tribunal in the 1590s following accusations about his beliefs and behaviour. Ralegh was not an atheist as we understand the term: his was a muscular unadorned faith, intense in its privacy and unbreachable in its force. But when his enemies reached for the accusation – which was deadly serious if proven and led to the stake – it was not Ralegh's personal devotions that they addressed but his public disinterest in such absolute categories. His kind of atheism was, in fact, viewed with perhaps even more distrust and disgust by the Protestant establishment than recusancy, and their horror of such indifference was shared across the religious divide.

To the modern, more secular sensibility there is something refreshingly undogmatic about this aspect of Ralegh's persona. But it also reflected a kind of immaturity. Ralegh never lost a slightly adolescent pleasure in fostering intellectual and moral discomfort in others – it suited his subtle, sharp, probing intellect, undulled by platitude – and it was surely what attracted him to Oxford and his circle.

Oxford was, when you first met him, splendid company. Powerful and rich enough to shrug off social restraints that would have daunted or repressed others, his conversation was a heady, transgressive mix of scurrility and sedition. He and his friends drank heavily, gambled and affected a sniggering disdain for convention which they mistook for intellectual adventurousness: they delighted in dangerous, unseemly, contrarian talk, at once posturing, vain and provocative.

As a series of interrogations and libels from the first years of the next decade reveal – made by key members of the circle after it had very publicly and acrimoniously imploded – nothing was off limits.

We find Oxford angrily arguing in favour of armed rebellion and deriding the acquiescence of the Catholics in their own subjugation, being content, he said, to lay down their heads till they were taken off – a tasteless remark at the best of times, but particularly spiteful when talking to a man, Henry Howard, whose older brother had suffered just such a fate a few years before.[8] We hear him mocking the holy trinity as an old wives' tale, and boasting that given six days he could make a better and more orderly set of scriptures. He is fond of claiming the Bible did more to justify licentiousness and obscenity than the works of Aretine, sixteenth-century Europe's premier pornographer, and swears he could use scripture to prove there was no life after death and that 'the rest was devised but to make us afraid, like babes and children, of our shadows'.[9]

Yet more outré were his claims of occult experiences. Oxford was in the avant garde of intellectual fashion here: John Dee, the queen's mathematician and later Ralegh's friend and colleague, spent several futile decades attempting to map proto-empirical techniques onto the search for spiritual enlightenment by seeking dialogue with angels. But even so there was something troublingly hallucinatory about Oxford's brags, such as the suggestion that he had frequently had sex with a female spirit; or that when Stevens held mass Oxford could see the crucified body of Christ between the priest's hands; or that he could conjure Satan and speak to him, and had frequently done so in a little house by the tiltyard at Greenwich.[10]

But Oxford's favourite theme was himself, and in particular his exploits during his travels in Europe. He led the Duke of Alva's troops to victory over a major Flemish town, he claimed.

He was offered the government of Milan; the Pope had offered him over £10,000 a year to stay in Naples; he had attacked Genoa with 15,000 men; he had lectured at the university of Strasbourg; he had seen St Mark's in Venice paved with diamonds and rubies; he had seen a mantelpiece in Genoa worth more than all the treasure in the Tower of London; an Italian countess had travelled fifty miles to sleep with him.[11]

In sum, there was not a little of Baron von Munchausen in Oxford, and it is no wonder that Ralegh stayed. The grandiose lies, the delicious offensiveness, the baroque threats of violence, the incoherent scheming all 'made much sport to the hearers', as Arundell later confessed.[12] Ralegh could indulge his youthful taste for contrarian positions while also seeking preferment from one of the court's most prominent noblemen: it was a self-indulgent, easy choice, oblivious to – or merely in denial about – the obvious and quite possibly mortal dangers that attended Oxford's favourite themes. Events might serve to mask the threat for a year or so, but they would surface eventually and destroy the careers, reputations and lives of several of Ralegh's friends.

Oxford himself, however, was intermittently ambitious and bitter enough to take his position seriously: as early as June 1577 he had approached the French ambassador, Mauvissière, and offered to head a Catholic revolt, albeit with unspecified aims. The following month he used Mauvissière to arrange a safe passage out of England for the priest Stevens, but by late autumn the authorities were scenting sedition in the wind and spies were set on the ambassador's house in Salisbury court, at the western end of Fleet Street close by Ralegh's lodgings in the Temple. The conspiracy, such as it was, evaporated, but the government's interest in Oxford did not.[13]

As for Ralegh, it is unclear how tainted he was with such activities, but his lifelong fondness for extravagant gesture, which no doubt also coloured Oxford's appeal, together with his impetuosity and impatience, would also lead him elsewhere in the summer of 1578.

While he had surely looked to Oxford for preferment and the possibility of income as much as the pleasures of entertainment, there were other paths to wealth and celebrity in London that were less dependent on incremental advances in favour, and by May Ralegh was busy alongside his brother, Sir Humphrey Gilbert, preparing ships for a high-profile voyage to the New World.

The attraction was two-fold. The young gentlemen who habitually flocked to such voyages expected some return on their investment. But fame – the glamour that attached to enterprise and endeavour – was a valuable commodity too: it could be parlayed into greater commissions and further rewards. When aspiring courtiers sought to forge careers, however briefly, in the fire of warfare or fights at sea, they were not absenting themselves from court politics to do so: they were pursuing their courtly ambitions by other means.

The impetus for the project had come from Gascoigne. In the winter of 1575–6 he had been leafing through some papers in Gilbert's study at his house in Limehouse – then a prosperous and populous hamlet on the northern banks of the Thames – when he came across the *Discourse of a Discoverie for a New Passage to Cataia*, which had been languishing in manuscript on Gilbert's desk for a decade. It was a treatise on the possibility of a maritime passage north-west over the Americas to the rich markets of China and the east. Gascoigne had a journalist's instinct for news and a need for ready cash: he borrowed the manuscript, dashed off a preface and sold it to a printer without troubling Gilbert for approval. He knew that his kinsman, Martin Frobisher, was preparing a voyage of his own in search of the same fabled route to riches, and Gascoigne's actions ensured that when Frobisher set off from the Thames in June with a modest complement of thirty-four men in three small ships, Gilbert's pamphlet was there on the bookstalls to profit from Frobisher's celebrity.

Whatever the reason for its publication, the reception of the *Discourse* gave renewed impetus to Gilbert's plans, and on 6 November 1577 he presented Elizabeth with a new discourse entitled 'How her Majesty may annoy the King of Spain'. The proposal was simple and bold: that Elizabeth should send out a fleet of warships which, under cover of a voyage of discovery, would target the Spanish dominions in the West Indies and use the conquered bases to launch attacks on enemy shipping – most notably the Spanish treasure ships out of South America, but also French and Portuguese shipping in the Caribbean and beyond. It was, in many respects, the template on which Ralegh modelled his entire maritime career. There was nothing wrong with the analysis – the vulnerability of Spain's South American empire was matched only by its strategic importance – but whether Gilbert was the man to exploit such weaknesses is another question. As events would shortly reveal, whatever his skills as a military leader, he was incapable of asserting authority where he could not command it.

Nevertheless it is a powerful and persuasive text, which Gilbert closes with an exhortation to swift action:

> If your majesty like to do it at all, then would I wish your highness to consider that delay doth often times prevent the performance of good things: for the wings of man's life are plumed with the feathers of death.

The startling final image captures something of both Gilbert's own oppressive fatalism and the morbid pressure of the times:

lives daily stalked by death, the undoer of ambition, the spy at the table, the traitor in the room.

Although he did not formally receive his commission until 11 June, Gilbert's project must have been tacitly approved early in the year, almost certainly under the patronage of Walsingham. Secrecy was vital, and we can see from a later voyage of Gilbert's in 1583 the lengths he went to to keep his intentions hidden. Gilbert's instructions for the ships in his fleet on that occasion were contained in two sealed documents: the first, sealed in yellow wax, was 'to be broken at the land's end of England and not before, for that is for their course only'; the second, sealed in red wax, was 'not to be broken up before they come upon the coast of America or within a hundred leagues thereof'.[14] In other words, most of those on board, including the captain and pilot, were meant to leave England without knowing their destination – or the purpose of their voyage. As a *modus operandi*, it had the complex impracticality of many of Gilbert's best conceits.

However imperative the need to hide the voyage's objectives from the Spanish, Gilbert's final fleet would dwarf that of Frobisher, ultimately carrying some 500 gentlemen, soldiers and seamen. Inevitably rumours of the voyage and Gilbert's intentions flooded London and by May, news of it had reached Bernadino de Mendoza, the deft and resolute Spanish ambassador in London, who reported to Philip II on the sixteenth that Gilbert had four fully armed ships in the river preparing to sail. Two weeks later, a source in the Earl of Leicester's chambers at court provided Mendoza with details of Gilbert's intentions, and before they sailed he could report contentedly that he also had an English spy on board too.[15] So much for secrecy.

One of those four ships on the Thames was under Ralegh's command. He was given the 100-ton *Falcon* – the name a discreet nod to the Boleyn family emblem – which is described in the state papers as being the queen's ship. If the historical record seems to tease here at a closer connection between Ralegh and Elizabeth at this early date, it cannot be further substantiated. Indeed, another document suggests the ship in fact belonged to William Hawkins of Plymouth, who leased it directly to Ralegh.[16]

When the whole fleet was finally assembled there would be any number of familiar faces for Ralegh: Henry Noel and George Whetstone were onboard *The Hope of Greenway*, under Gilbert's vice-admiral and Walter's older brother Carew Ralegh. Whetstone had been forced to send his play *Promos and Cassandra* to press uncorrected in order to join the voyage on time. Edward Denny captained his own ship, the *Bark Denny*; Charles Champernown, another cousin, sailed with Ralegh himself. Charles Arundell may have sailed, too, although it is more likely that his role was limited to investment.[17]

Ralegh chose a somewhat pretentious motto for his ship: *Nec mortem peto, nec finem fugio* – I do not seek death, nor do I fly from it – which seems to advertise the very sense of hesitancy and ambivalence that characterizes his early years in London. Gilbert was in his flagship, the *Anne Auger*, named for his rich Kent wife, whose fortune he spent on speculations like this voyage; his chosen motto was the attractively careless and brisk *Quid non?* – Why not? It might stand for the flexible ethics of the period, the casual morality of convenience and advantage. It was the first time either Ralegh or Gilbert is known to have captained a ship.

Little fanfare attended their departure from London, some time in mid-August while Elizabeth was being entertained in Norwich. But people in town were talking, and Thomas Churchyard, like Gascoigne a man with a journalist's eye for news and a hack's hunger for copy, was quick to capitalize on the moment, spicing up his *Discourse of the Queen's Majesty's Entertainment in Suffolk and Norfolk*, registered on 20 September, with 'a commendation of Sir H. Gilbert's ventrous journey'. It was the first time Ralegh and Elizabeth would be associated together in print.[18] Churchyard's poem is more press release than actual news: if Churchyard knows where the ships are headed, he isn't telling.

But Churchyard is too good and truthful a poet – and too experienced a soldier – to deliver the bland panegyric the occasion might otherwise demand. He is particularly good on life on board ship: the stink of pitch and tar; the diet of hard biscuit, simple beer, salt beef and dried stockfish; the hot flush and sweaty chill of seasickness retched up on the surging, swelling sea. He is good too on the physical experience of the weather, sudden winds blowing the unwary over the hatches or out of the rigging, and gales assaulting the shrouds and sails, their blows shuddering through every rib of the ship's hull. Most of all he knows what a sea-battle really entails, when shot fills the air as thick as hail and maimed men lie groaning on the hatches, limbs gone, waiting to die.

The poem is an attempt to answer the obvious question: why would indolent men with comfortable, sometimes glamorous lives, seek out such experiences? Churchyard rehearses the possibilities – wealth, fame, nationalist pride, a thirst for knowledge, the spirit of adventure – without really being persuaded by any of them. But then, he allows for every explanation save one: desperation.

Nevertheless, he captures perfectly the contradictions and ironies inherent in the enterprise: the ambivalent motivations of pampered young gentlemen seeking out the privations of life at sea; how private hunger for wealth and celebrity could be draped in providential patriotic tropes; how ideals of honour and glory measure against the brutal truths of war at sea.

Despite all this, Churchyard is careful to identify the leading lights behind the voyage individually; 'Rawley ripe of sprite,/ And rare right many ways' is sixth on the list. It is Ralegh's first true moment of public recognition, given that the commendatory verses in *The Steele Glas* were really exercises in self-promotion, and perhaps this iconizing memorial was in part the kind of public glory that Ralegh sought.

VIII: THE FORT OF FAME

When she did ill what empires could have pleased?

SIR WALTER RALEGH

The omens for the voyage were not good, but neither, it transpired, was the planning. Ralegh most likely slipped the *Falcon* quietly down the Thames and out to sea with Gilbert in mid-August – what Churchyard called a 'strange adieu'– and beat down the coast to Dartmouth, then still one of the major ports in Devon, where they made harbour on 25 August. On 8 September, someone stole one of the fleet's supply ships: hardly auspicious for a voyage that itself intended theft against Spain. Two days later another partner, Henry Knollys, brought his ship, the *Elephant*, into port. With the benefit of hindsight, the fact that Knollys was already sailing separately may have been symptomatic of the rifts that were about to occur. Indeed, on the twenty-second, presumably frustrated by the interminable delays, Knollys sailed alone for Plymouth, to be followed by Ralegh and the rest of the fleet four days later.

Ralegh did not reach harbour there until 15 October, struggling with contrary winds which dispersed some of Gilbert's ships as far east as the Isle of Wight. It was some two months since they had left London and many men on board were understandably becoming restless. Whatever objective had persuaded men to join the venture, eight or so weeks struggling to reach Plymouth would certainly have been a long way short of it.

Waiting for Gilbert's ships to arrive, Knollys' men rampaged through the town, killing a local man, John Leonard, and almost killing a constable; Knollys refused to give up the guilty parties to the local justices. Tempers were getting short. Gilbert asked Knollys to surrender the two murderers and Knollys again refused. By the beginning of November, other tensions in their relationship – almost certainly longstanding – were coming to the fore and Knollys was seeking to break the partnership. Ralegh was in prime position to watch as his brother's command – and with it his own ambitions – unravelled.

They attempted to leave Plymouth on 29 October, but were driven back into the harbour by a storm. The situation festered and Ralegh himself was called upon to bear witness to the recriminatory breakdown in relations. It must have been with a certain dispiriting sense of familiarity that on 5 November he found himself in front of another justice of the peace, less than a year after his encounter with Jasper Fisher.

Ralegh affirmed Gilbert's version of events and, although the timeline may be obscure, the rancour between Gilbert and Knollys was already poisonously open. At its heart was the question of pride. Knollys publicly affected to despise Gilbert's knighthood – claiming in fact to have refused one for himself on numerous occasions – and told everyone who would listen how shameful it was to serve under someone like Gilbert. He himself was, he said, 'equal in degree to the best knights and better than the most in England', and whoever those best knights were, it is clear Knollys didn't regard Gilbert as one of them.

There seems to be something calculated and malicious in Knollys' contempt, an evident pleasure in the open and public humiliation of his admiral; in other circumstances – at Oxford's table, say – Ralegh might have rather enjoyed the entertainment. But you can still hear the sting of the insult and Gilbert's wounded recoil in this piece of testimony:

> when Sir Humphrey Gilbert bad Mr Knollys to dinner, he answered that he had money to pay as well as [Gilbert], and that he would leave his trencher for those [beggars] that were not able to pay for their meals, which thing made Sir Humphrey Gilbert judge that Mr Knollys esteemed of him very little considering the place he held by her Majesty's commission.

Gilbert's injured self-regard and sense of baffled, ineffectual superiority echoes throughout his attempts to defend his own conduct, but he comes across as a man out of his depth militarily, socially and politically. If the squabbles were all somewhat childish, as Gilbert rightly observed in a letter to Walsingham – Knollys being 'moved by such trifles or toys as . . . were meeter to break amity among children rather than men', he said – then the very triviality of the issues was one of the ways in which Knollys was belittling Gilbert.[1]

For Ralegh, a man who aspired to the kind of freedom from restraint enjoyed by Knollys, he must – as Gilbert's brother – have shared in, and smarted at, his shame. But if he saw something admirable or to be envied in Knollys' liberty, that privileged status was impossibly out of reach for a man with as few familial connections as Ralegh. Henry Knollys was, as Mendoza had noted, the son of Sir Francis Knollys, Elizabeth's treasurer and a member of the Privy Council. Sir Francis was one of the few surviving servants of Elizabeth's brother Edward

VI: he had spent at least some of Mary's reign in exile on the continent, probably with Henry in tow. He was also one of the few stridently ideological Protestants whom Elizabeth tolerated in her inner circle, a man with the self-righteous confidence to censure everyone, up to and including the queen.[2]

Although an excess of self-regard hardly seems atypical at Elizabeth's court, Henry Knollys' bloated pride still seems inexplicable – unless, that is, you know that his mother was the daughter of Mary Boleyn, Elizabeth I's aunt, and sometime mistress to Henry VIII. Indeed, Knollys may very well have been the grandson of Henry VIII, since his mother's birth coincides with the period in which Mary Boleyn was Henry VIII's mistress. As if to cement his family's supremacy, Knollys' sister Lettice had married the Earl of Leicester at Wanstead the day before Henry had sailed from Dartmouth. Henry Knollys was close to untouchable, and he knew it. If Ralegh wished to escape the sort of humiliation being meted out to his brother, he would have to aim high indeed.

Gilbert sought to explain away Knollys' behaviour – and to avoid the conclusion that the attacks were deliberate reactions to his leadership – writing to Walsingham that Knollys must have always intended 'to break off from the beginning and . . . run some shorter course', by which phrase Gilbert means piracy. This was not implausible: like many of his peers, Knollys had a marked tendency to elide the distinction between personal promotion and the good of the realm. His morality was conditional – again, as with many contemporaries, it was commonly trumped by expedience or advantage – and there is ample evidence associating him and the *Elephant* with piracy throughout the 1570s.

But by drawing Walsingham's attention to the 'store of notorious evil men' around Knollys, Gilbert was being rather more disingenuous – and in pretending surprise and distaste not a little dishonest. There were in fact numerous pirates among the various crews, often in senior positions, a fact of which it is impossible that Gilbert and Ralegh were unaware. Indeed, it must have been policy.

The most prominent of these men was John Callis, the pilot of the *Elephant*. Born in Monmouthshire, Callis generally worked out of the south Wales ports of Penarth and Cardiff, where the local justices received stolen goods at bargain prices and in return released on bail any pirates who were unlucky enough to get arrested. Not without wit – one of his early ships was called the *Cost Me Nought* – Callis nevertheless had a reputation for exceptional brutality, which had led him to a spell in Marshalsea earlier in the year. Powerful connections spared him and he was freed on 14 July 1578; Knollys must have hired him almost immediately.[3]

But Callis was not alone: the master of Richard Udall's galleon, Court Heckenborg, a Dutchman whose name proved a particular challenge for Elizabethan orthography, was a long-term associate of Callis' and almost as prolific a criminal. Two other masters, John Granger on the *Bark Denny* and Richard Derifall on the *Francis*, had also been involved in piracy, as had Edward Denny himself. Francis Rogers on the *Galleon* was being investigated for, at the very least, receiving stolen goods from Heckenborg and Callis. Another man on Knollys' ship, Ferdinando Fielding, had sailed with Callis throughout the 1570s.

Perhaps their recruitment was a practical matter: the allure of riches from piracy, privateering and trade would draw many landsmen to England's ports and harbours whose utility at sea was strictly limited. Later, Ralegh would complain of 'these poor fishermen and idlers [who] are so ignorant in sea-service as that they know not the name of a rope and [are] therefore insufficient for such labour.'[4] Moreover if the aim was to counterbalance the inexperience of the gentlemen adventurers it was an astute, if amoral judgement: pirates, whatever their other qualities, were first and last experienced men of the sea.

Their presence also makes the status of Gilbert's voyage more uneasy and ambivalent and makes the wider claims made for it in terms of exploration and national interest difficult to sustain. Piracy was never regarded as a legitimate business; the hanging of pirates at Wapping and elsewhere was a regular occurrence through the reign. But the combination of naked self-interest and technological superiority – English ships being typically faster, more manoeuvrable and more heavily and more efficiently armed – was irresistible to many, and complicity, connivance and corruption served to give the practice a social acceptability it rarely claimed elsewhere. After all, *quid non?*

The most significant pirate on Gilbert's voyage was undoubtedly the master of Ralegh's ship. He was a Portuguese seaman named Simon Fernandes and he would have a major impact on Ralegh's career over the next decade.

Born towards the end of the 1530s in Terceira, one of the islands in the Azores – known among English sailors as the Isles of Pickery, pickery being a slang term for stealing[5] – Fernandes trained as a pilot and had sailed with the Spanish in the West Indies, probably also serving with them on expeditions up the eastern seaboard towards what is now Chesapeake Bay. He claimed to have left Spanish service following a conversion to Protestantism, but expedience is the more likely answer. He too first turns up in the records in Knollys' service, being invited by the latter to join the *Elephant* at Michaelmas 1574, but a reputation for piracy seems to have preceded him.[6] One charge has him killing seven men with his bare hands.[7] He had been arrested the previous year and brought to London in one of the government's periodic efforts to show it took the issue of piracy seriously – the same sweep that had caught Callis. But seamen with detailed first-hand knowledge of the Spanish West Indies were rare in England – Mendoza immediately identified him as a threat to Spanish interests – and someone brought Fernandes to the attention of Walsingham, who effected his release from prison and took him on to his payroll. From henceforward Fernandes would be 'Walsingham's man'.

Fernandes' conversation, it was said, was 'offensive to god, and nothing Christian-like, for yet he rejoiced in things stark naughty, bragging in his sundry piracies'.[8] He was known to claim that he was engaged in a one-man war with Philip II that transcended the legal niceties of Anglo-Spanish diplomacy; England may be at peace, he said, but he was always at war. He boasted too that he had a free pardon from five members of the Privy Council for any attacks he carried out against Spanish interests.[9] The sense of enmity with Spain in his talk is ferociously personal, but it is smothered by a self-righteousness which served to mask an easy elision of thievery into war and transformed every petty act of larceny into a principled blow against the empire. In this, Fernandes could exemplify a great many English seamen, Ralegh among them.

Fernandes' personality, his violent solipsism and unabashed greed, even when clothed in hatred of the Spanish, did not find universal favour among fellow crew-members: many grew to loathe and distrust him in more or less equal measure. Nevertheless, Ralegh must have been impressed; but then Ralegh was always ready to be seduced by the idea of secret knowledge. More importantly for their relationship, Ralegh had something Gilbert did not have: the ability to impose his authority where he lacked the social status to command it.

Coupled with a genius for persuasion, it made him a natural leader of men.

Knollys left Plymouth on 18 November, but he did not go alone. Gilbert had contrived to insult Edward Denny's pride, too, berating him for pulling his sword on an unarmed sailor to quell an argument, and Denny chose to sail with Knollys, as did the *Francis*, under Gregory Fenton. The *Red Lion*, captained by Miles Morgan, later slipped away to join him too.[10] Gilbert's lack of authority – and status – had cost him near half his fleet.

Gilbert and Ralegh took advantage of the good weather and finally took what remained of the fleet out to sea the next day. The records speak of a year's supply of food: peas and beans, bread and bacon, salt fish and biscuits – at three per man per day – and enough beef for three months.[11] A year was a long time to be away: Gilbert's grand ambitions for the voyage remained undimmed. The principal drink on board was beer, although as Ralegh unhappily noted, victuallers habitually cut costs when selling seamen beer, using any old casks to hand, even those previously used for herrings or whale oil.[12] There would too have been wine; gunpowder and shot; goods for trading. And, for the gentlemen aboard, personal effects: Ralegh himself habitually took a trunkful of books to pass the tedious hours at sea.

Gilbert's small fleet soon fell victim to the winter seas; one ship – the *Hope of Greenaway*, captained by Ralegh's brother Carew, began to leak badly and was forced to return to Plymouth, reducing the fleet to five, and the others were forced to take refuge the following month in Ireland for both repairs and supplies. Ralegh's ship the *Falcon* seems to have been a particular concern, proving difficult to handle and somehow poorly victualled, despite the lengthy preparations.[13]

Given the time of year at which he ultimately chose to sail, however, Gilbert must bear considerable responsibility for the difficulties he now faced. Summer was the safest season for crossing the Atlantic; Frobisher's three voyages to North America in the late 1570s had all departed England in May or June and returned in the autumn. It is no surprise then that by mid-December, when Gilbert and Ralegh were laid up in Ireland, their reputation at court, such as it was, was already beginning to sour, their celebrity fading. Another brother – Sir John Gilbert – was compelled to write to Walsingham to defend Gilbert against accusations circulating that the voyage had been ineptly and inadequately planned and equipped.[14]

According to Mendoza's sources, Gilbert was forced back into Irish waters in early February and by the end of the month was back in England with most of what remained of his fleet. It was an abject humiliation. One ship was missing, however: Ralegh, relishing the freedom of his first command, had ideas other than home for the *Falcon*.

He and Fernandes – the gilded young jade and the renegade pirate – made an effective if unlikely team. Supplies were low but the two worked hard to eke out what they had among the crew to extend the length of the voyage to its furthest limit. Ralegh, in a related law suit in 1581, went out of his way to praise Fernandes' diligence and good government; given that neither were qualities that most who met Fernandes noted in him, Ralegh's leadership must have brought out the best in him. But they were also qualities that Ralegh was discovering in himself.[15]

With almost nothing on board left to drink, Ralegh took the *Falcon* to Gran Canaria, where they took on 14 or 15 tonnes of canary wine and a quantity of sweet meats. From there, the ship's actions are clouded in unknowns. What little record there is comes from not one but two references – slightly contradictory though they are – in the 1587 continuation of Holinshed's *Chronicles* by Ralegh's friend John Hooker, which almost certainly derive from Ralegh himself. One account speaks of Gilbert's failure to make a planned rendezvous with Ralegh, the other of Ralegh purposely striking out for the Americas on his own 'desirous to do somewhat worthy [of] honour', reaching towards the golden shores of his imagination, a heaven just beyond his outstretched grasp. One refers to Ralegh leading more than one ship, the other to Ralegh's ship as on its own. One emphasizes terrible storms at the sea, the other a 'dangerous sea fight, when many of your company were slain and your ships therewith also sore battered and disabled'. Only one has any detail on the actual route taken, noting that Ralegh intended to sail for the West Indies but got no further than Cape Verde, off the coast of Africa – not very far west but a good deal to the south of the Canaries.

The discrepancies in these accounts are problematic. There is no record of any such sea-battle with, presumably, Spanish shipping, although Mendoza back in London continued to make considerable trouble over the transgressions of Knollys and other parties related to Gilbert's voyage, and would certainly have complained if news of another skirmish or attempted robbery came to his attention. Ralegh did not have the command of more than one ship. Cape Verde was too far south for a practical attempt on a crossing to the West Indies, which typically took advantage of the south-easterly trade winds to travel from the Canaries or the Azores.

Great heroism is certainly implied, but corroborative detail is withheld. It is in some respects a classically Raleghan moment, a sleight of hand: the great gesture shadowed by silences, by things discreetly not being said. Indeed, it is possible to speculate that the *Falcon* sailed further than the record implies. The following year a conquistador named

Pedro Sarmiento de Gamboa, crossing back home from South America and stopping at Cape Verde, heard that some time in 1579 the Portuguese had captured five Englishmen who came ashore in a boat near what is now Salvador da Bahia on the north-eastern coast of Brazil. The details of their story are hard to reconcile with any known English voyage of the period – except for the fact that they claimed to belong to a fleet of ten ships, and that the only known such fleet to have left England for the Americas at the right time was Gilbert's broken fellowship.[16] Fernandes certainly knew the coast since he had a Portuguese permit to trade in Brazil.[17] It may be relevant that Ralegh, when he came to write his *Discovery of Guiana* nearly twenty years later, does not say that his 1595 journey to the Orinoco delta and beyond was his first to the continent.

This is scant evidence, for sure, but given the pervasive secrecy surrounding the voyage, motivated in part by security concerns but later also driven by embarrassment and shame, it is hard to know if the vagueness of the accounts in Holinshead reflect concerted silences or merely the absence of significant things to say. However, their simple presence in the *Chronicles* suggests that Ralegh, at least, in 1587 at the very peak of his power and influence, still had an itch to scratch about his role in the enterprise, perhaps chafing at the strategic need for quiet over any reconnaissance that he may have done. It may be objected that it is implausible that no record survives of such endeavours, but clearly there was an English ship off the coast of Brazil in 1579 for which there is no other extant data.

An alternative, less generous explanation for the presence of these accounts is that they reveal a Ralegh pathologically keen to expunge memories of a significant failure. We do not need to say that the facts as laid out by Hooker are untrue to note that such trivial action as is described has little place in a major work like Holinshed's except to burnish the reputations of the actors in it. What is said may be personal propaganda of a sort, selective and distorted in the selection, and still materially accurate. Ralegh on this reading is the upstart favourite, attempting to reframe his public persona, establishing for himself a hinterland of heroic idealism, a claim to status in the nation's history. It is the calculated mask of the intelligencer allowing an audience, private or public, to understand him in a particular, sympathetic context.

There was nothing sympathetic about opinion when Ralegh and Fernandes brought the *Falcon* home in May 1579. Since November, Knollys and his associates had been busy pursuing their own objectives, and complaints rolled in to the authorities over the following months as a result of their activities. The *Francis*, in particular, was the cause of a considerable commotion: it took some £4,400 of linen cloth from two French ships, the *Mary* and the *Margaret*, some of which was sold at Torbay. The remainder was disguised in hogsheads and other barrels and stored by Knollys at Castle Cornet on the Isle of Guernsey, courtesy of his sister Elizabeth and her new husband Thomas Leighton, the island's governor. It must have been particularly galling for Gilbert that the only apparent material returns from his ambitious voyage were derived from Knollys' piracies.

Ralegh may have thought he had done enough to earn himself a hero's welcome back in Plymouth, but if that were the case he must have been quickly disabused of the idea. By May the primary tone of correspondence and comment had become hostile and accusatory, and the Privy Council had already gone so far as to revoke Gilbert's licence to travel on 26 April.[18] The following month, in a pointed letter to Gilbert's brother Sir John, the Privy Council noted that it had asked for bonds and sureties of good behaviour from Sir Humphrey, which he had failed to offer, despite remaining along the coast. Some of his men then stole a Spanish ship laden with oranges and lemons from the port at Dartmouth. The government demanded redress and Gilbert and Ralegh were stayed in port. It was the first time Ralegh's name would be discussed at the Privy Council, and the circumstances could hardly be less flattering.

Just a few days later, the council's tone hardened further. It wrote to the sheriff, vice-admiral, commissioners of piracies and justices of peace in the county of Devon requiring them:

> to make diligent enquiry of all piracies by seas and robberies by land committed by any such persons which heretofore pretended to accompany Sir Humphrey Gilbert, knight, Walter Rawley ... and others in their voyages, and to either commit them to prison, or if they shall so see cause, to take good bands of them to be forthcoming to answer to such things as they shall be charged with according to law.[19]

In a little over a year, the promise of maritime and martial glory had faded to ignominy, embarrassment and shame.

The plain fact was that the voyage had not only failed to achieve any of its objectives, it had failed even to get itself into a position to achieve them, having divided in two and proved itself incapable of crossing the Atlantic. Churchyard had promised his friends a prose celebration of their triumphant voyage; it would go unwritten. Rewards went ungiven, reputations unwon. Ralegh was forced to skulk back to London, his tail between his legs: the sea was forbidden him by the government, which again wrote to the juridical authorities in Devon that:

> Walter Ralegh [and others are] to remain on land, in her Majesty's name charging every of them to surcease to

proceed in that their enterprised journey, and to meddle no further therein without express order from [the Privy Council][20]

The gulf between hopes and reality yawned wide, stretching to breaking point the most precious commodity an aspiring courtier like Ralegh could have: usefulness.

By mid-1579 then, Ralegh had reason to be concerned about the way he might be defined at court, and he must have viewed the damage to his reputation, such as it was, by the voyage's striking lack of success as inherently desperate. Piracy was one thing – especially as practised against the Spanish; Henry Knollys had a perfectly successful, if less than stellar, career at court despite his criminal proclivities. Failure, the enemy of ambition and hope, was altogether worse. Gilbert had aimed high and lost and Ralegh, who had achieved more than his fellow captains, was associated in that failure by the Privy Council. He had good reason to feel aggrieved.

It was an inauspicious beginning to his public career. There were certainly personal rewards for him in the voyage – his first command, his ability to lead, a renewed sense of discipline and purpose – but if he was to continue seeking public rewards he would have to go further and achieve more. But Ralegh was about to make things worse.

IX: EXCESS OF DUTY

Never think Fortune can bear the sway
If virtue watch, and will not her obey

ELIZABETH I TO SIR WALTER RALEGH

For Ralegh to have absented himself from London and the court for eight months was a risk, but it also reveals how little he had to lose. In that absence events had changed the political landscape in ways that both empowered and imperilled his circle of friends around the Earl of Oxford. In short, Elizabeth had decided to pursue the Alençon marriage proposal made to her in the summer of 1578.

For Elizabeth, the same reservations that had stalled the match earlier in the decade still carried weight: Alençon was childishly short, disfigured by smallpox scars and some twenty years younger than the queen. He was, too, no less Catholic than he had ever been. But there were other, more personal considerations that led her to revive the idea of matrimony one final time. She had been deserted by the Earl of Leicester, and this was the last opportunity she would have to savour the idea of marriage; Burghley – optimism for once trumping a pragmatic approach – persuaded himself she could still bear children. Elizabeth may have concurred.

More importantly, there were political calculations: the prospect of marriage kept Alençon in the field as England's proxy in the Low Countries' struggle against imperial Spain. The promise of an alliance between France and England, meanwhile, was intended to check the ambitions of Philip II's increasingly hostile and aggressive government in Spain, which – having long ago decided that Elizabeth had no intention of marrying – looked on the negotiations with a mixture of incredulity and alarm.

At home, the possibility that she might marry a Catholic weakened the cause of Mary Stuart, still in her prison at Tutbury, but created other complexities. Country and government were divided on the issue: Puritan fellow-travellers like Leicester and Walsingham were hostile and fearful of the consequences of a foreign Catholic consort for the queen, while moderates saw an opportunity for the healing of political wounds, for renewed stability and – just possibly – a settled succession. The English Catholics, meanwhile, had high hopes of the marriage: the negotiations coincided with greater toleration for their religious practices – or less overt repression, at least – and those active in court politics saw in it an opening to overturn the upstart Protestant hegemony of Elizabeth's key advisers, and to restore the older, more entitled order of families. Among those with such hopes were the Earl of Oxford and the extensive Howard family.

To some extent they were put up to it. Mauvissière, the French ambassador, tasked with building support at court for the match, recognized that the opposition of Leicester and Walsingham would have to be neutralized or over-ridden if the case for marriage could make headway politically, and for that he would need proxies of his own to promote the cause. He allowed the Howard/Oxford axis to believe that Alençon was seeking liberty of conscience for the English Catholics as part of his price for marriage, whereas his only interest was in seeing that he himself would be free to practise Catholicism in public.[1] It wasn't difficult to persuade them that fortune's wheel was finally turning in their favour, and the force of their hope swept caution aside.

This then is how the English body politic presented itself when Alençon's envoy, Jehan de Simier, arrived in London on 5 January 1579 to negotiate the politics of the marriage contract. It was a member of Oxford's cabal Edward Stafford – accompanied by another, Arthur Throckmorton, Ralegh's future brother-in-law – who was sent on the ninth to meet him. Stafford, a well-connected man whose self-belief and ambitions were unmatched by his abilities, was one of London's premier spendthrifts, but he had established a good rapport with Simier and his master when an envoy to France the summer before. He took the entourage up the Thames to Syon House, which belonged to the Earl of Northumberland, another Oxfordian, at Kew, and then further upstream to the court at Richmond the following day, where a magnificent ball was held that evening in Simier's honour.[2] The entertainment was a mock tournament between six gentlemen and six ladies, the latter pointedly surrendering to the former; Leicester, it was said, had to scheme to get an invitation.[3]

Simier himself was Alençon's chamberlain, and a man of exquisite charm and judgement; Elizabeth took to him immediately. She unashamedly enjoyed the company of charming, attentive men, and Simier was adept in the games and rituals of courtly love, but that enjoyment does not necessarily equate to seduction: Elizabeth was quite capable of relishing immersion in the experience while deferring judgement on its purpose. Hatton and Leicester, however, were jealous of the time and attention she lavished on him, and

Leicester muttered darkly about 'amorous potions and unlawful arts' having been used to suborn her to Simier's will.[4]

Simier stayed at court: through a bitter, snow-filled February and on into spring, he moved between private conversations with Elizabeth – accompanying her as she walked her gardens – and negotiations with Burghley and other privy councillors, singly and collectively, formally and informally. The tide of opposition was rising, however, strengthening Leicester and Walsingham's hand and weakening that of the English Catholics, if they deigned to notice such things. Popular opinion was not the sort of cause they cared for.

By the time the chastened Ralegh returned to London – most likely in early summer – the politics of the moment were becoming increasingly fractured and confrontational, even as official talks had moved on to the subject of a meeting between Alençon and Elizabeth, something she claimed to regard as essential before anything further could be agreed. It was another kind of deferral, of course. And there were also those disfiguring scars to consider.

Was she seriously considering marrying Alençon? Many of those around her certainly thought so, and no one denied the enthusiasm with which she embraced the process. More cynical onlookers like Leicester and Mendoza doubted that she was any more sincere now about marriage than she had ever been – but her compelling performance, wielding the blunt power of the royal prerogative with a certain wistful reticence and charm, made them fear that she might be. That doubt was enough to keep them, nervous and uncertain, in the field. The Oxford/Howard axis meanwhile, with Ralegh back in their midst, were increasingly confident of their impending triumph and imprudent with it. They began passing intelligence about Elizabeth's plans and intentions to Simier: one of them would creep into the garden of his house at Greenwich and leave marks on a particular stone to indicate where and when they should meet. And it was more than court gossip that they had to pass on to him: with the connivance of a number of Elizabeth's ladies in waiting, they contrived to have letters and other papers lifted from the queen's pockets while she slept, to be read, shared and returned before morning.[5]

Was Ralegh involved in such dubious practices? It is certainly possible. Oxford later implicated both Charles Arundell and Henry Howard – and also, by virtue of the accusation, himself; Ralegh however was certainly close to several ladies of the privy chamber, a fact that belies – or perhaps explains – his later bitter comment that 'they were like witches: they could do no hurt, but they could do no good'.

One of the few early poems of his to survive is, in one of the two extant manuscript versions, titled 'A poem put into my Lady Leighton's pocket by Sir W. Ralegh'. Leighton was the younger sister of Henry and Lettice Knollys, and was newly-wed to the nearly fifty-year-old Sir Thomas Leighton the year before.

It is by no means a strong poem, being by turns formulaic and opaque. While it was clearly written in response to a particular set of circumstances, it is now adrift of the referents that would help us make sense of it, and it never manages to transcend the moment: too much has been lost. Ralegh sounds unsure of himself: a man observing and learning from the world, rather than participating fully in it, and its phrasing is awkward even for juvenilia. It flirts with both self-assertion and reticence, yet seems curiously unresolved at the close.

As a love poem, too, it appears singularly lacking in focus, but then perhaps it is really about something other than love. The context may be sexual in nature but is not unambiguously so. Of the poem's characters – I, thee and they – Ralegh refrains from suggesting an identity for the last, and figures himself as a man cast out from the grace of Lady Leighton's presence for indeterminate reasons. Although the description attached to it, then, seems at first sight a salacious nod to clandestine impropriety, in the context of the activities of Oxford's circle during the Alençon courtship it may take on other meanings too, hinting both in its content and its method of transmission at a more troubled birth, and at other kinds of covert acts.

Oxford's circle was also responsible for warning Simier of an impending knife attack, an event that has otherwise gone unrecorded. In response to the warning, Simier borrowed a 'privy doublet' – a light piece of body armour worn beneath the shirt – from Oxford himself. Whatever the details of the knife attack, the precautionary advice seems to have been timely. It was rumoured that Leicester tried to have Simier poisoned and, when that plan failed, that he employed his man, Robin Tider, to lie in wait and shoot him as he came out of a garden gate at Greenwich. Tider balked when he saw how well guarded Simier was.[6]

Alençon's passport was signed on 6 July and dispatched the following day. The arrangements for his arrival were so secret that a month later Walsingham was still in the dark, writing to Burghley from court – Burghley being away in Northamptonshire – that no one aside from Elizabeth, Simier and a handful of others knew what was being planned.[7] On 17 July, as Elizabeth was being rowed in her barge near Greenwich accompanied by Simier, Hatton and Lincoln, the anxious calm that had settled over events was riven by a gunshot from a nearby boat and one of her bargemen fell, a few feet from Elizabeth, bullet wounds in both arms.

Ever since the discovery of the Ridolfi plot a decade earlier many had feared this moment: an attempt on Elizabeth's life.

Assassination, aside from its obvious horror, held a particular dread for the creatures of Elizabeth's court since the queen's apparent disinclination to wedlock, and the peculiar circumstances of her inheritance, meant that if she died there was no clear succession. The most plausible candidate under the rules of primogeniture, Mary Stuart, was also among the least acceptable politically on account of her Catholicism. England was a heartbeat from civil war and anarchy, its most powerful men always on the cusp of ruin.

The culprit, a servingman named Thomas Appletree, was quickly sentenced to death, but Elizabeth, who had mastered herself almost immediately after the initial shock, reprieved him at the foot of the gallows, happy to be persuaded by his protestations of incompetence rather than malice. It is unlikely her belief in his innocence was anything other than genuine – Elizabeth was bloodily vindictive when genuine threats against her person were revealed – and accidental though the shooting was, Appletree's reprieve did little to ease the tension or the uneasy awareness that the Alençon match was increasingly unpopular in the country.

Oxford, if Henry Howard is to be believed, responded to the scent of violence in the summer air with planned attacks of his own. Howard claimed that Oxford considered having Hatton killed as he made his way one night to his chamber, and that he plotted Leicester's death twice – once as an assault from Oxford's 'cutters' as he travelled back to Wanstead and a second as he landed at the river stairs at court. Under pressure, Arundell later associated Ralegh's name with the putative murders of Leicester, explicitly inviting him to provide supportive testimony, but perhaps also implying that Ralegh was being asked to take an active part in the killings.[8]

The details are unverifiable and, if any such assaults occurred, no records survive, but violence – against enemies

and as a reaction to perceived betrayals among his friends –
was certainly one of the ways in which Oxford routinely
attempted to correct life's imperfections, and the accusations
are plausible, if unproven. If too there is something repetitive
and tiresome about Oxford's many threats, at the very least
they reveal the climate of thought of those in his circle, and tell
us something about the culture of unexceptional viciousness
that held sway.

Henry Noel, for instance, had been arrested a couple of
months earlier, in May 1579, for his part in a fight with one
John Parker, a gentleman, and his servants, in which one of
Parker's servants died. Ralegh's transgressions were less griev-
ous at this point, but they still reveal an ugly strain of cruelty:
Aubrey tells a story about how the young Ralegh, tired of the
railing of his friend Charles Chester, 'one time at a tavern . . .
beat him and sealed up his mouth . . . with hard wax'.

As for Oxford, the only thing that held him back from the
execution of his plans was the same flaw that crippled his
career – an inability to pursue anything with any seriousness
for long. Nevertheless, there were those for whom he could
sustain his hatred long enough to wound its target; in time,
Ralegh would be one of them.

The atmosphere in 1578 was further heightened in August by
the publication of *The Discoverie of a Gaping Gulf Wherein
England is Like to be Swallowed*, an excoriating attack on
Alençon and the marriage – and to a lesser degree Elizabeth
herself for entertaining the idea – by the Puritan lawyer John
Stubbe. Many suspected Stubbe had been briefed by Leicester
or Walsingham directly, and the book hit a nerve with both the
public and with Elizabeth, who wanted to hang its author and
his associates. In the end she had to settle for having Stubbe's
right hand amputated, a punishment that was met with

disturbing silence by the crowd at Westminster who saw it exacted. Stubbe called out 'God save the queen' before collapsing. Not one person took up the cry.

On 17 August, Alençon himself arrived – to nobody's particular surprise but Simier, who was still in bed when his master burst in. For eleven days, Alençon's presence at court would be an open secret, and the gestures towards pretence that he was not – hiding behind a tapestry to spy as the queen laughingly danced for him one evening – were somewhat less than persuasive. Elizabeth liked him immensely, his energy, charm and enthusiasm; his company was almost as pleasurable as Simier's, in fact.

Shortly after Alençon appeared at court – and perhaps inflamed by the heightened stakes his presence represented – the suppressed rivalry between Leicester's coalition against the marriage and the ascendant Oxford set burst rancorously into the open on the tennis court at Greenwich. It was in part a very Elizabethan conjunction of two highly combustible elements: sensitivity to perceived slights of honour and aggravated status anxiety, horror at transgression of the established hierarchy. It took only a childish insult to ignite the affair.

Philip Sidney was a cultured, well-travelled and extraordinarily self-possessed young courtier; his only obvious flaw at a court that privileged beauty was his looks, since his face had been scarred by smallpox in childhood. At twenty-four he was an exact contemporary of Ralegh's and if his literary reputation had yet to be won, then his intellect, talents, education and birth all seemed to destine him to greatness. Why that promise perennially failed to mature into major office and reward, despite the influence of his uncles, the Earls of Leicester and Sussex, remains unclear, although he evidently inspired a degree of ambivalence in Elizabeth, who seemed wary of rewarding him with her favour; he in turn could appear uninterested in according her the degree of submissiveness to which she was accustomed.

But whatever his connections, Sidney was still a mere gentleman. He was playing on the tennis court, when the Earl of Oxford strode on – 'swollen with the wind of his faction, then reigning' said an observer – and demanded that Sidney cede the court to him, his obvious social superior. Sidney, who was no less lacking in self-regard, stood his ground; his patronizing demurral – in essence telling Oxford to look to his manners – brought forth all the aristocrat's raging hauteur, and he called Sidney a puppy.

It seems to us rather tame as insults go, but both Oxford and Sidney understood and felt the force of its contempt. Some of Alençon's entourage, attending to business in the galleries overlooking the court, hurried over to see what the entertainment was. Noticing them, Sidney demanded Oxford repeat the insult, and when Oxford did so, Sidney – no doubt in part aiming to weaken Oxford's standing among the French – called him a liar and left the court.

Ralegh, for one, would be disdainful about those who gave the lie over obvious absurdities, thus aggravating trivialities until they became life-or-death issues. 'I will not deny but that it is an extreme rudeness to tax any man in public with an untruth,' he noted with urbane clarity, 'but all that is rude ought not to be civilized with death.'[9] It was the self-assured insight of a man habituated in childhood to shrugging off insult and slander, a man who had no use for respect.

Ralegh's cool rationality was not shared by either of the combatants in the tennis-court dispute, although if Sidney thought a duel was inevitable, then he reckoned without the Earl of Oxford, who, as a man given the lie, was the one honour-bound to issue the challenge. Sidney waited, but nothing came. It was not until Sidney prompted him a day later that Oxford sent two messengers over with a formal challenge.

The men he chose for the delicate role were Charles Arundell and Walter Ralegh. Of the two, it is Arundell who is most closely associated with Oxford, but at this moment Ralegh seems to have had Oxford's ear: it was Ralegh in whom Oxford confided that he had been offered an annual income of ten thousand crowns by Alençon if he followed him back to France, a promise reportedly sealed by the gift of a jewel after Alençon returned home.[10]

In meeting Sidney, however, Ralegh was coming face to face with a man widely regarded as the greatest of their generation. They were arguably men of equal talents and ambitions, if unequal advantages, and Sidney's stellar reputation – which flourished despite Elizabeth's ambivalence towards him – must have caused Ralegh to reflect with a certain bitterness on both his own unremarkable status and his failure to win reward. But the truth is that whatever hopes Ralegh had as a part of Oxford's circle, they were largely predicated on the actions of other people; little of his life in the 1570s, with the exception of the Gilbert voyage, showed much desire on his part to be actor in his own destiny. His failures thus far were failures of will as much as of achievement.

Sidney had a seriousness of purpose which Ralegh – and most of those with whom he had hitherto associated in London – entirely lacked, and while both men had a high regard for their own opinions, it was Sidney who spoke with a free and spirited candour that Ralegh could only have admired. When Elizabeth intervened over the tennis court squabble, reminding Sidney that deference to one's superiors was fundamental to an ordered society, he rather tartly replied that precedence did not excuse iniquitous behaviour, and proceeded to lecture her, politely but firmly, about a gentleman's liberty under the law. He would shortly write *A Letter to Queen Elizabeth Touching her Marriage with Monsieur*, an extensively circulated manuscript arguing against the marriage; even with his connections it was a courageous thing to do, and he was fortunate not to suffer a similar fate to Stubbe.

When Ralegh looked back on Sidney's brief career after his death in 1586, he was honest enough to admit what must have been apparent to those who knew both men: that he envied Sidney his greatness, acknowledging his virtues privately to himself, but withheld his praise – perhaps even denying it – in public. It was a brave admission at a time when veneration of Sidney's memory was at its height, and it reveals a degree of self-awareness and self-criticism, unmediated by rhetoric or dramatic gesture, that was new in Ralegh. After all, humility is not a trait for which Ralegh has ever been widely noted, but contemplation of Sidney's qualities drew it out in him all the same. If he only found the means and motivation to say so after Sidney's death, he did so in a way that acknowledged the fault retrospectively.

On the other hand, although such scepticism was against the tide of thought at court, he was not alone in it: he would have found a receptive audience for his doubts in Elizabeth, who evidently liked the ideal that Sidney represented rather more than she did the man himself. In any event, on finding Sidney, Ralegh and Arundell delivered Oxford's challenge, and received an eager verbal response in return. Reporting back to Oxford they were stunned to discover that Sidney's enthusiasm was not shared by their patron, who admitted to them that he had no intention of fighting. Instead he sketched out plans to Arundell, Howard and Ralegh to have Sidney murdered in his bed at Greenwich by twelve gunmen, whom Oxford would arrange to have slip away by barge down to Gravesend.[11]

Arundell and Howard later professed to considerable disquiet about such talk, and from the fact that Arundell named Ralegh as capable of supplying corroborative testimony, it seems reasonable to infer that they knew Ralegh to share their discomfort. Nevertheless, the events of the summer of 1579 make it quite evident that Ralegh was very much at the heart of the Oxford circle on his return from Gilbert's failed adventure, and perhaps far more so than he had been before his departure. When he had embarked on the *Falcon* the summer before, the group was an amorphous collection of individuals loosely cohering around an attitude of disaffection; it had vague aspirations and vaguer plans, but little impetus or direction. By the time of his return, however, its members had been propelled by the Alençon project into the ascendant, with favour, influence and power approaching fast over the horizon. It would be surprising, in the circumstances, if Ralegh did not cleave close to his friends, whatever his personal qualms: their rise seemed to offer the prospect of reward without effort or endeavour.

On 28 August Alençon left Greenwich abruptly after receiving news of the murder of his friend, Bussy D'Ambois, and Simier continued with the marriage negotiations, which would take a further three months to conclude. Elizabeth was seemingly no clearer in her own mind on the subject and sought the advice of the Privy Council. But, twenty years into her reign, no one on the council was rash enough to second guess her decision: after two days' debate at the beginning of October, the only thing on which it could agree was to support whatever decision she came to. Elizabeth was reportedly both disgusted at the lack of courage and devastated by the absence of unequivocal support for the marriage.

Nevertheless, by 10 November, if Mendoza is to be trusted, she had told her advisers that she intended to marry and that nothing they could say could dissuade her – although he later heard that she had also asked them to put in writing their individual opinions on the subject.[12] Knowing precisely where her counsellors stood – the quality, strength and direction of their thinking – was vital if she was to have any freedom of manoeuvre herself. Agreement on the marriage terms was finally reached on 24 November, and Simier left Greenwich the following day. It seemed as if Elizabeth's long maidenhood was over; Mendoza gaily predicted civil war in England and Catholicism triumphant.

Simier made his way slowly down to Dover, where Sir William Winter was in harbour with his ship the *Scout*, having been summoned back from service patrolling the seas around Ireland to ferry Alençon and now his envoy back and forth.[13] There Simier waited for his friend Stafford, who was again to act as Elizabeth's envoy to Monsieur; Stafford had secretly married Douglas Sheffield, Leicester's former mistress, on the twenty-seventh. Simier was still relentlessly wooing Elizabeth – writing six letters in five days as he dawdled through Kent's gentle hills, each letter carefully bound in pink silk. She sent back her replies via Henry Howard, a mark of trust which reflected her recognition of the status the Howard/Oxford axis was now enjoying.

But Howard and Stafford were not the only Oxfordians to accompany Simier as he crossed the Channel in what proved to be a brief window of fine weather at the end of the month: Arthur Gorges was there, too, as were the ubiquitous Arundell and Ralegh. Ralegh, happy perhaps to show off the circles in which he now moved, introduced both Simier and Stafford to his sometime bedfellow, Stephen Powle – only a little sickened, Powle confessed, by the pitch and yawn of the ship – who was coincidentally making the Channel crossing on his way to Geneva.[14]

That Ralegh was familiar with Simier is no surprise given what we now know about his role in Oxford's inner circle, although the only definitive evidence for it is one casual aside in Powle's private notebook. While it demonstrates the extent to which his effortless presence in Oxford's entourage had enhanced his network of potential associates, and therefore amplified his ability to project his talents, it also underscores the extent to which he had become almost wholly indebted to one particular faction. That was fine if Ralegh wished to remain a great man's attendant; but if he desired greatness himself, he would have to break free.

This bare twenty-mile sea-journey, accompanying Simier as he returned to France with the marriage settlement secured among his papers, was in many respects the high water mark for Oxford's set. There must have been a sense of victory, of vindication, as they surveyed the future. Even an attack by pirates operating out of Flushing on the return journey – they were pursued for some four hours through the narrow waters between England and France before the pirates gave up the chase – can have done little to dampen their ardour. They may even have regarded it as a backhanded compliment, since Arundell later alleged that the pirate captains, Clark and Harris, were serving under orders from Leicester.[15]

But there were already signs back at court, if they heeded them, that disaster was imminent. Oxford was not among those accompanying Simier, primarily because he had been confined to his chambers at court in Greenwich – a form of house arrest – following a quixotic attempt to libel the Earl of Leicester.[16] It was a foolhardy idea in any circumstance: Leicester's star may have been for the moment obscured, but he was still the most powerful man at Elizabeth's court and it would take a well-substantiated charge of extraordinary gravity to eclipse him entirely. Yet the most striking aspect of Oxford's libels against Leicester was their weakness. Oxford himself seems to have realized this, albeit after the event, and tried without success to manipulate Howard into supporting him.[17]

In fact, the accusations tell us as much about Oxford's prejudices as Leicester's pride and ambition. Leicester was alleged to claim that 'he was able to make the proudest subject to sweat ... and that he made the Duke of Norfolk stoop notwithstanding all his bragging'. This was no more than the brutal truth, whether Leicester said it or not, but the palpable shock is Oxford's not ours: the seventeeth earl is affronted that the son and grandson of traitors could say such things about England's only duke.

Similarly it is hard to imagine Elizabeth being particularly offended by Leicester's supposed revelation that 'the queen was of the hardest disposition ... and that no man in England had gotten anything but by his labour'. Only those who did not know Elizabeth well believed she dispensed her favour and goodwill for no return, and only those from the old-established Norman aristocracy believed that they deserved reward for their mere existence. The new rising men of England – the Cecils, the Dudleys, the Hattons – expected to sweat. The only charge with any bite was the claim that Leicester had told Oxford, four days before the queen heard of the death of the Earl of Essex that the earl 'could not live past such a certain time prefixed'. Leicester's reputation as a man willing to murder to achieve his ends was longstanding, if unsupported by anything other than circumstantial evidence.

As an accusation it was vague enough to give Leicester room for manoeuvre, but it was nasty enough to wound, and no less cruel in its reminder of Leicester's recent marriage to Essex's widow, with all that it entailed for Elizabeth. But compared to the rich seam of vilification mined by Arundell in *Leicester's Commonwealth*, Oxford's effort is poor as invective goes. In comparison, too, to the fertile inventions of his private boasts there is something sterile and unimaginative about them, as if they were goaded out of the accuser extempore, a bitter expurgation, rather than a coherent recitation of failures and frauds.

Howard's dismissive summary – 'my Lord of Oxford was put to bed for want of proof' – nicely captures the adolescent inadequacy of the episode.[18] It did, however, have unforeseen consequences. Oxford, confined to his chambers as he was for some weeks, continued on a confrontational path, his naturally acid disposition sublimating into something darker and altogether more corrosive for all concerned.

He had always had a taste for misogynistic invective against Elizabeth. One of his boasts from his travels was that 'the meanest shoemaker's wife in Milan ... is more gallant and delicately suited every common working day than the queen our mistress is at Whitsuntide'; on another occasion he upbraided Francis Southwell for praising Elizabeth's singing, swearing 'by the blood of God that she had the worst voice, and did everything with the worst grace, that ever any woman did'. Oxford could never brook any compliments of her wit or beauty; he himself was, he said waspishly, only ever at a loss for words when asked to speak in praise of her.[19]

But under house arrest at Greenwich, Oxford's assaults on Elizabeth's reputation went further. Howard later wrote to Elizabeth of Oxford's

> slanderous and hateful speech against your Majesty at Greenwich where he was restrained to his chamber ... where I willed him before with Rawley to forbear such speech as nobody could endure with duty to your majesty ... This beastly blindness which possessed him so far as it dispossessed him both of wit and reason was the cause

why they forsook him that made more account of your
good look than of his life and feared still lest your majesty,
discovering this fraud with time would thereupon dis-
countenance all those that by depending on his train
might seem to be partakers of his folly.[20]

What exactly did he say? The explicit answer is coyly withheld
by Oxford's accusers, Howard referring to Oxford having
'vaunted some favours from your Majesty which I dare take
mine oath upon the sacred sacrament were never yet imparted
unto any man that lived on this earth', but the implication
was clear enough, echoing the slanders that Elizabeth had
attracted throughout her adult life. Both Arundell and Howard
cited Oxford's claim that Elizabeth 'must be caressed for the
pound and another for his pleasure': he reluctantly flirted and
worse with Elizabeth for money – but looked elsewhere for
gratification.

It is instructive, after all the seditious, troubling things said
at Oxford's table, that it is comment on Elizabeth's person, on
her quasi-sexual relationship with courtiers such as Oxford,
that drove men like Ralegh from his table. They understood its
dangers. Indeed, the episode looks forward to, and may
inform, Ralegh's later observation at the end of her reign that
the young Essex sealed his fate not by insurrection but by his
insolent remarks about Elizabeth's body, the one unpardonable
sin at her court.

In any event, judging from Howard's description of the
group's reaction to these latest outbursts of Oxford's, this is
clearly the moment the Howard/Oxford axis began to unravel.
From his trajectory thereafter, this must be the moment Ralegh
too began to steer a different course, fearing a future as
collateral damage in the apparently looming wreck of Oxford's
career. The decision may have been forced upon him, but he

had opted for freedom at last; as Howard implied, in choosing his queen he was also choosing himself.

The irony is that, compelled to decide between Oxford and Elizabeth in December 1579, Ralegh's final choice of Elizabeth was at once an assertion of independence and a commitment to a life of dependency on her favour, her 'good looks'. But it was also his first demonstrable personal act of loyalty to her – and it almost cost him his life.

X: THE RIGHT-FLOURISHING MAN

The right-flourishing man in study is nothing but study;
in love, nothing but love; in war, nothing but war.

GABRIEL HARVEY

If 1579 had proved a turbulent year, it served merely to presage the storms of 1580. Elizabeth entered the year with evidently cooling enthusiasm for the Alençon marriage now that Simier and his master were back home in France and the gaudy, quotidian thrills of courtship were receding. The strategic need for some form of alliance was no less pressing, but perhaps she felt that she had done enough to solicit French support without entangling herself any further, although she would continue to relish the emotional highs of diplomatic seduction – its feints, flurries and raptures – for several years yet. Burghley, less sanguine as always, warned her to plan for the perilous likelihood of foreign invasion: building up military capability, strengthening naval defences and grubbing up the last roots of English Catholic power.

Ralegh, meanwhile, never a man with much patience for incremental change, abandoned Oxford and sought support from the Earl of Leicester. How introductions were effected is unclear; it is possible, for example, that Ralegh's cousin Edward Denny, a close friend of Philip Sidney's, played a significant role. Leicester would almost certainly have viewed Ralegh with suspicion given the company he had been keeping – the Howards' mistrust of Leicester was entirely mutual, and Leicester had marked out Charles Arundell for a troublemaker some years past[1] – and it is difficult to see what Ralegh had to offer in the short term aside from a ready stream of intelligence about Oxford's cabal and its intrigues with the French. But for Ralegh, the decision was without doubt an unambiguous repudiation of the last few years of his life. What is important about it is the humility, courage and clarity of thought that it must have taken; by breaking with one circle and choosing its antithesis, Ralegh was radically asserting his own autonomy and will. He would never be Leicester's man in the way that he had been Oxford's.

It is commonplace to talk of politics at Elizabeth's court being built around competing factions – Oxford, Cecil, Leicester and so on – and it would be foolish to deny the impact of patronage on political muscle; but these groupings were nevertheless always more fluid and contingent, the oppositions less absolute and stable, than is usually allowed. The intriguing point about Ralegh's move is that after he left the Oxford/Howard circle he never really belonged to another. Henceforward, he could no longer be found in any one set; he was too supple intellectually, too expedient, too self-aware to be so defined. He moved between the different worlds with characteristic indifference to their boundaries and to the bonds of loyalty and deference which they were supposed to imply; indeed, that indifference was necessary to enable him to move at all. Ralegh aspired to be of no particular party now but his own, and showed little interest in developing a following of his own at court. He will always be himself: a faction of one.

Nevertheless, the move must have been driven by fear as much as ambition: it was by no means certain, despite Elizabeth's havering, that the Alençon courtship would not lead to marriage and therefore to the diminution of his new-found patron. The fact was that Ralegh had seen the future with Oxford and it scared him. Leicester may have been the obvious – if not the only – candidate if he wanted to put distance between himself and his recent past, but it may also have been an attempt to gravitate closer to Elizabeth, a way of displaying his true loyalty to her.

The question was, how to prove it?

Oxford, Ralegh's erstwhile friend, had been released from house arrest when the court moved on from Greenwich to Whitehall towards the end of December 1579, an event he seems to have celebrated with the pursuit and seduction of Anne Vavasour, a young new maid of honour in Elizabeth's bedchamber. His relationship with Ralegh, already strained, cannot have been improved by Ralegh's dedication to her of one his best early poems, sometimes known as 'The Advice'.

True to its adopted title, the poem advises Anne not to submit to the seductions of an unnamed, unworthy suitor, whom it is not difficult to identify in the circumstances. It may also be true, however, that Ralegh was unconsciously address- ing his own fears and insecurities as he sought to distance himself from Oxford's unstable slanders. Couplets like 'For this be sure, the fort of fame once won,/Farewell the rest, thy happy days are done' have a certain applicability for a man contemplating the ruin of his reputation – at this point arguably the only commodity at his disposal.

Elizabeth had always been tolerant of Oxford's faults, despite her loud contempt for his profligacy, and she now attempted a rapprochement with him: the two were seen walking together in private conversation in the gardens at Whitehall on Wednesday 27 January. But Oxford was still intent on nursing the previous year's enmities back to life: the same day as he spoke to Elizabeth, he sent a new written challenge to Philip Sidney, probably using Arthur Throckmorton as his messenger. Two days later, and no doubt as a result of his letter, Elizabeth again commanded him to keep to his chamber. A week later the lord chamberlain, Sussex, ordered the same of Throckmorton.[2]

Ralegh had problems of his own to contend with, however. On Wednesday 5 February, two days before Throckmorton's house arrest, he found himself walking through the wet grass of the Sermon Court at Whitehall, where courtiers came to watch and listen when the Bishop of London preached to Elizabeth. Ralegh climbed the stone steps which led to a balustraded wooden terrace running along two sides of the court. In one direction the steps led east to Elizabeth's private rooms overlooking the Thames, but Ralegh had no place there as yet. At the top of the stairs Ralegh turned south and made his way to the council chamber, formerly Henry VIII's bedchamber; with him walked a fellow courtier named Sir Thomas Perrott. The young men had been summoned by the Privy Council to answer for a fight between the two of them in the precincts at Whitehall, both no doubt quickly rehearsing in their minds the necessary balance of contrition and swagger.[3]

Winter daylight came through wide mullion windows which opened on to the courtyard; on better days royal guests stood here to listen to the lesson and look down on the fine, square russet-painted wood-panelled pulpit and the courtiers gathered around it. Across the room the chimneypiece bore Elizabeth's coat of arms, crisply carved, supported by two lions. The fire in the hearth warmed the chamber but there can have been little warmth in the welcome Ralegh and Perrott received:

membership of the Privy Council was an onerous duty, made irksome by having to deal with sometimes lethal trivialities like this. Most of the councillors present had served Elizabeth for decades: waiting were Burghley; the Earls of Leicester, Bedford, Lincoln and Sussex; Sir Henry Sidney; Sir Thomas Bromley, the Lord Chancellor; Thomas Wilson, one of the queen's two principal secretaries; and Sir Christopher Hatton.

The council's distaste for Ralegh had already been aroused by his activities in connection with Gilbert's voyage. Now he was before them for the first time, they had little sympathy to spare. Perrott's father, Sir John, counted Leicester, Sidney and Sussex as patrons. Burghley can have had little reason to favour the dissolute friends of his son-in-law, while Lincoln was the grandfather of Harry Burgh, the young member of Oxford's drunken, violent entourage who had been killed in a brawl two years earlier, which probably differed little from Ralegh's fracas with Perrott. As for Leicester, whatever overtures Ralegh had made to him, this was surely not the kind of service either had in mind.

Ralegh failed to persuade the council that he was the injured party – faith in his bona fides can hardly have been widespread – but at least he took no more than equal share of the blame. Both men were dispatched for a week to the Fleet, a late-fourteenth-century prison on the banks of the river which gave it its name; there the council required them to reflect on how, in its lovely, weary, pointed phrase, they were 'in the mean season to demean themselves quietly'.[4] They were then bound over to keep the peace for an unspecified sum before being finally released.

What lay behind the brawl is unclear, although the fact that it coincided with the house arrest of other members of Oxford's circle, including Oxford himself, suggests that its members and former members were living under extreme pressures as the set fragmented. But there may also be an explanation for the Perrott episode that reaches back to Gilbert's ill-planned enterprise the year before last. Perrott's father, primarily a military man, had been tasked with pirate-hunting in the seas around Ireland in the late summer and early autumn of 1579. Returning home in October, he had happened on the pirate Richard Derifall of the *Francis*, who as already noted, had sailed under Knollys on Gilbert's voyage.

After a lengthy chase, Perrott finally ran Derifall down on the Flemish coast only to run aground himself on the sand-banks known as the Kentish Knocks some 20 miles east of the Thames estuary, as he brought his prisoner back in atrocious weather. The ship looked likely to break up in the storm – Perrott told his son Thomas, who was sailing with him, to prepare for death – and even when refloated after the tempest eased, it was barely seaworthy. Finally they turned to Derifall's experience and expertise to get them safely back to port in England, an act of generosity, solidarity even, for which Perrott promised to intercede on Derifall's behalf and plead for mercy before the queen.

If he ever did so, he was unsuccessful. Perhaps, given that no record survives, he never did: Perrott was considered even by his contemporaries to pursue his interests with unwonted ferocity, and was not a man for quiet acquiescence; another son remembered him as one who was 'more apt to give offence unto great ones than to creep or crouch unto them'.[5] Such hard dealing would, eventually, be the death of him. Yet on 24 October, a few days after Derifall had guided them to harbour and despite whatever protestations Perrott made, the pirate was brought before the Admiralty Court concerning the thievery of the *Francis*, subsequent to its role in Gilbert's voyage. A curt note, a single word, beside Derifall's name at the head of the examination reveals the sequel: *hanged*.[6]

It is not difficult to imagine Ralegh, increasingly untroubled by deference and no less aware of the bonds of mutuality and trust which English seamen owed each other, having something to say on the lack of charity and justice in the fate of his fellow adventurer. Gilbert, too, would quarrel with the navy official William Borough over the latter's arrest and execution of ten pirate captains in the summer of 1582.[7] But equally, Perrott may have had something to say about the kind of company Ralegh kept; insecure as he was, Ralegh would have felt compelled to respond.

But if the February brawl with Perrott was due to a lack of circumspection on Ralegh's part, its sequel would have another cause entirely. This time, it would be Ralegh's own life that was at risk.

On 17 March, little more than a month later, Ralegh was attacked as he walked along a narrow, busy thoroughfare in Whitehall called The Street, through which all road traffic between Westminster and the City had to pass. The walled gardens and orchards of the palace lay to the east, beyond which ran the river; to the west were the buildings housing the royal tennis courts, the palace bowling alleys and cockpit. Movement was further constricted by the way The Street was book-ended by two great Henrician gatehouses: one at the King Street aspiring to a smooth Italianate elegance; the other, the Holbein Gate up towards Charing Cross, a more distinctively Tudor creation, with two fine tall polygonal towers and a wide oriel window overhanging the gate behind which ran the queen's privy gallery. Indeed, with the queen, watchful or at ease, able to look down on it privately from the gatehouse, the crowded, claustrophobic space of The Street could stand as a synecdoche for the court itself.[8]

The official record is predictably dry: 'Walter Ralley and [Edward] Wingfield committed to the Marshalsea for a fray besides the tennis court in Westminster'.[9] But the testimony of Charles Arundell and Henry Howard is more revealing: Ralegh had been ambushed and forced to fight for his life. Wingfield had been commissioned to murder him by the Earl of Oxford. 'Thus for a recompense for Ralegh's service,' Howard recalled, 'his life should have been latched between both the walls . . . and suits of apparel given to those that should have killed him, for seeking my Lord of Leicester's favour.'[10] Oxford, lashing out at Ralegh's betrayal, had not lost his wit at least: there is something nicely judged in the reward of clothing for killing Ralegh, the penniless fashion-plate.

Ralegh seems to have been shaken by the episode. Thirty years later, as he wrote his *History of the World* in the Tower, he delicately parsed the degrees of depravity inherent in murder. Killing a man by guile was more shameful than to do so in open combat, he wrote. But of the varieties of guileful killing he anatomized, the least redeemed, he concluded, was 'lying in wait for blood privily, for the innocent, without a cause, in hope of spoil'.[11]

The Marshalsea was across the river in Southwark. As well as being the preferred place of confinement in Tudor London for pirates and debtors, it was second only to the Tower as the government's destination of choice for its political – primarily Catholic – prisoners. As those caught up in the aftermath of the Ridolfi plot had discovered, it was also therefore an easy target for government spies, solicitously drawing confidences from the unwary. The selection of the Marshalsea for Ralegh may have been happenstance, or it may suggest that his trajectory was increasingly being viewed with alarm by the authorities.

Superficially the circumstances of his imprisonment may not have concerned Ralegh, particularly since the following day he was joined there by his friend, cousin and fellow Oxfordian

Arthur Gorges, who had been committed for giving the lie to Lord Windsor, another man with strong Oxford connections, in the presence chamber – a further sign of how the force of the group's rupture had flung its members fractiously apart. But he was too intelligent and self-aware – and too insecure – not to have sensed that his career was unravelling fast. He had been drawn to the Privy Council's attention three times in the previous twelve months, none of them favourably. Indeed collectively they revealed him for what he was: irresponsible, feckless and untrustworthy. He had been assaulted twice in the last six weeks, once murderously. One of the most powerful men in England wanted him dead. He had been party to the ignominious collapse of Gilbert's American venture and all too closely associated with the treacherously Francophile Catholicism of the Oxford set.

Ralegh no doubt had Leicester's influence to thank for the fact that, while Wingfield was still experiencing problems with the council some four months later, his own release seems to have been swift.[12] But reflecting on his recent experiences, he must have noted that thus far he had been a failure in areas where he had subordinated himself to others, and that the only small measure of success he enjoyed had been as captain of the *Falcon*. He had attempted to drift on other men's tides, and they had failed to raise him; now he realized that, deference be damned, he would have to do it for himself.

It must have also been apparent to him that he had no immediate future in London: the risk was too great. With the cloud of the Gilbert voyage still not long past, his choices were few. Indeed, arguably he had no real choice at all.

The Spanish had long recognized Ireland to be a strategic weakness in England's defences. The former ambassador de Spes, contemplating England's brazen interference in the

Spanish Low Countries, had outlined the case in detail back in 1572:

> It will be easy to pay them back in their own coin both in Ireland and in England, as the Irish are Catholics and wish to shake off the yoke of the English who cruelly tyrannize over them . . . The task is an easy one, and with three or four thousand men and a competent fleet the island would be mastered [. . . and] if Ireland were ours first, it would afford great facilities for the subjection of England.[13]

The analysis was impeccable, but despite grander ambitions being sketched out in Madrid and Rome, the first fruits of Hispano-papal meddling in Ireland – a force of just fifty Spanish and Italian soldiers led by James FitzMaurice, exiled nephew of the Earl of Desmond – were pitifully thin. FitzMaurice landed his small party in Dingle Bay on 17 July 1579, the same day Thomas Appletree had shot Elizabeth's bargeman. From there they marched the few miles north-west along the Kerry peninsula to Smerwick, the westernmost harbour in Ireland, where they took over a fort named Dún an Óir above the town and awaited reinforcements.

FitzMaurice himself was dead within days, but Ireland was ripe for revolt and rose without him, fired by the rhetoric of a renegade English priest named Nicholas Sander, who had come over with FitzMaurice: the rebellion burst out across the province, burning towns across Munster and terrifying the English and their dependants.

The Tudor response to Irish unrest had always been bestial, as if the province were a place where all the savage terrors of Protestant eschatology had to be appeased on their own terms. Policy amounted to little more than the choice of starvation or slaughter: the Irish careers of Gilbert and Carew, among others, attest to that. Four years earlier, in July 1575, the Earl of Essex at the head of the English army in Ireland had hunted down and butchered four hundred women and children of the M'Donnell clan at its Rathlin Island redoubt some miles off the northern coast of Antrim; a few made it down to the caves by the sea but Essex's men followed them and smoked them out, cutting them down there on the summer shore.[14]

The English fought back against Sander's insurrection with the only tactics they knew and by the early months of 1580 had regained much lost ground; but with insufficient numbers and uncertain supplies they were not confident of victory, and everyone expected further support for the insurrection to arrive over the horizon from Spain. Burghley's fears had been realized all too soon.

Yet there were reasons to be cautious for all concerned. Experience had taught Elizabeth that victories in Irish affairs were both largely illusory and hugely expensive. For precisely the same reason, it had often proved the graveyard of reputations: very few men came home with their status enhanced and fewer with any semblance of financial return to show for their travails. As Ralegh would note, looking back on Elizabeth's reign:

> All her old captains by land died poor men [and those] who have done as great honour to our nation (for the means they had) as ever any did: those ... with many other brave colonels, have left behind them (besides the reputation which they purchased with many travails and wounds) nor title nor estate to their posterity.[15]

It is all the more remarkable, then, that Ralegh managed to parlay his service into the very highest favour possible; indeed, the brutal chutzpah and self-promotion of his Irish campaign displayed a kind of genius at work.

By the spring of 1580 Elizabeth was increasingly concerned about the situation in Ireland, and alarmed at the prospect of a significant Hispano-papal force arriving in Irish waters, something that everyone expected imminently. Mendoza did his best to stoke English fears at court: when Elizabeth raged at him that further Spanish interference in Ireland would compel her to engage against Spain in the Low Countries, he replied that if Philip did decide to send an army against her, it would hit her so hard that she wouldn't have time to breathe, never mind meddle in Flanders.[16] His aim was to frighten her into withdrawing English support for the rising in the Low Countries and reining in her privateers, but he mistook, as many men did, Elizabeth's apparent indecision for timidity.

Instead, Elizabeth responded decisively, as she always did when faced with what amounted to a personal, physical menace. Winter was hurriedly dispatched back to Ireland in March with four ships at his command to prevent any such landing and otherwise harass the rebels. Through late spring and early summer details of the county musters taken of men able to do military service came rolling in daily to the Privy Council. Lord Grey of Wilton, Gascoigne's old patron and a client of Leicester's, was offered the post of lord deputy of Ireland, a position he accepted with some reluctance, complaining privately about the lack of notice and the sudden urgency, almost implying an unseemly panic; but he was in Dublin by 15 July to take up office.[17] Ireland was finally getting what it needed: money, men and, above all, royal attention.

Nevertheless, it may be a mark of how seriously Elizabeth took the situation that Leicester – still out of favour – could be found once again putting out feelers to Spain, implausibly offering both his own service and the possibility of a secret agreement between Philip and Elizabeth. Mendoza did not take the bait.[18] Rumour amplified the dangers and there was talk that Spain was preparing for a massive invasion, a fact that seemed to be confirmed by intelligence reports.[19] On the day that Grey took office, Elizabeth issued a proclamation against seditious talk about either the approach of a Spanish fleet or a projected Hispano-papal invasion of England.[20] It was primarily aimed at the Catholic English gentry, who were now being subjected to greater restrictions on their liberty and higher penalties for non-conformity than ever before. The government had also been alarmed by the clandestine arrival of two English Jesuit priests, Edmund Campion and Robert Parsons, in June, who shared Sanders' papal authority and proselytizing zeal. A new aggressive strain of counter-reformation Catholicism had come to England, stretching Elizabeth's tolerant spirit perilously thin. Plans were drawn up for a dedicated prison for the leading recusants at Halton Castle in Cheshire to keep them out of the common gaols and away from their comfortable circles of influence.[21]

This then was the charged atmosphere in which Walter Ralegh and Edward Denny stood, most likely on Finsbury Fields a few days after the fifteenth, reviewing the three hundred fighting men levied by the City of London for service in Ireland. They had both been appointed as captains by Grey, no doubt at Leicester's suggestion, with a hundred men each under their command. Ralegh would have certainly known of Grey through Gascoigne, and it is possible that the two men had already met. For Leicester, who would have had reason to doubt Ralegh's loyalties, Ireland was the perfect crucible: it was certainly a safe place to send a potential enemy. Ralegh and Denny had their pick of the muster; the remainder were to see action on board ship.[22]

Oxford's threats followed Ralegh across the water: both Arundell and Howard attested that he had bribed some soldiers to kill Ralegh, Denny and another man named John Cheke over there, but this was nevertheless a pivotal moment in Ralegh's life. Over the next eighteen months he would fight two campaigns in Ireland: one was the government's against Catholic insurrection; the other was his own unremitting campaign to shake off his former associations, to erase the public memory of his failures and friendships, and to make an irrefutable case for his own deserts. He was relentless in his pursuit of both, and it is hard to say in which he was the more brutal.

It took over a month for Ralegh to get his small force over to Ireland. One of his very first acts was to sit with Captain Warham St Leger, the provost marshal of Munster, in judgement of Sir James Fitzgerald, brother of the rebel Earl of Desmond. It was an ideal opportunity for Ralegh to show he had the sensibility and unwavering focus for the trials ahead. Fitzgerald had been mortally wounded in a pitched battle on 4 August; subsequently trussed up and imprisoned, he was brought to Cork where Ralegh and St Leger, acting under martial law as judge and jury, sentenced the already dying man to be hung, drawn and quartered, his broken body set on the city gate to feed the birds of prey. Ralegh the cool-thinking rationalist had no mercy to spare for the Irish.[23]

Most of the details of Ralegh's Irish exploits, including this one, are to be found in the *Chronicles of Ireland*, which was published as part of the second edition of Holinshed's *Chronicles* in 1587. Its author was Ralegh's friend John Hooker, and the likelihood of Hooker's source being anyone other than Ralegh himself is remote: the details are too personal, the focus too close. Indeed, some of the anecdotes have the tone and shape of dinner-table talk, smoothed and polished by repetition, as when Ralegh lingered behind after the English broke camp to ambush the Irish foot-soldiers who came to scavenge. He challenged one of those he captured about the stack of withies he was carrying. The prisoner replied he was taking them to hang some Englishmen. 'Is it so?' said Ralegh. 'Well, they shall now serve for an Irish kern,' and ordered the man to be hanged.

The point is not that this happened. In itself it is unremarkable: summary executions under martial law were so widespread that they even turned the stomach of the loyalist Earl of Ormond, the general of the queen's army in Munster, and a man who could *name* 5,650 Desmond clan members and clients whose deaths he had overseen in the eighteen months from December 1579.[24] It is not even that Ralegh and his fellow soldiers thought it amusing at the time, in the heat of a desperate and brutal hand-to-mouth campaign. It is that the story is meant to be witty in recollection; in the context of the story, Ralegh's response to the man is almost a punchline.

This is the personal background to the defining moment of Ralegh's military career in Ireland: the bloody aftermath of the siege of Dún an Óir at Smerwick on the morning of 10 November 1580. Politically the events of that day and those that led up to it were the culmination of the existential fear and anxiety Elizabeth had felt since the beginning of the previous decade with the discovery of the Ridolfi Plot, the Northern rebellion and the publication of the papal bull against her. That Ralegh was instrumental in relieving her, for the moment, of that fear, can have done her regard for him no harm at all.

The English had been expecting a large Spanish force for many months. Unfortunately, when it came, England's principal defensive fleet was elsewhere: Sir William Winter had taken his ships back to the Chatham dockyards in September for refitting and supplies. He must have missed the Spanish by a matter of days: the mayor of Waterford alerted Walsingham to the arrival of eight Spanish ships into Smerwick harbour, where hundreds of troops were disembarked and stores unloaded, on 18 September. Winter made it to the Medway yards on the twenty-fifth; by the twenty-eighth he had new orders and he sailed on the twenty-ninth with nine fighting ships under his command.[25] The seriousness with which the threat was perceived was in little doubt; but the terror excited in the English by this modest incursion on one of the westernmost extremities of Ireland speaks volumes about the nature of their insecurities and their paranoid distrust of all things Irish.

There were some 800 Spanish soldiers in Smerwick now – not the 1,500 which the English feared had landed – under the leadership of an Italian, Sebastiano de San Joseppi, who was content to wait within the fort for the arrival of Desmond's promised Irish force, which numbered 3,000.[26] With them, however, was the nominal Catholic bishop of Dublin, Mateo de Oviedo, who was impatient for battle. When it became apparent that no significant number of Irish troops was likely to find its way to Smerwick, Oviedo decided to sail back to Spain to drum up more military support from Philip. He took with him the remaining ships together with some 200 men to form his embassy, thereby both fatally weakening the invading Catholic force and removing any chance they might have had, slim as it would have been, to escape to sea.

Whether they could have held out until the arrival of Desmond's army or – less plausibly – a significant number of reinforcements from Spain is a moot point. The English had control of the sea, Winter's fleet beginning to gather in the harbour beneath the fort on 7 November, the same day that Ralegh came to the promontory alongside Denny and Zouch as part of Grey's 800-strong army. Two artillery pieces were brought ashore from the ships in the still of the night, and trained on the fort while trenches were begun to undermine its walls, despite several desperate sorties by the Spanish to disrupt them. The only English casualty was John Cheke – one of whom Oxford had threatened – who was shot in the head by a sniper.

Out in the bay Winter's ships rode in deep water relentlessly bombarding Dún an Óir with their bow guns; Winter himself probably drew the map of the action in the bay that now sits in the Public Records Office at Kew, showing smoke belching from six of his ships gathered around the fort on the headland where it juts out into the bay. The battery thundered and deafened for two days, filling the air with the dry rasping stench of sulphur and nitrate, shrouding the peninsula in thick dusky smoke. The Spanish were still hoping Desmond's army would come over the brow of the hill on the ninth, but unbeknownst to them, the only other troops in the area were those of Ormond, marching to support Grey in the siege. They called for a truce that evening, lowering the black and white flags with which they had tried to signal Desmond and replacing them with the single white flag requesting parlay; San Joseppi came out of the fort as the sun was setting and surrendered before Grey on his knees.

What happened next, however, is still the source of fierce debate. The official account from Grey – written by the poet Edmund Spenser, later a close friend of Ralegh's, who was at Smerwick as Grey's secretary – says that Grey demanded that the Spanish 'should render [him] the fort and yield their lives to [his] will for life or death'. But there are reasons to doubt that. One is the practical point that the English did not have the resources to maintain a long siege, particularly with winter fast approaching, whereas there were enough supplies in the fort to last several months. So why such a quiet and abject surrender. Another is the extent to which the English reinforced and elaborated their defence of Grey's actions over the years. The suggestion that Grey offered favourable terms and then reneged on his word once the Spanish had been disarmed has always seemed a plausible counter-narrative. Nearly twenty years later, in response to contemporary but unrecorded challenges to the English story, Spenser felt the need to write that 'Some say he promised them life; others, at least he did put them in hope thereof . . . This is most untrue – myself being as near them as any'.[27]

Nevertheless it is possible that Grey did not intend events to fall out quite as they did. On the morning of the tenth, Ralegh and another officer named Mackworth were sent into the fort to oversee the surrender of weapons and to ensure that none of the spoils were looted. The official account then says that Grey sent in bands of men to kill all but the most senior of the enemy men, those being kept aside for ransom – a cruel decision ruthlessly executed. The soldiers were put to the sword, the Irish men and women – some of them pregnant – were hanged. But things may not have been so efficient and ordered.

Richard Bingham, captain of the *Swiftsure* out in the bay, wrote to his friend Ralph Lane in Kerry the following day claiming that, once the English had taken possession of the fort, some of the sailors from Winter's fleet joined the soldiers and 'fell to revelling and spoiling and withal to killing' until every last person in the fort was dead.[28] Three men – two Irishmen, one a priest, and a Catholic Englishman – were dragged off to the local blacksmith before being hanged, where their joints and bones were smashed with a hammer on the anvil and the priest's thumb and forefingers were hacked off. When their bodies finally swung on the gallows in the fort, the English used them for target practice, literally shooting them to pieces. The picture of a chaotic and unplanned explosion of bloodlust, rather than cool military calculation, is the more persuasive. Even Grey admitted that much of the enemy's stores were wasted in the confusion and disorder as the English forces rioted through the fort; why there should have been such disorder he doesn't say.

Interestingly, Camden looking back on the events at Smerwick some thirty years later in his *Annales* suggests that Grey was in fact overruled by his officers – principal among them Ralegh, Denny, Macworth and Zouch: 'it was decided, the Viceroy disagreeing and weeping, that, the leaders being spared, the rest should as a warning be promiscuously put to the sword, the Irish to be hanged'. This doesn't say much for Grey's leadership, of course, but it does strengthen Bingham's implication that the driving force behind the slaughter came from the English officers – key among them Ralegh – and their troops inside the fort. There were so many dead in fact that the English couldn't count them; the fort was some 350 feet long and 100 feet wide, little room for the slaughter of 600 men: the carnage in such a confined space, the blood and terror, must have been horrific. Several accounts note cries of *misericordia, misericordia* – mercy, mercy –being heard over the walls of the fort during parlay. But there was no need to ask for mercy when negotiating the terms of a surrender from no particular position of weakness. It is more likely that the recollected cries for mercy were those of the men and women in the fort as Ralegh and Mackworth and their men began the killing.

Ralegh had surely killed men before, but the Irish campaign of 1580–1 was the first time he had done so in Elizabeth's name, in defence of her person. Indeed, it may be memories of the slaughter at Smerwick that explained the presence in his great unfinished poem to Elizabeth, *The Book of the Ocean to*

Cynthia, of an image of how 'a body violently slain/Retaineth warmth although the spirit be gone/And by a power in nature moves again' as if the recollection of hundreds of human carcasses cooling on a cold Irish autumn morning could not be dissociated from the push and pull of their relationship.

Certainly there is good reason to think that Smerwick represented a defining realignment for Ralegh, earning him access to the highest circles at court and redeeming the faith of those who had supported his appointment of command in Ireland. Searching the bodies and belongings of the dead in the hours and days after the massacre, scouring them for anything of value, Ralegh discovered a cache of letters which revealed 'some matters of secrecy' regarding Hispano-papal intrigue against England. He recognized them immediately as a passport to favour, a gift of good fortune, if he could ensure that he and he alone were considered responsible for their discovery. It is a tribute to his persistent and forceful eloquence that Grey allowed him to take them personally back to London.[29]

But Grey's acquiescence may well have had its roots in his growing unease about the fate of the garrison. There is an undoubted defensiveness about Grey's own account, a sense of events being rationalized after the fact rather than a considered policy explained, which is absent elsewhere in the Irish records when the English are discussing their brutal suppression of rebellion. Certainly when the news broke it horrified continental Catholicism, and Burghley, for one, mindful of the wider political struggle, was unimpressed. Alongside his written report, Grey had already sent Denny back to court to defend himself to Elizabeth directly; Ralegh with his treasure trove of intelligence – at once bearing witness to the necessity of the killing and being evidence of its fruits – must have seemed a further level of insurance.

Ralegh arrived back in court at Whitehall on Saturday 17 December, two weeks after Denny. He must have quickly discovered that Elizabeth did not concur with the reservations of her principal minister. Although she chided Grey that his decision to spare the officers should have been hers, not his, she was in fact ecstatic, writing at the head of the official dispatch to Grey on the twelfth, which itself offered great thanks and commendations: 'you have been chose[n] the instrument of [God's] glory.' It was, of course, personal, all about her: 'The mighty hand of the Almightiest power hath showed manifest the force of his strength in the weakness of the feeblest sex and minds this year to make men ashamed hereafter to disdain us.'

She also found time to thank 'such captains and soldiers as in this enterprise did assist you for their great forwardness and courage showed in performing this so acceptable a service to us . . . so much the rather for that we have been informed what great penury they have sustained in our service there'.[30] Camden, mindful that such enthusiasm for bloodshed did not wholly accord with the image of the Virgin Queen, later wrote that she 'would have preferred that [it] had not been done, for she loathed cruelty, however necessary, on prisoners, and she had difficulty in admitting the reasons for the slaughter'. This was not true: when faced with a personal threat – and she considered invasion of her territory almost indistinguishable from physical assault – she was wholly uncompromising. Grey's fault in sparing the Spanish and Italian officers was one of excess mercy, she thought: they should have died with the rest.

Precisely what Ralegh's letters contained is unknown; some at court gossiped that 'the bishops of Spain and Italy are detected', others that 'Alva, the king of Spain's lieutenant . . . is found faulty'.[31] Given that there is no reference to these documents in the national archives – and their arrival in London caused no discernible diplomatic ripples or intelligence efforts – it is reasonable to suppose that their contents did not merit the hyperbole that Ralegh generated on their behalf. It cannot have been too much of a surprise to anyone, whatever court gossip said, that Italian and Spanish soldiers were present in Ireland because imperial Spain and the Catholic church wished it so, and there must have been more to the letters than that. More likely they hinted at future plots and interventions in Ireland, threatening generalities to which Ralegh could apply his talent for speculation and projection and display his new-won local knowledge. The precise details of the documents, in other words, were almost beside the point: Ralegh at last had a hand of his own to play. This time as he entered the presence chamber, its high gilt ceiling inscribed with the dates of great English battles, and made his way through the press of people gathered there, the rush-strewn floor swallowing the sound of his steps, he must have known he had been gifted a moment to remake himself, free of his former reputation, a means to prove his personal and political worth. Not many English captains returned to court from Ireland with their reputation enhanced and the swagger of a clearly defined victory in their gait. Ralegh now had that opportunity.

There is no doubt that he used his discovery of the letters, reinforced by the brutal practicality of his actions at Smerwick, as a means of impressing his talents, judgement and loyalty on men such as Burghley and Walsingham who hitherto had reason to be sceptical of him on all three counts. Given the tone of his letters to them in the months that followed, which while not informal are certainly familiar, he must have spent enough time in private conversation with them through the Christmas and New Year revels at court to presume a little on their friendship and favour. As for Elizabeth, Denny had inadvertently laid the groundwork for Ralegh by ensuring that she was warmly disposed to the captains who had effected her glorious victory at Smerwick and in any event she liked men who showed judicious initiative in her cause, and the fact that he was Kat's nephew must have been a particular satisfaction for her.

The rise in his status was signalled by the reward of an appointment as an esquire of the body extraordinary under the lord chamberlain, Sussex – a role that in principle required Ralegh to sleep in the presence chamber and protect the privy chambers after nightfall, and which brought a modest but welcome annual salary of £33 6s 8d, but which in practice, for him at least, was largely honorary. But if they spoke privately, Ralegh kneeling before her to talk, his soft voice ideally suited to being overheard by no one but the queen, it would still have been in the very public arena of the presence chamber. Ralegh's real reward, in fact, was to gain an audience, to be heard at last. It was his first experience of such favour and no doubt he rejoiced in it: he had seized her attention, and that of her key ministers. He was not about to let go.

Events conspired, however, to make the timing of his return to London potentially catastrophic. The day before, on Friday the sixteenth, the Oxford cabal had finally collapsed – messily and publicly – in the presence chamber. Oxford, bitter at the way in which his friends – Howard in particular – had distanced themselves from him, denounced Howard, Arundell and Southwell to the queen as seditious malcontents. Prostrating himself before Elizabeth, Oxford confessed that he and his friends had been party to a Catholic conspiracy for several years. Howard, he said, had reconciled.[32]

Oxford's timing was exquisite. The Jesuits Campion and Parsons were still at liberty and there were moves afoot to make those responsible for converting others to Catholicism guilty of treason, and to introduce heavy fines and prison sentences for those attending mass. Just days earlier, on 1 December, the Privy Council had issued a letter proclaiming its intention to 'make some example of [Jesuits] by punishment, to the terror of others'. Mauvissière, the French ambassador, was present and Oxford turned to him to confirm his story. Unsurprisingly, Mauvissière flatly denied any knowledge of the matter; he could hardly do anything else. But, with such dangerous accusations in the air, the government was highly unlikely to accept the word of the French ambassador as final.

On Christmas Day, a Sunday, Oxford used Anne Vavasour to arrange a meeting with Arundell on the lower terrace at Whitehall where he tried to persuade Arundell to support his accusations against Southwell and Howard, offering him £1,000 and safe passage out of England if he would do so; Arundell refused.[33] Before the week was through, he and Howard were arrested, Leicester apparently increasing the stakes by spreading a rumour that they had been plotting to murder Elizabeth and, perhaps a conscious echo of the Smerwick action, slaughter as many Protestants as they could.[34] Out of the depositions and interrogations of these two quickly came the tawdry history of Oxford's circle, its follies, hopes and fractures. The heretical railing, the seditious plans, the treasonable prophecies, the violence, the sleazy and malicious innuendo about Elizabeth: it all came out.

When news of their arrest reached Ralegh it must have seemed a catastrophic blow. He had single-handedly engineered a reversal in his fortunes and contrived to create a new image for himself of a man of military professionalism and political acuity: the exposure of his erstwhile friends and inquisitorial exploration of their activities threatened to reopen associations in his life he had attempted to close for ever, a fatal undertow dragging him back down even as his tide was rising. But worse was to come.

Of the men in question, Arundell was undoubtedly the most exposed: Howard had family, connections, wealth, tradition, history to protect him. Arundell's principal protector had just accused him of treason in front of the queen. He was right to be fearful, and his terror is audible in the surviving transcripts of his interrogation. *Jhesus*, he begins. It is at once a supplication, a prayer, an exhalation, a comfort, a kind of curse. As if to say: what is this the start of? Where Howard is pompous, blustery, unctuous, Arundell is direct, anxious, angry, afraid. There is a show of defiance – 'Thus I answer,' he says of the first accusation – but the questioning beats him down.

> I protest before God . . . it is most true . . . I take God to witness . . . I never saw . . . I have declared and will avow on my oath and maintain with my sword . . . I never knew . . . I know not . . . I know not . . . I never saw . . . I do not remember . . . the time is long since . . . I have clean forgotten . . . it is most true . . . he never declared any such thing . . . neither has it passed my mouth nor did I ever hear it spoken . . . I never spoke with . . . I never saw . . . as God knows both [Oxford's] intent and mine, so I beseech him in his justice to reward us.

Arundell, of all those in Oxford's circle, seems a decent man born in an unlucky time.

The problem was, however, that most of those whom he and Howard could call on as independent witnesses to Oxford's excesses were also Catholic and, by default, suspect. It was a problem they solved by turning to one of the few men in

Oxford's circle who did not fit that description, and a man who, moreover, seemed absolutely of the moment: their old friend Walter Ralegh.

The question facing Ralegh now was: whom should he betray? Oxford was temporarily under the wings of Ralegh's current patron, Leicester. Few can have had any illusions about the rapprochement lasting, but between them the two noblemen wielded formidable power and influence. But to accept Arundell and Howard's version of events was to place him uncomfortably close to seditious and perhaps treasonable talk. Moreover, Oxford had tried to have him murdered at least once and Ralegh's decisive rejection of him almost a year earlier left little room for second thoughts. Ralegh's conscience was unlikely to have been cluttered with moral considerations, but he can have had little stomach for what looked like a poisonous, even deadly choice.

Arundell and Howard's depositions belong to the very last days of December and the first two weeks of January, and may go some way to explaining why Ralegh remained in London for some six or seven weeks. If Ralegh was formally asked to bear witness, as requested, to Arundell and Howard's depositions, then his testimony has not survived; more likely the questioning was informal, particularly given his new-found amity with Walsingham, and Ralegh's answers were sufficient to dampen inquisitorial enthusiasm rather than inflame it. Indeed, the government seems ultimately to have come to the conclusion that the accusations were not worth exploring to the full extent of its powers, the implication being that the players in question were fundamentally unserious. Is that Ralegh's handiwork? It has some of his hallmarks – being asked to choose sides and instead finding an angle of his own; judgements on the failings of others that are at once belittling and acute – and it is certainly a plausible explanation for the way the investigation withered in the new year. It may possibly also be a reason for Howard's pathological hatred of him in years to come: Howard was an intensely serious and self-important man and to be characterized as an irrelevant fool – particularly by a man of no particular social cachet – may have been enough to goad him into loathing.

Whatever Ralegh said, however, his aim was unquestionably to free himself from the shadows that hung over his past. It was a mood that extended through his stay in London, which lasted until at least 3 February, when he gave a deposition for a Chancery lawsuit arising from the failed 1578 voyage. Ralegh offered singularly tepid support for Gilbert in his statement: in the close, familial world of late Tudor England it was an act of surprising disloyalty.[35] Elsewhere, if Ralegh knew it, his family was about to change for ever: a little over two weeks later, his father would be dead. Ralegh was back in Ireland by then, and his feelings about the loss have gone unrecorded. If he contrived to visit his family during his return to England the visit left no trace in the archives, but then why would it? The centre of his life was not the West Country anymore. Perhaps he saw it as merely another shadow lifting from his past; certainly he must have felt more alone, and his own man more than ever.

Landing back in Dublin towards the end of February, Ralegh rode back to Cork, accompanied by just six men – a fact that in itself perfectly illustrates how great was his appetite for risk in Ireland, how much he had to prove. The road took them through hostile territory and he quickly found himself in the hardest fight of his life. Riding ahead from his men, Ralegh and his guide forded a tidal inlet a few miles west of Cork between Ballinacurra and Midleton, where he was ambushed by John FitzEdmund FitzGerald, the seneschal of Imokilly and a key figure in the rising, who had been lying in wait. FitzGerald burst from cover, spurring his horse hard and catching Ralegh as he entered the water. Ralegh made it across the ford but Henry Moile riding behind him, but still several hundred yards ahead of the rest of the men, was thrown by his horse in mid-stream, and called out to Ralegh to come back and save him. Ralegh pulled his horse round and plunged back across the ford, gathering up Moile's mount and returning it to him. Moile leapt into the saddle but in his fear and haste overshot, falling into the mire the other side – no doubt to Ralegh's incredulity – and startling his horse away entirely. With the rest of the company still some distance behind, Ralegh stayed by his man, pistol cocked in one hand and staff in another, facing off against the enemy, hoping to buy enough time to retreat to the relative safety of an abandoned castle a long mile away. Ralegh's resolution unnerved FitzGerald, who was expecting the English to flee and he offered little more than invective by way of attack until the remainder of Ralegh's small company arrived. Nevertheless, Ralegh's lack of caution would leave three of his men behind him dead with their horses as he pulled back from the ford.

The ambush was evidently a story that Ralegh liked to tell; it became part of his myth. His friend Spenser wrote a fictionalized version for the Ralegh character, Timias, in the *Faerie Queene*, and Ralegh himself left two further variations on the theme of his courage. To Hooker, five or six years later, he spoke of being attacked by some twenty men, most on horseback. But just a few days after the encounter – in a letter written on the day his father was buried in an Exeter church – Ralegh wrote a braggishly modest account of it to Walsingham. Here he records slightly fewer horsemen – fourteen in fact – but fully sixty men on foot ranged against him.[36] Given the discrepancy it is hard to take either figure seriously, although it was true that the English customarily fought and won battles in Ireland against what ought to have been unthinkable odds, a fact Ralegh on reflection ascribed entirely to their superior armaments.[37]

That should not detract from the plain courage that Ralegh displayed that day, the fierce indomitable will required to face down any significant number of men alone. The force of personality – a kind of hard, disconcerting charisma – is obvious, as is the absolute loyalty to his men and his unquestioning willingness to defend their lives with his own. Ralegh had learned how to lead.

Nevertheless the episode also highlights weaknesses in his military abilities, in particular a recklessness which, while attractive as a personal quality, was likely to prove a liability in command, and a lack of preparedness which suggests a surprising indifference to discipline. Perhaps, buoyed by his reception in London, his negligence was borne of over-confidence, but even his friend Hooker felt compelled to note that Ralegh was travelling openly through enemy territory with insufficient men to fight off a serious assault; moreover they were strung out carelessly along some distance of road. Against better equipped and trained combatants he would not have been so lucky.

Bloodied and battle-hardened as he was by his years in France, Ralegh could hardly claim inexperience, and his organizational skills had already been tried on board the *Falcon*. Indeed he was better placed than many of his fellow officers to recognize the quality of enemy he was fighting. It may follow that if Ralegh elected to embrace outsize risks in Ireland, it was a positive choice, pushing at the limits of the possible for the sake of a greater cause, but it may also be true that his carelessness came from a sense of hopes realized, a glimpse of destiny, his relief proportionate to his desperation.

His recklessness, then, was not rooted in mere courage: it was driven by a starving ambition but complicated by fear and insecurity. Ralegh had spent too long trying to avoid responsibility for his own career; in Ireland, he was making amends with a vengeance.

Camden's suggestion that officers such as Ralegh may have overruled Grey at Smerwick – either in argument or de facto through their actions – makes increasing sense in light of Ralegh's behaviour over the following months, which showed growing disregard for both social deference and the discipline of military command, a young man's easy contempt for his elders that resonates with us, perhaps, rather more than for Ralegh's contemporaries. February saw him writing over the heads of his superiors to both Burghley and Walsingham, the latter being in receipt of two letters, one of which contained Ralegh's faux modest account of his own valour already referred to.

In the other letter, Ralegh attacked the Earl of Ormond, who, as an Irish nobleman, found the scorched earth and starvation policies of Grey et al difficult to stomach. *This man*, Ralegh calls him, an extraordinarily contemptuous phrase for a minor gentleman to use of a peer in a letter to one of Elizabeth's senior ministers. 'There are at this instant a thousand traitors more than there were the first day [Ormond became general]. Would God the service of Sir Humphrey Gilbert might be rightly looked into, who, with the third part of the garrison now in Ireland, ended a rebellion not much inferior to this in two months.'

Ralegh's animus against Ormond was probably inspired by the fact that Ormond had refused to support him in his depredations of David Barry's estates at Barry's Court in County Cork, which Ralegh – greedy for tangible reward –

coveted in their entirety. But he may also have had an eye on developments at home. Ormond was part of Oxford's circle – and that would have been reason enough to keep his distance.

Indeed, the early months of 1581 saw him strenuously trying to prove to Walsingham, Burghley and Leicester – at whatever cost – that he was wholly committed to the English Protestant cause. If smearing the loyalty and judgement of a Catholic superior officer – who also happened to be an associate of Oxford's – was what it would take, Ralegh was in no mood to demur.

With Elizabeth's comments on the penury endured by her soldiers no doubt in mind, Ralegh also told Walsingham that, 'God is my judge, it grieveth me to receive her Majesty's pay . . . to see her so much abused, and I will rather beg than live here to endure it. I would most willingly give over my charge . . . if I could, and serve her Majesty privately with a dozen or ten horses during the wars.'[38] It is indicative of how self-consciously histrionic – not to say dishonest – such grand-standing was that his surviving letter to Burghley – as treasurer, the man with the purse-strings – is not remotely that of a correspondent expatiating on how much it grieves him to be paid, but a detailed and business-like accounting of expenditure and monies-owed since embarkation the previous July.[39] Ralegh's later reputation as a spendthrift may be deserved, but he was always assiduous in his search for ready money. Thus it is that now he wrote to Burghley first, almost certainly as soon as he returned to Cork, waiting until the following day to tell Walsingham about the ambush. Heroism was one thing; cash flow was quite another.

If Ralegh felt his career to be finally cohering into some version of destiny, then he had some cause: he was one of three men promoted to deputize as the governor of Ireland in the summer, from which position, still bitter about his failure to secure Barry's Court, he continued his vociferous campaign against Ormond, enlisting or otherwise bullying Grey into supporting him in his lobbying. Elizabeth eventually ordered Ormond to stand down in June, apparently having been persuaded by his enemies at court that he had been responsible for the deaths of just three rebels in the previous eighteen months, which insult led Ormond to produce the list of his 5,650 named victims.[40] At which point Ralegh turned his attention to Grey. Grey had had enough and was already asking to be discharged. Ralegh, who probably knew that Grey had conspicuously failed to mention him in his official accounts of the action at Smerwick, wrote to his sometime patron Leicester in August that, 'I have spent some time here under the deputy [Grey] in such poor place and charge as were it not for that I knew him to be one of yours I would disdain it as much to keep sheep.'

Again, the disrespect is shocking, and it is not altogether clear that Ralegh's contempt for Leicester's client is not also an implied criticism of Leicester himself. Certainly Ralegh makes no attempt, as it were, to excuse Leicester's patronage of Grey, to disassociate him from the charges he is levelling at his commanding officer. Indeed, the tone of the letter overall, despite the odd gesture in that direction, is barely supplicant at all, and quite different from the tone of those to Walsingham and Burghley. Grey, well aware of Ralegh's insubordination, wrote to [Burghley] that, 'I neither like his carriage nor his company; and, therefore, other than by direction or commandment, and what his right can acquire, he is not to expect [anything] at my hands.' But Ralegh, eager to return home and capitalize on the reputation he had forged in Ireland, did not care. On the closing days of the year, he was back at court carrying official correspondence for Elizabeth from Ireland.

This was his chance.

XI: THE SACRED ANCHOR

Then must I needs advance my self by skill
And live to serve, in hope of your goodwill.

SIR WALTER RALEGH

Elizabeth had spent all of her reign and most of her life fighting
the imperative to marry, intent on preserving a vital pale of
private freedom for herself, seemingly at any cost, personal
liberty and independence of action being the root of her
emotional security. With marital pressures all but extin-
guished, then, it might be thought she was more free than ever,
but in a sense the fight itself had been what sustained her, a
rare source of human certainty as well as a vital diplomatic
tool, and without it the burdens of her role were more starkly
apparent. Moreover, if she thought she could escape the
suffocation of captivity – in the form of fear and its
precautions – while her cousin Mary Stuart lived, she was
mistaken, although the only practical solution to that problem
– Mary's death – still seemed unthinkable. Yet what would
happen if Mary outlived her? Elizabeth had always managed
both people and policy through the strategic use of deferral,
but that required time to be on her side, and, truth be told, it

was no longer clear that was so. Even Leicester had grown tired of waiting.

There is a portrait of Elizabeth from the early 1580s – attributed to Quentin Metsys the younger – which seems to capture this sense of physical and emotional exhaustion, of things at an end. Elizabeth stands in a simple black velvet gown beneath a fine, translucent silk mantle. Her wan, drawn face is framed by a white ruff, pearls around her neck and a large golden brooch with a single vast pearl pendant beneath it on her breast above her heart. The ennui is specifically articulated in the principal motto, written on the base of a column on which she rests, gently, her right elbow: *Stancho riposo e riposato affano*, 'Wearied rest and rested weariness'. She is of course alone, but her isolation is amplified by the riotous scene in the colonnade outside her chamber where courtiers and guards mingle, talking.[1]

The painting sits within the family of sieve portraits – her favourite symbol, according to Camden – using the familiar classical image to connote Elizabeth's purity, the reference being to a vestal virgin who filled a sieve with water from the Tiber and carried it, without spilling, to her temple to prove her chastity. But in place of clarity, the symbolism of the painting as a whole is complex, ambiguous and contradictory. The sieve is positioned close to her thigh and seems to draw attention to the very aspect of her behaviour that it seeks to deny, and while the myth of the virgin is explicitly about containing water, that is precisely what sieves do not ordinarily do, a fact which the motto written around the rim of the sieve emphasizes: *Terra ilben/Al dimora in sella* – The good falls to the ground while the bad remains in the saddle. What, the painting seems to ask, has chastity achieved for her? Has her freedom, her isolation, really been worth it?

Behind Elizabeth, however, between her and the door,

Metsys has placed a globe. It echoes visually the O of the sieve, and ships can be seen on its surface, sailing west to the Americas. The globe's motto, *Tutto vedo et molto mancha* – I see all and much is missing – seems to conflate imperial exploration and discovery with Elizabeth's identity, as if Elizabeth might somehow be fulfilled – completed even – by such conquests. It reaches out towards the idea that she has an imperial destiny in which exploration promised is being offered as a palliative for her fatigue, empire as a surrogate for marriage. What else did she have to look forward to?

Ralegh's entrance, on this reading, was perfectly timed. Indeed, if Ralegh ever did lay his cloak at Elizabeth's feet it was now. This is the story as it comes down to us from its source in Fuller's *Worthies of England*.

> [T]his captain Ralegh coming out of Ireland to the English court in good habit (his clothes being then a considerable part of his estate) found the queen walking, till, meeting with a plashy place, she seemed to scruple going thereon. Presently Ralegh cast and spread his new plush cloak on the ground; whereon the queen trod gently, rewarding him afterwards with many suits, for his so free and seasonable tender of so fair a foot cloth.[2]

Perhaps it is just that: a story. We do not know the facts of the matter: Fuller is the only source, and he is by no means a contemporary – compiling his *Worthies* some seventy or eighty years after the event in question – and as a consequence, most biographers downgrade the information from fact to anecdote, despite often reprinting as truth other pieces of information or Raleghana which have no greater claims to veracity. It seems too good, too self-consciously styled a moment, to be true.

But the historical truth of the story may not ultimately be important, because its survival suggests that it memorably articulates something of the dynamic between queen and courtier in general, an iconic moment that marries deference – the very quality he so conspicuously lacked in his Irish dealings – to an exaggerated courtesy that shouts for attention: a display of both wealth and subservience that is at the same time a claim for preferment. It does all these things. But it also defines something particular about Ralegh – the extravagant rhetorical act, the ostentatious gesture: the self-seeking, self-publicizing butterfly.

We are so absorbed by Ralegh's attention-seeking self-abasement that we do not fully acknowledge Elizabeth's role, quietly treading on her young courtier's cloak – not merely the embodiment of his status and place in society but, as Fuller is at pains to note, a large part of his actual estate, his wealth – pressing it, howsoever daintily, down into the dirt. In a sense, it is the archetypal Elizabethan move: dispensing favour, the warm sun of her attention, while also reinforcing the rules under which such heat was expended, a none-too-subtle reminder of where the power lay in the relationship. Rewards were expressions of gratitude but also a means of control.

Ralegh's complaints about how much she exacted as the price of her favour are enacted in the anecdote, something that Fuller was certainly aware of but which seems to have been forgotten in the dazzle and glamour of Ralegh's charisma. Fuller continued:

> It is reported of the women in the Balearic Islands, that, to make their sons expert archers, they will not, when children, give them their breakfast before they had hit their mark. Such [was] the dealing of the queen with this knight, making him to earn his honour, and, by pain and

peril, to purchase what places of credit or profit were bestowed upon him.[3]

We might also pause to reflect that some echo of the sexualized phenomena of Simon Forman's dream about Elizabeth may be latent in Fuller's Raleghan myth too. Indeed, the elements that the two narratives share – the association of clean, fair clothing with Elizabeth, the dreamed of object, and the protagonist's role in protecting her from dirt – are striking. Although Ralegh's role is not overtly sexualized in the way that Forman's dream is, it may be that there are sexual nuances to the story that are now lost. There are similar tensions at play in the story that, while Dudley and Norfolk were playing tennis, with Elizabeth looking on, 'Lord Robert, being hot and sweating, took the queen's napkin out of her hand, and wiped his face, which the duke seeing, said that he was too saucy, and swore that he would lay his racket upon [him].'[4] Norfolk's discomfort and anger arises from the conjunction of disrupted social hierarchies, intense familiarity with things of the queen's person, and the hot sweat of Dudley's body – in a sense the inevitable tension between the abstract concept of the sovereign's body and the real human presence with all its complex possibilities.

But such things aside, we should not miss the truth about Elizabeth's response to Ralegh embedded in the myth: feelings of surprise and relief; the sense of something fresh and new, a kind of liberty.

Absent the cloak it is impossible to identify now a precise catalyst for Ralegh's rise from high regard to royal favour; perhaps it is foolish to look for one. Clearly there must have been a day at Whitehall, a moment, when Ralegh was first invited to attend Elizabeth in the relative intimacy of the privy chamber, primarily a female domain for a regnant queen, to talk beneath Holbein's great, intimidating portrait of Henry VIII, his favourite wife, Jane Seymour, and Henry's parents, Henry VII and Elizabeth of York, which was painted straight on to the wall there. Holbein had drawn Elizabeth's father so that he glared with disconcerting belligerence out of the painting at anyone who dared look at him – it was not a room in which one could forget the deference a subject owed to his queen, the woman whose need for freedom had ended the Tudor line. Beyond it lay more private areas still: Elizabeth's withdrawing chambers and ultimately the ill-lit, airless room in which she slept, its single window facing east over the Thames above the river stairs.[5] But the modest drama of Ralegh's first steps into that world are less important than the emotional drama of the affection he found waiting for him there.

Ralegh was seduced by her power, of course, by the mere fact that he could consume the attention of a prince through whom flowed the eternal divinity of kings. He later wrote regretfully of 'those marvellous perfections,/The parents of my sorrow': the idea of her as someone who 'outflew the fastest flying time', possessed of 'A beauty that can easily deceive/Th'arrest of years, and creeping age outclimb', whose presence seemed a 'fire that burns, but never wasteth,/That looseth nought by giving light to all'. This is Elizabeth as queen, arguably the central certainty of his life, an absolute, true as touch, the moon to his tides. But Ralegh was close enough to see the human cost of that certainty, and he was seduced and ultimately sorrowed too by her teasing tender subtleties, lovely in their unpredictability and impermanence: 'I love the bearing and not bearing sprays/Which now to others do their sweetness send,/ Th'incarnat, snow-driven white, and purest azure', he wrote. Nothing is as fleeting as the scent of a flower, nothing epitomizes drab melancholy better than their fading colours.

Ralegh's emerging love for her, then, had to reconcile both resolute immutability and a haunting, dream-like evanescence; the impossibility of such a task may not yet have dawned on him.[6]

That Elizabeth should turn to him at this point in her life should occasion less surprise than it does. He was not as unknown before Ireland as his biographers have traditionally suggested, notwithstanding the fact that his reputation tended more towards the disreputable and infamous than he would later care to recollect – something that he contrived to have painted otherwise in contemporary histories with the conniv-ance of his friend Hooker, in particular. But his bearing in Ireland had transformed his standing at court – Ralegh claimed to be embarrassed by the praise and favour he received from Walsingham – and he had learned from his association with the Oxford circle the virtue of standing apart. For Elizabeth, it had been four years since Ralegh had first been introduced to her; now, she must have felt, he had at last begun to prove his worth.

Elizabeth was, after all, a cool judge of character, of men and their uses; she had done it her whole life, not infrequently with her life itself at stake. Ralegh's public profile thus far showed him to be an often undisciplined and volatile man from an unimpeachable Protestant background but of negligible social status, whose lately discovered appetite for recognition and reward did not wholly disguise a more profound ambivalence towards the personal cost of ambition and power. He had, after all, seen how failure at court had destroyed his friend Gascoigne. His religious upbringing may have given him a sense of self-righteousness which was often indistinguishable from entitlement, but that could be undercut by a vicious and debilitating self-doubt which he disguised behind swagger and bluff.

He was well connected with both the legitimate and illicit seafaring communities – moving quietly between the two, in fact – and had a range of interesting, if not dangerous, relationships amid the Catholic underground and the wider demi-monde of malcontents and contrarians who scrounged their gilded livings on the fringes of the court. He had quasi-imperial ambitions for himself and England abroad – those westward ships on her globe – but had certainly shown himself to be ideologically flexible at home. His contempt for custom meant he brought fresh thinking, an aggressive novelty, a liberty of mind to bear on issues. In most, if not all of these things, he was entirely unlike the other men whom Elizabeth tended to favour. He had proved himself useful in Ireland and she could no doubt see other ways in which he could be of greater use in the future. But he was a wild card nonetheless.

Ralegh was, perhaps surprisingly given the force with which he expressed himself, a soft-spoken man, with what one friend called 'a bold and plausible tongue';[7] words flowed easily, eagerly from him, cloaked in rough West Country vowels he never shed. But with the fluency came a talent for blunt-speaking, for tart judgement and pleasurably brutal honesty, delivered as much for effect as for accuracy. 'In all that ever I observed in the course of worldly things, I ever found that men's fortunes are oftener made by their tongues than by their virtues,' Ralegh would later write. He, more than anyone, knew the truth of that observation.

Ralegh was no Iago. He offered the illusion of integrity, a riveting matter-of-fact directness that contrasted violently with the deferential, self-defensive tone of much court discourse: he was the antithesis of a diplomat or statesman, something he himself – seduced by his own talk – never seems to have recognized. If the archetypal Machiavellian strategy was to say one thing and do another – the kind of unremarkable deceits with which Leicester was regularly charged – Ralegh's rhetorical strategy was something like the opposite: to say what he thought and to mean what he said. Every statement was an implicit challenge to his interlocutors to disagree. He was not a man for subtle half-truths or dissimulation: when he lied, his lies were big, flat and absolute, as if he could force people to accept his version of reality merely through the force of his speech. But more than anything he had the gift of often being right, or rather of saying things that people thought to be true, but didn't dare articulate for themselves. His judgements were a combustible mix of wisdom, insight and acuity, leavened where necessary with breathtaking expedience – a quality he had learned from his father, as well as the likes of Cobham and Knollys.

To the disgust of many at court who found his manners abrasive, Elizabeth – no stranger to the language of deceit herself when the moment demanded it, nor to the pleasures of shocking and offensive speech – loved to hear him talk:

> true it is, he had gotten the queen's ear in a trice, and she began to be taken with his election, and loved to hear his reasons to her demands: and the truth is, she took him for a kind of oracle, which nettled them all; yea, those that he relied on began to take this his sudden favour for an alarm and to be sensible of their own supplantation, and to project his [fall]

But Elizabeth had always enjoyed challenging those about her, questioning their judgement, the consistency of their positions, their information – it was essential to her control, her freedom of manoeuvre. It is not difficult to imagine, therefore, a certain relish at Ralegh's ability to do the same so effectively: his presence as a proxy widened the scope of her liberty. Those around them sensed this connectedness and found it inexplicable: it was a different kind of relationship from those she had shared with Leicester and Hatton, and its difference, defined by Ralegh's apparent independence from other courtly and societal constraints, was a threat.

That there was an almost immediate intimacy between Ralegh and Elizabeth seems incontrovertible, perhaps ultimately rooted in the shared and private community of Champernown education and care, where humanist scepticism met Protestant certainty. Ralegh writes revealingly that he 'loved her both, by fancy, and by nature,/That drew even with the milk in my first sucking/Affection from the parents breast that bare me', weaving together a subject's love for his queen with both familial affection and more seductive pleasures. But it is also true that their attraction also found root in their very different singularities: they were both people apart.

Elizabeth was fond of giving nicknames to her confidants: Simier was her monkey; Alençon her frog; Burghley her spirit; Walsingham her moor; Leicester her eyes; and so on. Her name for Ralegh was Water. In part it affectionately referenced his ties to the sea and perhaps nodded at the elemental ebb and flow of his ambitions and energies, with playful implications for her favoured sieve iconography too. Elizabeth herself was Diana – or Cynthia – the goddess of the moon, to whom all tides were subject. But what no one seems to have commented on is that it was also actually his name, not merely a clever pun on it. Water was a common and accepted variant spelling of Walter – and many people, Ralegh included, pronounced it in such a way that the two words were indistinguishable. She loved him as himself.

Ralegh was, of course, tall and handsome, physically magnetic with a raw libidinal energy that his peers, as already noted, commented on. In this he was more than matched by Elizabeth's flirtatious tactility, which seemed to promise or imply intimacies which, like Elizabeth's favours generally, were more powerful and seductive for being withheld. That energy of his was therefore displaced into the dizzying metaphorical games of his love poetry, where complex, layered conceits overlap one another, seeming to enact in themselves the very unresolved contradictions and uncertainties of Ralegh's own position, not least the impossibility of talking directly about such things.

None of Ralegh's poems were published in his lifetime and his corpus is one of the most fluid and uncertain of any major English poet, depending as it does on variable transcriptions and often debatable attributions in a wide range of private collections. We must assume that was a personal choice on Ralegh's part: those he wrote for Elizabeth, or with her in mind, were essentially positional – statements of how he wished to be understood, as much if not more than declarations of feeling or intent – and to publish them would be to diminish their effectiveness, to deny one of the very things that gave them power, the implied gift of intimacy and insight.

Stephen Powle, Ralegh's friend and Middle Temple bed-fellow, ascribes to him a poem written, Powle says, 'to Queen Elizabeth, in the beginning of his favours'. It catalogues apparent contradictions in nature, beginning 'The lowest trees have tops', but resolves itself in the idea that those who declare their feelings least, are those who feel most deeply:

The firmest faith is in the fewest words
The turtles cannot sing, and yet they love.
True hearts have ears, and eyes, not tongues to speak
They hear, and see, and sigh, and then they break.[8]

Unstated is the implied contradiction that a man whose influence on her is attributed to his eloquence cannot say the things he most wishes to say, the things that are most true; the question of whether those things relate to love and fidelity is likewise skilfully elided.

The articulacy of silence was a conceit Ralegh evidently liked, perhaps because it contrasted well with the operatic intensity of Hatton's eloquence. But as a trope it also clarifies for us Ralegh's persona as he presented himself to Elizabeth in these early months and helps explain why he never joined in the elaborate gift-giving rituals which so enlivened and enriched the new year for Elizabeth, nor the tilts and other heraldic exercises in splendour and rhetoric. Not for Ralegh the riotous heat and colour of such displays: his identity instead was rooted in the cool, the detached, the playfully dispassionate; if he seemed arrogant it was, he implied, because he required distance to sharpen his judgement.

He reworked the trope of silent speech again in the poem 'Our passions are most like to floods and streams', which survives in multiple manuscript collections, including one, interestingly, belonging to the Champernown family and stamped with the royal coat of arms. Here again arguments from nature lead again to the conclusion that the deepest passions are those that are unspoken, and that 'They that are rich in words must needs discover/That they are poor in that which makes a lover'. He goes on to chide Elizabeth for '. . . thinking that he feels no smart/That sues for no compassion . . .' and, in a moment of self-revelation, claims that 'I rather choose to want relief/Than venture the revealing' of his true feelings. The revelation is manufactured, of course, but that is not to say it does not also reflect a deeper uncertainty for Ralegh about his goals, his future: the yearning for certainty, embedded in a plea for love, is real enough.

As well as being a positional statement in his challenge for Elizabeth's favour against the gilded rhetoric of other courtiers, then, this is also Ralegh's artful way of foregrounding an ambivalence about his newfound status at court, pleading for understanding of the impossibility of his position in the guise of a refusal to plead. Elizabeth, for her part, understood such rhetoric well enough – too well, in fact, to take it seriously. His aloofness was in some sense a mirror image of her indecision: both were ways of maintaining a wary distance from the pressure of the moment.

Ralegh had clearly been allowed direct access to the queen almost immediately on his return to court at the close of 1581, and the queen had liked what she had heard. This is not too surprising, since Ralegh told her, on this occasion at least, precisely what she wanted to hear: that she could have several hundred more troops in Munster without extra cost either to herself or to Ormond, whom she was keen not to antagonize further. Burghley wrote to Grey in Ireland on 1 January 1582 telling him of Elizabeth's enthusiasm for Ralegh's plan. Grey responded immediately with a furious assault on Ralegh's integrity: his ideas had a superficial plausibility, Grey said, but demanded the impossible of those tasked with their execution. A sympathetic witness might have said that Ralegh's swaggering certainties were both credible and credulous, heavily dependent on false or over-optimistic assumptions. But Grey was not sympathetic: he thought Ralegh was deliberately setting others up to fail. Ralegh, however, could not lose: as long as he had Elizabeth's support, refusal to implement his ideas looked like weakness, or worse, while the inability to do so successfully looked like incompetence.

No wonder Ralegh's elevation scared his peers at court: their relationship was uncharted territory, a new reality they would have to adjust to. Yet as far as Elizabeth was concerned, Ralegh still had work to do.

The slaughter at Smerwick notwithstanding, English fears about the Catholic threat had not abated. Indeed, it might be said that Smerwick was greeted so favourably not least because it was a rare symbol of resistance to the Hispano-papal menace. Campion had been caught the previous July; after months of torture he was charged, not under the recent treason statute against Catholic reconciliation, but under the old Edwardian law of 1351. When he was executed on the first day of December – around the time that news of the massacre reached court – he died, the government argued, a political traitor rather than a religious martyr.

Concern about renascent Spanish power had led Elizabeth briefly to re-awaken the Anjou courtship, and the duke had been in England since late October. By the turn of the year, and Ralegh's arrival at court, she had tired of the pretence, and had offered Anjou £60,000 to fund his military action in the Low Countries, where William of Orange, the de facto leader of the Protestant resistance, had offered him the sovereignty of the provinces – once they became independent of Spain. With characteristic caution, Elizabeth paid him £10,000 initially, with the remainder only payable once he was safely distant in Antwerp. The fact that she was now funding a French prince's conquest of the Netherlands was a minor point: Spain had to be weakened. Failing that, it had to be distracted.[9] With the departure of Anjou, and definitively liberated from the subject of marriage, Elizabeth became personally freer than she had ever been, but her political choices, her political freedom of manoeuvre, had never been more restricted.

Ralegh was among those in the Earl of Leicester's great entourage as he accompanied Anjou to the Netherlands. It was an honour, a mark of status, but perhaps not a particularly

significant one in itself since some 100 gentlemen went with
Leicester to Antwerp, among them Philip Sidney and the
ubiquitous Henry Noel. Moreover, Ralegh knew many of those
around Anjou well. Notable by their absence, however, were
Henry Howard and Charles Arundell: the two had been
arrested again just as Ralegh arrived back at court, first seeking
sanctuary in the house of a startled Mendoza around midnight
on Christmas Eve, fearing they would be sent to the Tower to
die.[10] Mendoza had never met either of them before, but he
knew an opportunity when he saw one and by the time they
left, he had ascertained that they were only to be placed under
house arrest, and Howard had already sworn an oath of loyalty
to Philip II. Ralegh would never see Arundell again, but he
would face Howard across a Winchester courtroom twenty-
one years later, in November 1603, by which time Howard's
former amity towards him had decayed into pathological
hatred. Howard would be one of the judges who sentenced him
to death.

Elizabeth was with Anjou's entourage as they left London on
1 February, dressed in black to demonstrate, lest anyone doubt
it, her sorrow at his departure, arrangements for which had
been rushed through in just eight days. Ralegh no doubt kept
a discreet and appropriate distance, perhaps reflecting on the
revolutions in his life since he had ridden the same road with
Simier a few years before. Elizabeth rode with Anjou for four
days as they made slow cold progress through Rochester, where
she showed him the thronging shipyards on the Medway,
implausibly promising him use of her entire navy, then on to
Sittingbourne and Canterbury, where they parted, amid
passionate displays of grief. In public she continued disconso-
late: she would give a million pounds, she said, to have her frog
swim in the Thames rather than the stagnant waters of the
Netherlands. 'It is all nonsense,' Mendoza reported back to

Philip, and he was right. It was said that in December the mere thought of his departure had made her dance for joy in the privacy of her chambers – much as her mother had done half a century before.[11] Ralegh was, at last, in the right place at the right time.

Across the Channel, Anjou landed at Flushing to a deafening welcome of gunfire, fireworks, trumpets and drums. Antwerp was perhaps the wealthiest city in northern Europe, and certainly the greatest centre for international trade and finance north of the Alps, acting as a clearing house for spices and silver from the new world, for metals from the mines of eastern Europe, fine wools and silks from Italy and English cloth, and there he received a welcome commensurate to its riches.[12] Many Dutch, however, were far from confident that a French Catholic was the right person to lead their struggle against Spanish dominion, never mind be their king. Most of the English returned home with Leicester after Anjou's reception in Antwerp on the nineteenth; Ralegh stayed behind, most likely at Walsingham's behest. He was still intelligence gathering in Antwerp a month later, on Sunday 18 March, when a Basque man attempted to assassinate William of Orange, shooting him in the face at close range as he rose from dinner. For weeks it was thought he would die: his doctors struggled at the limits of their knowledge and skill to staunch the flow of blood. It wasn't until the beginning of May that his recovery looked certain.[13]

There had been a price on William of Orange's head since 1580, when Philip II had issued a proclamation demanding his assassination; many in England reasoned that Elizabeth's life was under threat too. Ralegh, coming with news of the attempt, must have left almost immediately and raced back to London, since he delivered his package to Walsingham on the twenty-third. But he also had a message for Elizabeth, given to him personally by William, together with some letters, presumably before the attempted assassination: *sub umbra alarum tuarum protegimur* – we are protected beneath the shadow of your wings. Whatever meaning William had intended to convey, when accompanied by news of his attempted murder it seemed at once a challenge and a rebuke: Elizabeth was the defender of Protestant Europe, the only bulwark against the triumph of Catholicism, but if William was not safe in his own castle, how safe was anyone? Was Elizabeth doing all she could?[14]

With the pretence of interest in Anjou finally dispensed with, Elizabeth was free to relish Ralegh's company more and more. When the opportunity arose to award him another commission in Ireland, she gave it to him – while freeing him from the necessity of actually returning to the province. No one seems to have noticed before that, in the warrant for the appointment, made some time that April, she explicitly connected her care for him to her affection for Kat Astley:

> our pleasure is to have our servant Walter Rawley trained some time longer in that our realm for his better experience in martial affairs, and for the especial care that we have to do him good, in respect of his kindred that have served us, some of them (as you know) near about our person ... the said band may be committed to the said Rawley, and for that he is, for some considerations, by us excused to stay here, our pleasure is that the said band be ... delivered to some such as he shall depute to be his lieutenant there

Whatever other emotions she felt towards Ralegh, there is a gentle solicitousness hidden here, a sense of tenderness and concern, which she rarely, if ever, had cause to express elsewhere. The phrase 'for some considerations' is at once a regally dismissive refusal to explain and a need that she cannot, or will not, articulate. He had been in the Low Countries for nearly two months: she was not going to lose him again quite so quickly. It is hard to imagine the complexity of the feelings he, a young man not yet thirty, excited in her, a childless single woman approaching fifty, by reminding her so strongly of her governess, the only mother she had truly known, and one of the few things of permanence she could rely on in her youth.

Ralegh might have been surprised to discover that he gave Elizabeth a similar sense of certainty to that he found in her. For his part, his position in her favour probably seemed largely bound up in his Irish experience; that too seems implicit in her warrant. He had received £200 in back payment for his Irish service in February, while he was in Antwerp. It was a relatively large sum of money, but it is impossible at this distance to know how much of it was to pay for genuine and outstanding debts and costs incurred over the previous two years, the accrual of which was the common experience of English officers under Elizabeth. If most left her service considerably poorer – and more bitter – than when they entered it, it was usually not for want of trying. Profiteering was endemic: most augmented their own wages by creaming off money intended to pay either their men or their suppliers, and it would be surprising if Ralegh were any different. The reckoning he submitted at the beginning of the following year – which included payment for his command under the April commission – claimed he was owed over £800 in back pay.[15] What he eventually received is unrecorded.

The previous month, presumably while Ralegh was absent in Antwerp, although conceivably immediately upon his return, complaints against Ormond's government resurfaced in the shape of a document listing seventeen instances of his weakness, inconstancy and incompetence. Ralegh is specifically cited as a witness to Ormond's private comments on the treatment of traitors, after Ormond had executed two would-be assassins hired by unnamed Englishmen to murder the seneschal of Imokilly. From the context, Ralegh must have been one of those Englishmen; despite his later public disdain for assassination as a tool of government in the *History of the World*, it wouldn't be the last time he would privately recommend such a course. Ralegh had a finely tuned moral sense, but he did not always defer to it in his decision-making.[16]

Ralegh was also called on to support the charges. He may have been more involved in the drafting and circulation of the document than is now apparent; one of the charges concerned the spoiling of David Barry's castles 'which might have been kept for her Majesty's service' – still, evidently, a sore point for Ralegh.

While pursuing his campaign against Ormond, Ralegh was lobbying vociferously against Grey: the greater their discomfort and defensiveness, the more Ralegh appeared vindicated in his criticisms. Naunton, looking back on Ralegh's career from the early seventeenth century recalled that the two were summoned before the Privy Council to argue their causes, and that the council were impressed with Ralegh's plausibility. There is no evidence for this account in what survives of the council's records, but whatever the details the tenor of the anecdote is certainly true: the Countess of Bedford still felt the need to lobby on behalf of Grey, a relative by marriage, later in the year, writing to Hatton:

> my Lord Grey hath by his travails in Ireland done as well, and governed those parts as painfully, carefully, and justly as any man that ever exercised that place before him; yet

I fear me there hath not wanted some such as have extenuated his Lordship's good services: for this cause I could not but earnestly recommend unto you the preservation of his Lordship's well-deserved honour and credit with her Majesty against such as have, or may seek to impair the same.[17]

The idea of Ralegh as an enemy to the honour of others was present from the very beginning.

Elizabeth's insistence on Ralegh's withdrawal from Irish service did not mean that she wanted him for mere adornment, and the fact that she did not want him absent on extended service in Ireland did not preclude other kinds of service. It was part of the dynamic of their relationship – distance from her, temporary exile from her presence being an excellent way of sharpening the appetite for her favour, a reminder of her power and what absence from it entailed. Moreover, she clearly had meant what she said about Ralegh's need for military experience. We find him next in the Netherlands again, at the beginning of June, in the camp of Sir John Norris's English regiment outside Antwerp; his precise business there is obscure, as much of his work in these months was carried out at Elizabeth's behest, personal commands quietly delivered out of the hearing range of spies, most likely in her privy chambers, as she lay on her Indian couch beneath the open window, perhaps, or leaned wearily against a silver tapestry, animals picked out in gold upon it, which was fixed to the wall simply so she could rest against it. If Ralegh had been working for Walsingham or Burghley, say, there would have been a paper trail; ultimately we know little of what passed between them because those who watched them at court, who hung on every loose strand of rumour, knew little. We too have to watch Ralegh's actions and conjecture.

Norris was nominally a client of Leicester's, but was from a family long-favoured by Elizabeth, Norris's grandfather having been one of those courtiers executed alongside Anne Boleyn in 1536. Norris himself was a professional soldier, a stubborn, hard-drinking man deeply committed to the Protestant cause, utterly confident in his own judgement and his relationship with Elizabeth; rare was the man with the courage to report that he had not obeyed her instructions because he thought them ill-advised.[18]

He had seen active service in the Huguenot cause in France at Montcontour and elsewhere, and it is quite possible therefore, although unproven, that he and Ralegh were already acquainted. Not surprisingly, given that Anjou had led a Catholic army in France, Norris sided with many of the Dutch in being somewhat sceptical about Anjou's commitment to the Protestant cause in the Netherlands. The impossible politics of the situation were the subject of much diplomacy and low-level espionage over the months that followed, with Elizabeth affecting outrage at the idea that anyone should doubt Anjou's integrity or withhold their loyalty from him – a stance which had no discernible impact on the stubbornly intractable realities, revealing instead for her an alarming inability to extend her writ beyond her borders, or to influence events with significant implications for her personal safety. In this context, Ralegh – fresh and pliant, eager to please, and somewhat familiar with the principals – may well have seemed a good choice to carry messages from her to the recuperating William of Orange or indeed to Anjou himself.

In any event, while in the camp Ralegh became embroiled in a row between Norris and one of his colonels, Sir John North, another Protestant with links to Leicester, who refused to defer to Norris because he, North, came from an older family. No doubt there were echoes here for Ralegh of Knollys' dispute with Gilbert a few years previously, and Ralegh seems to have sided with Norris in what was an increasingly violent dispute: in one argument North stabbed his opponent, a Mr Webb, twice in the chest – a 'ticklish, dangerous and chargeable action' as Walsingham's correspondent describes it.[19]

Back in England, it was increasingly clear that, if Norris was already looking to Ralegh to defend him at court then he was making an astute bet: the circumspect Burghley was paying him the immense compliment of taking him seriously. Among the state papers for October that year are Burghley's hand-written notes of Ralegh's plan, given more or less verbatim, for subduing Munster. Ralegh's vision is a complex and brilliantly coherent construct of ifs, mights and maybes; but the image of England's greatest elder statesman, now sixty-three and ravaged with gout and other infirmities of age, quill in hand as the young Ralegh dictates his ideas, is a powerful testament to the seismic impact Ralegh was making at court.

Nor was there any falling away in Elizabeth's apparent favour to Ralegh, although there was also precious little reward as yet. It was enough, however, to inflame the envy of the volcanically sensitive Hatton, perhaps aware of how Ralegh's self-position-ing was a more or less explicit reproach of his own, and mindful too of Ralegh's talent for lobbying against those, like Grey and Ormond, whose own efforts and successes seemed to diminish his lustre. The difficulty was how to approach her with any degree of privacy: the last thing Hatton wanted was to make an outright enemy of his rival. But Ralegh was ubiquitous in the privy chambers now, loitering there at all hours of the day and night: 'My bound respect was not confined to days/My vowed faith not set to ended hours' he wrote. It was his habit to sleep no more than five hours a night, which meant that he could be at the door of her withdrawing chamber waiting for her to emerge each morning.

It was Sir Thomas Heneage, acting on Hatton's behalf, who found her one early autumn morning as she prepared to ride out to kill a cornered doe in the great park at Windsor, Ralegh not yet anywhere in sight. Heneage gave her a letter from Hatton, together with three small tokens – a bodkin, a bucket and a book. She fumbled with the bodkin, failing to fix it in her hair, and ignored the letter, but she understood what Hatton intended by the miniature bucket – a container for Water – smiling at his jealousy. After riding on for a few moments she took up the letter from Heneage and read it, her cheeks flushing at what Hatton had to say, her mood seemingly veering sharply between anger and amusement.

Hatton's letter has not survived, but given the hysterical tone of other correspondence of his to Elizabeth, its contents aren't too hard to imagine. Ultimately, flattered by the intensity of Hatton's insecurity, she bade Heneage tell him how dear he was to her still and that 'she had bounded her banks so sure as no water nor floods could be able ever to overthrow them'. To assure him that he was not in danger of drowning she promised to send him a bird, to remind him of God's covenant after the Flood 'that there should be no more destruction by water'.[20]

Elizabeth liked and encouraged such games: elaborate metaphors had an obvious attraction for someone whose whole life had been an extended exercise in the strategic possibilities of ambiguity. She liked too the implication that the Fortune she represented to men like Ralegh and Hatton was, if not precisely fickle, then certainly possessed of an implacable, divine unpredictability: as with God's will, theirs was to submit, not to question. What she would not have liked, and what no doubt sparked her ire, was the condescending implication, apparent even at second hand in Hatton's complaint, that she was in danger of submitting to Ralegh, of allowing him to submerge her judgement beneath his. Ralegh's personality at court was evidently regarded as overpowering, all pervasive in its force – Hatton's fear of 'drowning', while an obvious extension of the metaphor, is also a remarkable image of helplessness and impotence – but it held no fear for Elizabeth. She had no doubt she could control him and certainly made no effort to reduce the time she spent with him.[21] Hatton acknowledged as much by repeating the game two months later, sending her a 'fish-prison' – again via Heneage – which she responded to by saying she preferred flesh to the creatures of water. Elizabeth also professed herself pleased that Hatton's 'sour humour' was lifting, an optimistic assessment it is hard to agree with on the basis of the surviving evidence.[22]

The episode is trivial in itself, but the animosity and fear which that very triviality masks was profound. All favour at court flowed from Elizabeth and it was, by its very nature, finite: she did not dispense money out of the nation's treasury, and was parsimonious in the extreme in the offering of titles or significant offices of state. Her preferred gifts were in the form of land, or rights which the beneficiary could, with a certain amount of diligence and ingenuity, exploit. Ralegh's favour, his absorption of so much of Elizabeth's time and attention inevitably meant that she would have less of both for Hatton, which impacted on his ability to lobby her on either his own behalf or on behalf of his clients. It eroded his status, which in turn diluted his attractiveness as an intermediary for suits to the queen, a lucrative and influential role. Material preferment for Ralegh, deferred though it was for the moment, was necessarily a threat because it too deprived him of potential future income. Any gift to Ralegh was a gift not given to Hatton.

Ralegh, isolated by both temperament and his total dependence on Elizabeth, was rapidly accruing enemies but as yet had no recompense to speak of for his troubles. Without a meaningful role, he had the freedom to linger by Elizabeth's side; she welcomed his company wherever they were, but she also preferred her courtiers to be useful. His position was becoming extremely precarious; it is no wonder he did what he could to monopolize her time. He was trapped in a vicious circle: clinging to Elizabeth's company fuelled his enemies' envy and ire, while ceding ground to them would almost certainly mean allowing them to undermine him. He had always been ambivalent about the path to power, wealth and preferment, and now that uncertainty, that deep-grained self-doubt, resurfaced. There was a kind of claustrophobia to courtly ambition which he struggled to accommodate. The pressure of constant presence, of resisting the animosity of those all around, was taking its toll. Fuller records how Ralegh scratched on a window-pane where Elizabeth would see it the phrase, 'Fain would I climb, yet fear I to fall.' Elizabeth's response, scratched beneath, was teasing, its comfort elusive: 'If thy heart fails thee, climb not at all.'

She was not finished testing him yet; he still had much to prove. Did he have the tenacity and will to serve her? Was he a safe investment for her time, loyalty and love? Elizabeth was unpersuaded.

XII: A DURABLE FIRE

Love abideth not with want, for she is the companion of plenty and honour.

SIR WALTER RALEGH

As far as the documentary record is concerned, Ralegh seems to have spent 1582 desperately defending his position at court, waiting – patiently or otherwise – for the rewards that would cement his status. But while he clung to the centre he was also quietly exploring other avenues of self-enrichment, profitably investing and re-investing such capital as he had in mercantile and privateering ventures running out of Plymouth and other familiar ports.

That, at least, is the only credible explanation for the fact that, early in 1583, he could find the large sum of 2,000 marks to buy a 240-tonne ship from the Southampton ship-owner Henry Oughtred. A craft of that size was manifestly both a claim to significance and a statement of intent; Ralegh named it the *Bark Ralegh* and offered it immediately to his brother Sir Humphrey Gilbert as the flagship for his latest voyage of discovery to the Americas.

Gilbert had persisted with his vision while Ralegh had pursued his career in Ireland but it is likely that, given Ralegh's lukewarm support for his brother in the 1581 court case, Ralegh was ambivalent about Gilbert's prospects for success, wishing to share in any possible reward but unwilling to risk further personal taint in another Gilbert failure. In any event, Gilbert had dispatched Fernandes across the Atlantic again in the spring of 1580 to scout locations for a possible colony. On 11 September that same year he could have been found at the house of John Dee in Mortlake, where the two men indulged in one of the most absurdly arrogant acts in the history of the British Empire: they agreed to divide the whole of North America between the two of them, with Dee receiving all the land above the 50th parallel. The agreement speaks to the casual excess of their imaginations, their hubris; but it also reveals the limitless imperial horizons of the historical moment, unimpeded by knowledge of awkward realities. For some – Ralegh among them – the idea of America was a powerful, almost addictive counterweight to the impending European crisis, where England and Elizabeth's horizons seemed to be retreating before the terrible fact of imperial Spain.

Gilbert's urgency, however, was fuelled principally by the fact that his 1578 patent was due to expire the following year and he was desperate to monetize his imperial vision. Ralegh agreed to use his hard-won heft at court to support his brother. Gilbert could use his help: despite an impressive list of investors, which included most of the principal figures at court, his reputation for repeatedly failing to get out to sea in a timely manner – and when there to make a profit – continued to haunt him. Elizabeth had formed the clear impression that he was 'a man noted of no good hap by sea' and asked that he withdraw from the leadership of his own voyage. It was, however it was dressed, a humiliating request and Gilbert sent a grovelling list of excuses to Walsingham for his abject record, acknowledging that his endeavours had earned him 'the scorn of the world' – a desperate admission for a man so proud and sensitive to slights on his honour. 'I trust her Majesty, with her favour for my 28 years' service, will allow me to get my living as well as I may honestly (which is every subject's right),' he pleaded, 'and not to constrain me, by idle abode at home, to beg my bread with my wife and children.'[1]

Ralegh's record is silent on the matter, but he had a great deal invested in the success of the Americas project – in terms of his identity at court as well as his imposing new ship – and, having experienced Gilbert's leadership and organizational skills at close hand, he can have been little more confident than Elizabeth about Gilbert's prospects of success. It may also be true, however, that Ralegh's apparent indifference to Gilbert's travails at this point stems from the limited possibilities of the historical record; his modus operandi was almost exclusively verbal, relying on his plausible tongue and proximity to the queen to press or resist suits as he saw fit. Almost all of this vital aspect of Ralegh's life – and the dynamic of his relationship with Elizabeth, is lost to us. However, one surviving piece of evidence – a letter from Maurice Browne in London to John Thynne, the step-son of Walter's brother Carew, with whom Thynne was in dispute – does offer us a tantalizing glimpse of the intensity of the process. The letter dates from the following year and Thynne is enjoined to consider

[T]he great and especial favour that Water Rawley is in with her majesty, whereby you shall be sure that during the controversies between you and his brother, you shall [find] Water but your heavy friend wherein he may displeasure you . . . My lord of Leicester is the only man that can command or persuade with master Water

Rawley, who are supporters the one to the other. Wherefore coming to my Lord often and using his countenance with familiarity will greatly stay Master Rawley from doing you the hurt which otherwise having occasion he would.[2]

This unfolds the world perfectly: supplicant lives balanced between amity and degrees of coercion. But the words Browne chooses also forcefully convey what it was like to experience the oppressive pressure of Ralegh's attention – some might say malice – when it was turned against his enemies, or the enemies of his friends. *Heavy. Displeasure. Hurt. Inform against.* The sense is of an emotional and mental assault so intense it is almost physical. While it is no surprise to find Ralegh close to Leicester at this point, given the events of 1580 and the tone of Ralegh's surviving letter to the earl in 1581, the suggestion that Leicester has to persuade as well as command Ralegh – persuasion being no command at all – underscores Ralegh's apartness from the ordinary structures of court organization as well as the scale of his achievement over the preceding year or so: Robert Dudley, the Earl of Leicester, the man who patronized Burghley and boasted of making England's only duke stoop before him, is treating Ralegh as an equal.

Mr Water Rawley is in very high favour with Her Majesty, neither my Lord of Leicester nor Mr Vice-Chamberlain [Hatton] in so short time ever was in the like, which especial favour hath been but this half-year. But the greatest of all hath been within this two months.[3]

Browne's gossip, dispatched out of London in May 1583, is particularly noteworthy because he was part of Ralegh's rapidly growing circle. He gives us, as it were, the received opinion of

Ralegh's people – and perhaps of Ralegh himself – regarding his new-found status. Most significant is the extraordinary confidence it exhibits, the explosive self-regard: it may have been presumptuous, but it certainly wasn't delusional.

One reason for Ralegh's new confidence in the early months of 1583 was Elizabeth's offer to him of a London home – Durham Place, more commonly referred to as Durham House – although she declined to formalize the gift in a lease or otherwise give it any legal status. While he lived there, he did so at her pleasure, and if he felt secure, as he did, it was because of the strength of her affection for him, not from any rights he had acquired. In some sense then his confidence was mis-placed, founded on insubstantial and – as time would tell – unreliable truths, on emotional rather than practical certain-ties; but Ralegh could often be blinded as to his own best interests, failing to plan far ahead or otherwise tend to his or his family's future security, relying on the high tide of his success, the cavalier energy of the moment, to carry him over.

This disinterest in detail where his own private interest was concerned would ultimately prove highly self-destructive, but it is of a piece with his apparent refusal to build a coherent power base at court, to shore up his status with a Raleghan faction. To the extent that he would have a following, it would be exclusive of court life, built among sea-faring men, among poets, mapmakers and mathematicians. Perhaps his fiery, aggressively discomforting persona simply alienated too many people and therefore precluded the possibility of such a coterie. But he certainly feared failure; why then did he neglect to buttress himself against its impact? Was he so seduced by his own myth? There are times, after all, when the best form of defence is defence.

Durham House, one of the great medieval mansions that lay between the Strand and the north bank of the Thames, stood at the bend in the river above Whitehall. Built in the thirteenth century as the London residence of the bishop of Durham, it had been appropriated from the church during the Reformation – much to the chagrin of the bishop, who hadn't given up hope of restitution – and now lay in the crown's gift. But even in pre-Reformation times it had long been used as a kind of royal guest house: Henry V had stayed here in his youth; other temporary residents included Cardinal Wolsey; Leicester's father, the Duke of Northumberland; and Lady Jane Grey. Elizabeth herself had stayed here, as had her mother before her. Over the course of Elizabeth's reign De Quadra, the Spanish ambassador had lived here during his mission, and she had also lent it to Leicester and the Earl of Essex for extended periods; Henry Knollys had been married here. Now, as a mark of Ralegh's new-found status, it was his home; but even a brief glance at its history suggests that it was perhaps a less significant gift than he thought. After all, he didn't even have the whole building: a man named Edward Darcy lived on the ground floor.[4]

Unlike the other mansions along the waterfront, Durham House was built directly on to the river, a gate leading through from the small inner courtyard to the river stairs, which had originally constituted the property's principal entrance; those who approached from the street had to make their way through an imposing gateway which nevertheless abutted the stables. This unusual proximity to the river made even the high-ceilinged, marble-pillared great hall feel damp – the house had 'an ill air', some thought – but perhaps the gift of a home at the water's edge was another small joke on Elizabeth's part, a play on her favourite's name and proclivities.[5] We do not know if she visited Ralegh here – while certainly plausible it upsets the apparent dynamic of their relationship – but she could undoubtedly see the house from the window of her bedchamber a few hundred yards upriver. Ralegh chose as his study a top-floor turret-room built out of the river-frontage toward the eastern end of the house, with a view commanding a great arc of the Thames from Whitehall and Westminster across to Blackfriars and the City in the East – the most pleasant prospect in the world, Aubrey said. He may have slept in a field bed, but his was covered in green velvet woven with silver lace, and his rooms were hung with rich Arras tapestries.

Ralegh was already establishing a reputation for his sumptuous apparel – and, more generally, for ostentatious displays of wealth, of conspicuous consumption: it was said he had spent some £3,000 between November 1582 and April 1583. He ate off silver plate stamped with his own coat of arms, although most of his meals in fact came from the queen's privy kitchen, a rare and very personal act of favour, and one which attests to where he spent most of his time. By now he had some thirty liveried men in his train, half of them gentlemen, many adorned by Ralegh with gold chains. To his followers and friends, his life seemed one of abundant pleasure and delight which he was ready and eager to share; extravagance fulfilled an emotional need, an affirmation of worth, of arrival, but it was also a political statement, an assertion, in no uncertain terms, that he was already a man with destiny's weight upon him.[6]

The sense of goodwill which clearly animated Elizabeth's dealings with Ralegh in early 1583 was now extended to Gilbert. Ralegh wrote to his brother on 15 March from the court at Richmond with the queen's opinion of his voyage, which gracefully inverted the previous offer:

Her Highness willed me to send you word that she wished as great good hap and safety to your ship as if herself were there in person, desiring you to have care of yourself . . .

therefore for her sake you must provide for it according-ly.[7]

With the valediction came the gift of a golden anchor, set with diamonds and rubies, and inscribed, *tuemur sub sacra ancora*, we are safe under the sacred anchor. The anchor was held by a portrait of a queen.[8] The echo of Orange's message was no doubt unconscious, but Ralegh might have had pause to question what kind of security she could in fact offer.

Gilbert was not the only man to feel the warmth of Elizabeth's favour thanks to Ralegh. On the morning of 18 April, with the court starting its slow exodus east from Richmond to Greenwich through the lush green heaths and meadows that lay south of the river – and destined that night for Clapham – Elizabeth and Ralegh rode out together. They left behind them the distinctive cupolas and towers of the palace, itself receding in a sea of cherry trees, the blossom from its great orchards rising before it like a dazzling wave. But Elizabeth was barely in the saddle before Ralegh suggested a change to her plans. She should, he said, visit his friend John Dee, whose house was to the north-east by the Thames at Mortlake.[9] Dee, his ambitions far outpacing his rewards, was grateful for the favour. *Quod defertur non aufertur*, Elizabeth told him, giving him her hand: what is deferred is not lost. It might have been her guiding principle.

This was a small matter, of course, a minor diversion one spring morning, but it spoke both to Ralegh's attraction and to his growing hold over her. There wasn't much in Elizabeth's life that offered the opportunity for surprise – perhaps that was another reason for her inordinate fondness for presents – and a spontaneous gesture, a momentary freedom of movement, represented a glimpse of heaven. That Ralegh chose this moment to guide her to a man who, as much as anyone, was a prophet for the kind of imperial vision that Gilbert and Ralegh attempted to enact, cannot have been coincidence. As well as being a vehicle for his own ambitions, Ralegh increasingly believed a western planting, a colony in the Americas, was Elizabeth's only chance for genuine political – and therefore personal – freedom, for a bulwark against the tyranny of Spain and Rome. This brief morning flit from predictability offered Elizabeth consolation, a comforting artifice, the pleasing illusion of liberty, but it also held within it the proffered gift of the thing itself, a promise in the guise of a dream.

If Ralegh was now seeking to both exemplify and be the agent of her longed-for liberty, he was also seeking liberations of his own from her. It may be no coincidence that his first known financial rewards began to flow in the spring of 1583 too; indeed Browne's 'within these two months', written in May, is precisely right. The tendency in Ralegh biography is to enumerate the prizes that Elizabeth bestowed on her new favourite simply as evidence of that favour. That much, of course, is self-evident. But closer examination of specific gifts reveals a more complex, less passive relationship between the two – one in which Ralegh actively worked to target possible gifts and then lobbied to receive them. He had discovered that she could be quiescent, biddable. The process also illuminates something of Ralegh's own working practices: the dark underside of his charm and glamour.

On 10 April Ralegh wrote a brisk, friendly letter to Thomas Egerton, the solicitor-general, noting that 'It hath pleased her Majesty to bestow the leases of Scotney and Newland, lately granted unto her from All Souls College in Oxford, upon me'.[10] This is not untrue, but it elides the actual sequence of events, which were markedly less mundane than Ralegh liked to describe. The truth was that, while Robert Hovenden, All Souls College warden, was absent, one of Ralegh's new followers, a Catholic gentleman named William Langherne, practising the role of intelligencer, had used his position as a recent fellow of All Souls to sniff out the leases in question and pass on news of them to Ralegh.

When he received Langherne's information, Ralegh sought out Elizabeth at Richmond, where she often took the court in winter, perhaps for its many covered and glazed galleries and passages offering protection from the cold.[11] The leases still had six years to run, but after listening to Ralegh – no doubt somewhere with as much privacy as they could find, whether in the withdrawing room, its rich hangings concealing white-lime and checker walls, or out in the gardens and orchards which its wide bay windows overlooked – Elizabeth was persuaded to write to the college requesting they be granted to her, so that she could then gift them to him. Langherne, alongside Ralegh's cousin Arthur Gorges, then went to work on the college fellows to ensure support for the conveyance to Elizabeth – a difficult proposition to refuse politically in any case. In the meantime, Ralegh sold the leases on, no doubt receiving sizeable sums of money: the rents on Scotney, for instance, which was a twelve-year lease, were worth over £100 annually.

Ralegh had again proved himself a man in a hurry, looking for a short-term gain over long-term advantage: to put it bluntly, he needed the cashflow to maintain the impression of a status and wealth he had not yet achieved and was evidently sensitive to imputations of poverty. 'They are poor/That can count all they have', he would write, offering a key to his apparently insatiable appetite for wealth: no sum could ever be enough to assuage his fears. Indeed, he used the construction 'they are poor' more than once, as if to distance himself, subconsciously or otherwise, from the very thought of moneylessness.

Once Elizabeth's request had been granted, she simply demanded that the leases be made over to Ralegh's nominees. Her acquiescent role in all this, which is at best a scam by which Ralegh could appropriate her authority to his own financial ends, to the detriment of a not-insignificant institution, tells us something about their friendship and the degree of licence she was willing to allow him, but also perhaps something about their attitude to cruelty and abuse of power. For Ralegh it was a malign necessity, vital to his own prosperity; Elizabeth was merely indifferent to its effects. She was quite happy to sacrifice the comfort and rewards of others to keep the cost of her personal government and its favours off her own balance sheets.

To make matters worse for the college Langherne contrived to have himself appointed one of its attorneys on 1 April to oversee both the alienation and the original leases through Chancery, the college authorities still unaware of his role in the detaching of these properties from All Souls. It is a measure of Langherne's chutzpah – surely one of the qualities for which Ralegh had employed him – that he inveigled a lease for himself while all this was unravelling: his reward to himself was Halstow Mill, situated on the spur of north Kent between the mouth of the Medway and the Thames estuary, for a period of twenty-one years.

Elizabeth's next gift to Ralegh came on 4 May, with 'the farm of wines', a grant of the exclusive right to license vintners in England; that is, anyone who wished to sell wine had to pay Ralegh an annual fee of £1 for the right to do so. Although there is no evidence of the conversations that must have taken place around court, it is hard to believe that Ralegh did not engage in intense lobbying on his own behalf for this highly lucrative gift: the previous recipient, Sir Edward Horsey, a client of Leicester's, had only died five or six weeks before, while the court was at Richmond, and Elizabeth was usually deliberately slow in distributing such rewards when they reverted to her.[12] This was, by her standards, lightning fast. Certainly Ralegh would have had ample opportunity to promote his cause, both at Richmond and Greenwich, and indeed over the course of their journey between the two via Mortlake and Clapham. Perhaps he took advantage of the holiday spirit at court on May Day, when Elizabeth and her courtiers – Ralegh surely among them – climbed the hill behind Greenwich Palace and dispersed to walk in the meadows and woods, savouring the scents of spring flowers, the chatter and cry of birdsong. Turning, Ralegh and Elizabeth would have seen the palace laid out beneath them, the busy river thick with shipping of every kind, and on the far side of the water four miles to the north-west, the city itself, packed high and close on the shore like merchandise. The prospect must have seemed an apposite metaphor for his ambitions.

On receipt of the farm, Ralegh promptly sublet it to a man named Richard Browne for £700 a year, a sum that seems to have significantly undervalued the grant since within a few years Browne was contriving to extract some £1,100 a year, a fact Ralegh resented so much he used his power – or rather, the power of his closeness to the queen – to have the grant revoked and then reinstated in an attempt to break his contract with Browne. Nevertheless, the initial decision to appoint Browne reveals again Ralegh's urgent need for capital to fund both his newly extravagant lifestyle and the ambitions it embodied; perhaps too it reveals an impatience with the incremental processes of wealth accumulation. Accustomed since childhood to the potentially rich pickings of privateering, as well as the quasi-legitimate trade with the Huguenots of La

Rochelle, he was ill-equipped temperamentally for the accrual of rents and levies which were the basis for all traditional wealth. He was never a man to be incremental in anything.

Then, as his star at last seemed permanently ascendant, Ralegh's relationship with the Oxford circle raised its head again: Elizabeth suddenly decided to reopen the investigation into the Howard/Arundell accusations of two years before. What prompted her concern is unknown – it could have been a move against Ralegh, although he himself claimed to have no inkling what lay behind it – but it is more than likely that it was impelled by Walsingham's discovery in mid-April that Henry Howard was paying clandestine midnight visits to the house of Mauvissière, the French ambassador, and that Mauvissière was secretly corresponding with and sending money to Mary Stuart, queen of Scots, through the person of a man named Francis Throckmorton.[13]

Throckmorton, an exact contemporary of Ralegh's, was from a different branch of the family to Ralegh's future wife Bess and friend Arthur, and had been born into the old faith. He had not long returned from several years in self-imposed exile among the Catholic emigrés on the continent, where he had mixed with men like his cousin Sir Francis Englefield, a former Marian privy councillor, now blind in exile, who actively promoted a papal invasion of England to restore Catholicism, and Thomas Morgan, Mary Stuart's codemaker, who had first been picked up in the aftermath of the Ridolfi plot, before finally fleeing England in 1575. Elizabeth herself had noted Morgan as a troublemaker before his arrest, describing him, not too warmly, as a man with a 'fond busy head, always seeking to deal in other men's matters'.[14]

Oxford's father-in-law, Burghley, wrote to Ralegh in early May 1583 from his mansion at Theobalds in Hertfordshire, asking him to intercede with Elizabeth on behalf of the earl. Burghley, ravaged with grief at the recent death of his eighteen-year-old daughter, also named Elizabeth, had heard rumours of the queen's intentions and he wanted such a move quashed immediately. That Elizabeth's most loyal and most powerful servant for some thirty years at this point should have needed Ralegh's help is a significant indication of Ralegh's intimacy with Elizabeth. But it was a judicious choice, too: few people at court had more interest in keeping that dispute out of the public eye than Ralegh. Indeed, with the immense rewards of the last few months, arguably he now had as much to lose as any of the principal parties. That may also have been part of Burghley's motivation.

Notwithstanding that, Ralegh's account to Burghley of his conversation with Elizabeth at Greenwich is as close as we can get to overhearing them, and an insight into how seductive his logic could be, and – by extension – how powerful an enemy he could make himself. What is notable, in particular, is the fact that he nowhere seeks to downplay, apologize for, or otherwise minimize Oxford's offences. Quite the reverse. Indeed, he seems to be making a concerted effort to remind Elizabeth of Oxford's failings even as he argues against their prosecution, reminding her of his own involvement with Oxford almost as a way of affirming the seriousness of Oxford's sins. If Oxford was seeking forgiveness and forgetting, he would have to get it without the help of Ralegh, who seems to be pushing Elizabeth to a tactical rapprochement that allowed Oxford access to court while affirming that he deserved to be confined to its margins.

I spake with her Majesty, and ministering some occasion touching the earl of Oxford, I told her Majesty how grievously your lordship received her late discomfortable answer. Her Majesty, as your Lordship had written, (I know not by whom lately and strangely persuaded), purposed to have new repetition between the Lords Howard, Arundell and others, and the earl, and said it was a matter not so slightly to be passed over. I answered that being assured her Majesty would never permit anything to be prosecuted to the earl's danger, if any such possibility were, and therefore it were to small purpose, after so long absence and so many disgraces, to call his honour and name again in question, whereby he might appear the less fit either for her favour or presence. In conclusion, Her Majesty confessed that she meant it only thereby to give the earl warning, and that, as it seemed to me, being acquainted with his offences, her grace might seem the more [merciful] in remitting the revenge or punishment of the same.

If Elizabeth's apparently meek submission seems somewhat out of character, it only serves to emphasize the extent of his influence over her. Certainly it seems to bear out the observation of Ralegh as her oracle, with all the atypical passivity that image implies.[15] He continued:

I delivered her your Lordship's letter, and what I said farther, how honourable and profitable it were for [Her] Majesty to have regard for your Lordship['s] health and quiet, I refer to the witness of God and good report of her highness.

There is both kindness and courage in Ralegh's words here. The death of Burghley's daughter the previous month had been unexpected and Burghley had withdrawn to Theobalds, lost in mourning. The queen, however, tired of his absence, and Walsingham wrote to Burghley on her behalf on 20 April:

> Her Majesty hath willed me to signify unto your Lordship
> that as she hath been pleased for a time to permit you to
> wrestle with nature ... so now she thinketh that if the
> health of your body may so permit you, you should do
> better to occupy yourself in dealing in public affairs than
> by secluding yourself from access to give yourself over a
> prey to grief.[16]

Ralegh's rebuke to Elizabeth on this, gentle though it is, is
unmistakable – it is hard to think of another man from whom
she would have accepted such constraint on her actions.
Ralegh's letter concludes:

> And the more to witness how desirous I am of your
> lordship's favour and good opinion, I am content for your
> sake to lay the serpent before the fire, as much as in me
> lieth, that [he], having recovered strength, myself may be
> most in danger of his poison and sting ... Thus being
> unfeignedly willing to deserve your Lordship's good
> favour I humbly take my leave.[17]

There is little reason to doubt Ralegh's ongoing concern about
Oxford's 'poison'. In some sense, he had done Burghley a
genuine and selfless service here in advancing Oxford's cause
at the risk of his own personal safety; neither he nor Burghley
would have been under any illusions about the 'danger' that
Oxford brought in his wake. Nevertheless, the image of
Oxford, Burghley's son-in-law and one of the most senior
figures in the aristocracy, as a venomous snake is brilliantly
Raleghan: startling, brutal and true.

At the end of May, the court decamped to Burghley's
magnificent new palace at Theobalds, near Cheshunt in

Hertfordshire, which Burghley had largely designed himself at vast expense: its pleasure gardens were said to extend for two miles in every direction, and the gardens were themselves bordered by water, so that one could circumnavigate the entire estate by boat. However, the extent to which Burghley would have welcomed such an onerous level of attention so soon after such a catastrophic personal loss is debatable. Ralegh shared chambers – we might say a suite of rooms – with Fulke Greville and an unspecified number of other gentlemen on the second floor of the inner court, close by the queen's painted gallery and her privy chambers and those of her gentlewomen of the bedchamber.[18] Fairly evidently, despite physical proximity to the queen, Ralegh was some way removed from the kind of status accorded to, say, Heneage, Hatton and Walsingham in such hierarchies. But, in a sense, that was the point of their relationship: Elizabeth had plenty of public ministers, officials and servants, and to the extent that Ralegh aspired to be among them, his hopes were based on a misunderstanding of their affinity. Favoured he may have been, but Elizabeth preferred theirs to remain a kind of private understanding, intimate and discreet, and manifestly not the sort of thing she wished to advertise in the domestic sleeping arrangements.

At the end of her visit, on 1 June, Elizabeth acted on Ralegh's advice and summoned Oxford to her presence. 'After some bitter words and speeches,' Roger Manners reported to the Earl of Rutland the following day, 'in the end all sins are forgiven and he may repair to the court at his pleasure. Mr Ralegh was a great man herein, wherat Pondus is angry for that he could not do so much.'[19] The identity of Pondus isn't wholly clear. Burghley himself is sometimes advanced as a candidate, although given that he had himself asked Ralegh to intercede it isn't immediately apparent why he should then be irate at

Ralegh's success. A more likely candidate is Hatton, still sulking at Ralegh for outshining his own star at court.[20]

On 11 June, back at Greenwich, Ralegh would have been at once relieved and concerned to hear that Gilbert had finally set out for Newfoundland from Plymouth with his small fleet of five ships, among them the *Bark Ralegh*, which although no longer Gilbert's flagship was by far the biggest craft in the expedition, weighing almost as much as the other four ships put together. But once again, Gilbert's talent for delay and organizational incompetence had asserted itself over events; the year was already 'far spent', noted Edward Hayes in the only surviving account of the voyage, and the ultimate timing of the departure was as much as anything to ensure that their stores were not too depleted before they set out.[21] If Ralegh had been in contact with the captain of his ship, Michael Butler, a long-time associate of his, he would have been well-apprised of the situation on board. Nineteen men had deserted from the *Bark Ralegh* shortly before departure, and two days into the voyage, it turned about and sailed back to Plymouth, a devastating betrayal of Gilbert's project.

Hayes described the moment thus:

> when we hailed one another in the evening ... they signified unto us out of the Vice-admiral that both the captain, and very many of the men were fallen sick, and about midnight the Vice-admiral forsook us, notwithstanding we had the wind East, faire and good. But it was after credibly reported, that they were infected with a contagious sickness, and arrived greatly distressed at Plymouth: the reason I could never understand. Sure I am, no cost was spared by their owner Master Ralegh in setting them forth: Therefore I leave it unto God.

It is difficult not to read a degree of sarcasm into Hayes' parting comment, particularly since the reason ultimately offered for the *Bark Ralegh*'s desertion was precisely that: concern over the level of supplies on board. Although the record cannot be stretched to say that it had been Ralegh's plan all along to withdraw his ship – to gesture towards support while holding to a different course in private – it is difficult to construct a coherent narrative from the facts as they are. After all, if victuals were genuinely low, that fact cannot have suddenly been discovered after merely two days at sea; moreover, why go through the charade of signalling illness on board and then leave the fleet secretly in the dead of night? But if many of the crew were indeed struck down by sickness, why then suggest later that the problem was with the stores? Certainly if there were insufficiencies on board, that inadequacy – together with the evidently poor recruitment practices – could be laid at Ralegh's door; perhaps he simply lacked the capital.

Gilbert himself was unsympathetic: two months later he was still angry enough about the desertion of the ship to write to his friend Peckham that 'The *[B]ark Ralegh* ran from me, in fair and clear weather, having a large wind. I pray you solicit my brother Ralegh to make them an example to all knaves.'[22] Ralegh of course did no such thing – in fact, Butler would be one of his trustiest lieutenants for years to come. Why Gilbert did not write directly to Ralegh is open to speculation; perhaps their relations were indeed more strained than might otherwise be thought. As for Ralegh, he may have been caught in the same bind as Elizabeth – wishing the voyage a success but doubtful as to Gilbert's capacity to deliver it.

As it was, if he did entertain reservations about his brother, they were to be proved devastatingly accurate. Of the four ships that crossed the Atlantic – the *Delight*, the *Golden Hind*, the

Swallow and the *Squirrel* – only two would return. Ravaged by disease and plagued by a degree of ill-discipline that bordered on insurrection, let down by poor supplies and by Gilbert's lack of focus and leadership, and disappointed by the distinctly unparadisal landscape of Newfoundland, the voyage was another defeat for Gilbert. Had he lived, his return would have been humiliating, as would the cost – human and capital – of the failure. The *Delight*, captained by Thynne's charming correspondent Maurice Browne, went down off Sable Island on Thursday 29 August. Gilbert had some idea of wintering further down the coast, but the loss of the *Delight*, which carried much of the remaining equipment after the desertion of the *Bark Ralegh*, made such plans – implausible as they were – impossible. Gilbert's ship, the *Squirrel*, sank, all hands lost, on 9 September during the return journey. Elizabeth's promise of safety had once again proved hollow.

It was the *Golden Hind*, captained by Hayes, which brought news of the disaster back to Falmouth on 22 September.[23] Whatever their differences, Gilbert had been an immense influence on Ralegh's life, at once a role model, a visionary and a cautionary tale of how the desperate need for reward drove men to actions for which they were ill-equipped; the question was whether Ralegh wanted to acknowledge that debt and the warning it seemed to encode.

For the moment, however, Ralegh's thoughts were far from the north Atlantic and his brother's fate upon it. I wrote earlier that Ralegh was a faction of one at Elizabeth's court; it might be truer to say that, as she became increasingly confident of his loyalty and comfortable with his judgement, he and Elizabeth were becoming a faction of two. Another reason she was reluctant to offer Ralegh significant public office was that to do so would limit his utility to her: she did not want him to have a second power base at court, or to learn the interdependence of, say, Walsingham and Burghley, who for all their many disagreements on policy could find common cause in their exasperation with her. This way, Ralegh was something of a free agent – albeit one whose freedom was limited to her command. Trapped by politics, by patriarchy and custom, Elizabeth hated her enforced inactivity, and hated too her reliance on talk, perhaps precisely because of her genius for it. She understood command to be an active verb and she fought daily battles against those who would render her passive and reactive. Ralegh was one of her answers to the challenge of effecting policy directly.

She had in fact just dispatched him to Scotland to co-opt for England the two most powerful figures in the seventeen-year-old James VI's minority government: Sir William Stewart – widely known as Colonel Stewart in light of his extensive service in the Netherlands – and James Stewart, the Earl of Arran, for the moment James VI's favourite.[24] There was some sense in this strategy, in that James VI was at the time reaching out to the French, in particular, but also to the Duke of Guise, Philip II and the Pope – all of whom were of course vehement supporters of James' mother's claim to the throne of England. Indeed, James' outreach seemed to imply a willingness to allow the invasion of England through Scotland.[25]

But there were several unusual features to the plan, too, which made it counter-intuitive. The first was that the scheme was contrary to government policy as currently being pursued by Francis Walsingham, in alliance with Leicester. Walsingham's strategy to contain Scotland remains obscure in its workings, but he made its aim explicit: 'to play some such plot as [James VI] may be bridled and forced, whether he will or not, to depend upon your Majesty's favour and goodness'. It is not clear that his plan involved much more than England's usual strategy of wresting control of the pliant young king to more friendly councillors – but it made perfect sense.

In fact, the same day that Hayes had ridden into Falmouth harbour with news of Gilbert's loss, Walsingham had written to Leicester asking him to use his influence on Ralegh:

> I hear that there is a by-course in hand with Arran and the Colonel wherein Mr Ralegh is used for an instrument. I hope he is too wise to be used in any such indiscreet dealing. Your lordship may do well to give him advice to abstain from such by-courses.[26]

His irritation is still audible.

The other unusual feature of Ralegh's activity in Scotland is that Arran was strongly in favour of a Franco-Scottish alliance and in any case had a low view of England and the English: the country was, he said, 'a receptacle of all those that offend in Scotland, either in treasons or murders'.[27] Colonel Stewart, meanwhile, had been on a brief embassy to Elizabeth's court in May to assess the prospects of an alliance with England, and had formed so decisive an opinion that he had returned to Scotland to liberate his king from the close control of a Presbyterian clique and restore Arran to power.[28] It says something for Elizabeth's faith in Ralegh's abilities, in his plausibility, that she thought he could prosper on her behalf in such unpromising circumstances.

There is no doubt that Ralegh liked the intellectual swagger of the path less taken no less than the challenge to orthodoxy, and he and Elizabeth may have felt that unprincipled men, as Stewart and Arran certainly were, might be easier to influence than those motivated by ideology and power. Briefly, it looked as if Ralegh's charm had indeed effected a change in Scottish policy, but the fundamental flaw in his strategy was a failure to think through its implications for Anglo-Scottish relations going forward – a characteristic carelessness. Elizabeth, of course, disliked the restrictions that came with the kind of agreement Walsingham had in mind, which was likely to bind her in to commitments to Scotland – of money, in particular – which she had no desire to make. She also had no problem with a quick fix if longer-term solutions seemed unachievable or prohibitively expensive. Walsingham was both greatly concerned and deeply cynical, writing on the thirtieth to Bowes: 'I learn that the by-course goeth forward, and is well hearkened unto, great assurances are given that the King shall be altogether at her Majesty's devotion more firmly than ever before. I am sorry that Scotland should be able to abuse us with these vain entertainments.'[29]

He was yet more explicit in his bitterness to the Earl of Leicester in a letter written the same day:

I am sorry that the well affected in Scotland shall be left as a prey unto their enemies. The distrust of some such like issue as is now fallen out made them loath to give ear, for that by experience they have found that we do but coldly back our friends. Sorry I am from the bottom of my heart that I have been made an instrument of ambush, which beside the touch of my own poor credit, will make men both there and elsewhere loath to deal with any of her Majesty's ministers. The well-affected noblemen have no other way to save themselves but to make work unto Colonel Stewart and Arran, and to promise hereafter to forbear to have any other dealing with England, and to reconcile themselves unto the King's mother. Whether this be good for her Majesty I leave to your Lordship's consideration.[30]

Walsingham knew better than anyone that reconciliation – or any rapprochement – with Mary Stuart, James VI's mother, was soon to be politically impossible.

There had been an English spy in Mauvissière's house since April, communicating with Walsingham under the name Henry Fagot, but plausibly identified as the renegade Catholic priest and philosopher Giordano Bruno.[31] On 15 November he sat down at the Bull's Head Without Temple Bar with one of Burghley's intelligencers, William Herle – an old friend of Gascoigne's who had helped break open the Ridolfi plot – and passed on an explosive revelation: there was a well-advanced plot, directed by the Duke of Guise but with papal support, to launch an invasion of England to coincide with a Catholic uprising, with the aim of assassinating Elizabeth and placing Mary Stuart on the English throne.

Fagot had previously identified Francis Throckmorton and Henry Howard as being in active communication with Mary, and the two were arrested over the next couple of days. Fagot, who clearly disliked Howard intensely, did his best to blacken Howard's name with reports of his conversation that sound eerily reminiscent of those with which Howard himself charged Oxford, but Throckmorton – 'a party very busy and an enemy to the present state' Fagot said – was the catch. When he was taken at his home by St Paul's Wharf the authorities found a list of key Catholic nobles and gentlemen together with an assessment of which English harbours would be most suitable for landing a foreign army.

Throckmorton was on the rack early on the morning of the nineteenth. It was just a taste of what was in store: he was 'somewhat pinched, although not much' said the government propaganda afterwards; after three days he was quite himself again, they said. Between rackings he smuggled out messages ciphered on the back of playing cards, but tortured again on the twenty-second he broke down and confessed everything – most significantly, from the government's point of view, the fact that Mendoza, the Spanish ambassador, had been instrumental in co-ordinating the conspirators' communications with Mary, which – in a blow to his prestige and judgement – was certainly news to Walsingham, who had been focusing on the French. Indeed, while unmasking the Throckmorton conspiracy was undoubtedly an intelligence coup, it had the paradoxical effect of demonstrating vividly to the English authorities how little they knew, and how easy it was for the Catholic underground to evade detection – even to the extent of communicating with Mary, who was meant to be sequestered in the Earl of Shrewsbury's care at Sheffield.

While the conspiracy had the same essential outline as the Ridolfi plot of the decade before, that had been fairly clearly the product of Ridolfi's fantastic energies – despite Norfolk's treachery. This, however, was of a different order: more thoroughgoing, further advanced, and actively supported by those with the wherewithal to prosecute it effectively. The alliance of the Spanish, the papacy and the Guise family represented, in part at least, the very thing Elizabeth had fought for three decades to avoid: England's Catholic enemies in Europe united against her. Moreover, the apparent radicalization of Catholic gentry like Throckmorton, making good on the threat embodied in the papal bull of 1571, was deeply troubling: Elizabeth's enemies seemed to be multiplying; they could certainly be anywhere.

The shadow of the Oxford set fell on events again: there were many Catholics at court, and even more with close Catholic associations, who might have secretly reconciled. There were no doubt others who might be desperate enough and far enough adrift from their principles to be swayed by the prospect of reward. Ralegh himself could have been one of them. Where was her cherished personal liberty in that kind of world?

Shortly before Christmas, Mauvissière rode with Elizabeth from Hampton Court to Whitehall. He reported that the two of them had become separated from their escort and that as they rode on people knelt in the cold winter mud and blessed her as she passed. She turned to him and said pointedly, 'Not *everyone* wishes me dead'.[32] The bravado was characteristic, as was her refusal to be intimidated by the revelations into hiding from public sight. But the idea of others being delighted at her death held a morbid fascination for her: she repeated to Mauvissière one of Fagot's claims – almost certainly fabricated, as it happens – that there had been celebrations in Spain when rumours of her death were erroneously circulated. She was still acclimatizing to the fact that some – perhaps many – people in England did indeed want her dead. But who? Again, the gaps in the government's intelligence were painfully apparent.

After his confession, Throckmorton lamented, 'Now I have disclosed the secrets of her who was the dearest thing to me in the world ... and whom I thought no torment should have drawn me so much to have prejudiced as I have done by my confessions'.[33] But Mary still had one protector – Elizabeth, who would not countenance her prosecution yet. She found the idea of prosecuting and executing a fellow monarch instinctively abhorrent – no doubt due to a troubled mix of private emotion, given her family history, and a shrewd awareness that such a path weakened her own authority. Moreover she may have been right that the evidence was not quite conclusive: the documentary trail did not lead all the way to Mary's door, despite the obvious balance of presumption. Long ago, when Mary had first come to England, Cecil had written to Elizabeth, setting out the bare truth: 'The queen of Scots is and shall always be a dangerous person to your estate:

yet there are degrees of danger ... If her person be restrained here ... it will be less; if at liberty, greater.'[34] The Throckmorton plot revealed beyond doubt that mere imprisonment still left Mary with enough liberty to put Elizabeth herself – and the entire English Protestant settlement – at risk. Yet Elizabeth demanded more proofs; Ralegh, and others around her must have felt that, as well as needing saving from assassination, she also needed saving from herself.

It must have been apparent to all that the authorities needed more people on the inside, more double agents, more *agents provocateurs* – despite the fact that they would also, by their very nature, raise the level of fear and uncertainty, even as they promised the reassuring certainty of information. Sides were being drawn, but the loyalties of many men were obscure: who could anyone trust?

Mauvissière reported in December that 'Charles Arundell and several more noblemen and principal gentlemen of quality ... fled [...] and embarked at night on board a vessel at Arundel, which still more astonished the queen and her council.'[35] There is no evidence, other than his flight, that Ralegh's old friend was involved in the conspiracy; but he was highly unlikely to remain free if he stayed. Given his associations and his history, he was just the sort of man to be charged with the duty of assassination. Herle had reported to Burghley seeing him towards the end of November buying gloves and perfume from a new perfumier in Abchurch Street; Arundell was, Herle deduced, intending 'to use them to poison the queen, she having her senses of smelling so perfect, and delighted with good savours'.[36]

In that kind of paranoid atmosphere, who knew what represented safety?

XIII: HOLLOW SERVANTS

In silence there is safety but in speech there is peril and in writing more.
EDMUND PLOWDEN, MIDDLE TEMPLE

For Elizabeth, the heightened vulnerability that Throckmorton's discovery ushered in added greatly to her burdens. In a sense she faced a very modern dilemma: how to maintain the usual liberties and routines of daily life while living with the terror of an unspecific but real threat. One direct effect of Fagot's revelations, however, was the expulsion of Mendoza on 9 January, an act that Walsingham seems to have handled with ill-disguised pleasure: the demand that he leave the country, Mendoza wrote to Philip, was accompanied with what he called such impertinences that he didn't dare repeat them to his king. It is fairly clear from Mendoza's account that he didn't handle the meeting well, despite having ample warning of its subject: he lost his temper and declared that as he had 'apparently failed to please [Elizabeth] as a minister of peace she would in future force me to try to satisfy her in war', a bellicosity he seems to have regretted since he felt the need to apologize to Philip and note that he had spoken as an individual and his words did not therefore commit Spain to military action.[1] For the English, his words merely confirmed their worst fears. Mendoza would move only as far as Paris, where he fitted in, all too comfortably, the English no doubt thought, among the Jesuits and the English Catholic exiles.

But other former members of Oxford's circle continued to suffer. Henry Howard's nephew, Philip, the twenty-six-year-old Earl of Arundel, was brought in for questioning, while Henry Percy, eighth earl of Northumberland, was interrogated and sent to the Tower – on the same day Mendoza was expelled – for abetting the escape of Charles Arundell and Thomas Paget. It was suspected that Northumberland had been privy to details of the plot for some months, and that Arundell and Paget had fled because they knew enough to incriminate him.

Ironically, perhaps, the most compromised of the Oxford alumni was missed entirely; he would not in fact be identified as of interest until 1586. He was Ralegh's friend and follower George Gifford, a Throckmorton on his mother's side. A courtier by 1573, George Gifford was made a gentleman pensioner in 1578 and seems to have been a prominent one: he was among the Whitehall tilters in 1581, and again in 1583, 1584 and 1585.[2] He must have met Ralegh around 1578, whether through Oxford's circle or through other, now lost friendships or connections. It was also about this time that things began to unravel for him.[3]

Von Wedel's observation about young gentlemen being forced into highway robbery might have been made with Gifford in mind: in 1583 he was in trouble for aiding the escape from custody of a highwayman named Nix and only evaded punishment thanks to his court connections. Quite clearly, he was a man of few scruples, on one occasion cozening a Throckmorton kinsman into helping him defraud a friend of the latter of eighty pounds of cloth by promising to use the money raised to help pay for the manufacture of a philosopher's stone to turn base matter into gold.[4]

Nevertheless, despite everything we know of Gifford, what he did in late April 1583 still astonishes. Escaping scrutiny thanks to his connections after breaking Nix from prison, Gifford travelled to Paris and met secretly with Charles Paget and Thomas Morgan; he told them he was a Catholic and was prepared to assassinate Elizabeth – if the Duke of Guise would recompense him sufficiently. As a gentleman pensioner, he claimed, he would have no difficulty getting close to her.

Gifford does not sound much like anyone's idea of a subtle conspirator, and – to give the Catholics their due – much as their correspondence regarding his offer crackles with excitement at the premise, it is also cold with doubt as to his reliability; 'unfit to build on', was their eventual conclusion. Nevertheless, it was certainly rumoured that Guise did in fact pay him anything up to £5,000; another version of events had the duke depositing the money with Mary Stuart's agent in Paris, the archbishop of Glasgow, until such a time as the deed was done.

Gifford made no effort to fulfil his bond, and it is certainly not beyond the bounds of possibility, given what we know of his proclivities, his talent for spinning other men's dreams into gold in his purse, that he viewed the approach to Guise as the ultimate scam, selling the tallest tale in Europe, with risks and rewards to match. He would have been a fool to approach such a task without some kind of support at court, whether from Walsingham, Ralegh or Hatton – all three of whom he depended on at different times in his career – but perhaps Gifford was that fool.

Clearly, however, if anyone at court sanctioned such an approach to the Catholic exiles it would have had an aim beyond sounding their hatred of Elizabeth; after all, the depth of that was known. What needed to be mapped was Mary's complicity, and it is therefore revealing that the earliest surviving report of his offer, from the papal nuncio in Paris, notes that Gifford first made his pitch to Mary, who – presumably suspicious at Gifford's bona fides – refused to listen to him.[5] Was this then an early attempt to smoke out Mary, the government feeling awkwardly for the shape of the plot which she and Throckmorton, among others, were developing? Or was he serious when he made the offer but ultimately found it impossible, on whatever diffidence or scruple, to prosecute it?

There is no record that anyone at court knew of Gifford's precise deal at the time, but everyone was familiar with the idea of it: Elizabeth had much more to fear from an enemy within than she did from an invasion force. Hadn't someone almost assassinated the Prince of Orange two years earlier? The number of people who had the same degree of access as Gifford was large, and policing them all was impossible.

While Elizabeth considered such threats, Ralegh was beginning to show increasing signs of ambivalence about his position again. In February he joined another Gilbert brother, Adrian – considered by some contemporaries a buffoon and, perhaps not coincidentally, a good friend of Dee's – in The Colleagues of the Discovery of the North-West Passage, alongside another sea-faring man, John Davis. Ralegh, in fact, took Dee's place in the triumvirate.[6]

The fellowship was explicitly formed to exploit Gilbert's recent patent, granted on 6 February, for discovery of a passage to the east and to trade and settle in any countries discovered along the way. It was a classically Elizabethan reward structure, the gift of something that with hard work and good fortune could be turned to private profit, but which required no outlay from the crown at all. But in joining himself formally to Gilbert's venture – a much greater commitment than that he offered Humphrey Gilbert – Ralegh was signalling an intent to build a power base, a second centre of gravity outside the court, one that sought to unite a range of conflicting aspirations and ambitions. 'To seek new worlds, for gold, for praise, for glory,/To try desire, to try love severed far', was how he characterized his hopes in a later poem, bundling together personal freedom, the hunger for wealth and power, imperial outreach and intellectual discovery. That intention was underlined the following month, on 25 March, when he received a new patent himself from Elizabeth at Whitehall, which in essence superseded that offered to Humphrey Gilbert. It was a very public expression of personal faith on Elizabeth's part in Ralegh's vision and his abilities – all the more so, perhaps, because Ralegh was her favourite and his brother had proved so incapable of success.

Ralegh left Whitehall that day with a very particular burden of expectation. Gilbert's responsibility had been to his investors, and to those who shared his vision; Ralegh also carried the private hopes of his queen, and a need to validate her trust and judgement. As for Elizabeth, while the terms she offered Ralegh were similar, indeed largely identical, to those offered to Gilbert, what was different is the context: when Elizabeth offers Ralegh, her favourite, her oracle, the liberty

> to embark and transport out of our realm of England and Ireland, and the dominions thereof, all or any of his . . . goods . . . with such other necessaries and commodities . . . for the better relief and supportation of him the said Walter Ralegh[7]

she is engaging in an act of extraordinary personal generosity. When she had offered the same terms to Gilbert it was merely a business proposition. Indeed, she had a proposal of her own for Ralegh with regard to the new country's name: Virginia. On one level, this gift of a name was a tacit affirmation of his work, and a statement of affinity, of shared enterprise, between them; but it was also a reminder of ownership, of the fact that however wide the freedoms he might enjoy personally or politically in the Americas, he did so on her licence. Virginia would be her kingdom if it thrived, but his failure if it did not.

Whatever Ralegh's motives or emotional need to assume his late brother's troubled legacy with regard to the Americas, it is quite apparent that he did not do so without thinking deeply and critically about his brother's failure. He must have been aware, despite the propaganda that was circulated in public by men like Hayes and Peckham, that most of those who had sailed to Newfoundland were dismayed by the distinctly hard and uninviting landscape, quite different from the paradisal land of plenty they had expected. 'Now I ought to tell you about the customs, territories and inhabitants,' one of them wrote to Hakluyt, 'yet what am I to say . . . when I see nothing but desolation?'[8] Ralegh instead decided to focus his attention further down the eastern seaboard towards more temperate climes – and closer too to the Spanish sphere of influence.

It was a considered decision, marrying bare practicality to an aggressive imperial strategy, and one that reflected Ralegh's style of thought, which, sceptic though he was, found its most comfortable expression in clean simplicities at the expense of grubby complexities, while still clinging tenaciously to an epic scale: he was a minimalist with a maximalist heart. In this, he was almost an embodiment of England's new-found Protestant nationalism, with its stripped-down intellectual aesthetic and providential sense of destiny.

The decision also bore the hallmark of the cabal of men that Ralegh was gathering around himself at Durham House, a radically different society from that which existed at the court, or indeed from those coteries to which he had previously belonged. They were not men with connections, but with aptitude, sharing Ralegh's sceptical temperament but applying it as a practical proto-scientific method to the challenges of his hoped-for imperium.

In this, as in so many things, he was trailing in Gilbert's wake – or rather, finding a way to give Gilbert's ideas a life beyond the airy perfections of the imagination. A decade earlier Gilbert had proposed to Elizabeth the creation of an 'Academy of Chivalric Policy and Philosophy' in London to educate England's young nobles and gentlemen youth in utilitarian subjects such as politics and law, natural philosophy and medicine, mathematics and geometry, and how they applied to civil and military policy. Learning was to be driven by practice and example, not by what Gilbert dismissed as 'bookish circumstances': 'men shall be taught more wit and policy than school learnings can deliver . . . for the greatest school clerks are not always the wisest men.'[9]

In his own self-made world, Ralegh exhibited a confidence and security he could only aspire to in the exposed arena of the court. He took Gilbert's brilliant and innovative, but hugely ambitious and impractical concept and distilled its essence to suit his current needs:

> The . . . mathematician shall read one day cosmography and astronomy, and the other day tend the practices thereof, only to the art of navigation, with the knowledge of necessary stars, making use of instruments appertaining to the same; and also shall have in his school a ship and galley made in model, thoroughly rigged and furnished, to teach unto his auditory as well the knowledge and use by name of every part thereof, as also the perfect art of a shipwright . . . Also there shall be one

who shall teach to draw maps, sea charts, etc, and to take by view of eye the plot of any thing, and shall read the grounds and rules of proportion and necessary perspective mensuration belonging to the same.[10]

Out of Gilbert's fantasy Ralegh conjured a working reality. At the heart of it was a mathematician named Thomas Harriot – a reticent, intense young man who wore only black – arguably the most brilliant Englishman in that field before Isaac Newton. Ralegh paid him an exceptionally generous salary to teach his sea-captains navigational theory, the practical application of mathematics and astronomy.

Information was a kind of power and, perhaps aware of how tenuous his political power was, how fragile his fortune, Ralegh revelled in its ownership and display. Harriot was given a modest room at Durham House on the top floor close to Ralegh's and with access out on the leads, where he conducted experiments at night. Also active in related fields as optics, natural philosophy, algebra and astronomy, Harriot's reputation has been fatally damaged both by his strange diffidence about publishing his work and the posthumous loss of many of his papers, but in his lifetime he was highly regarded in the scientific community across Europe: visionaries like Kepler wrote to him for advice.

In employing Harriot to lecture and advise on every aspect of his planned voyages – including ship design and construction – Ralegh had given navigation perhaps the most brilliant and original mind ever to work on its problems. It is not difficult to see how well the two men worked together: they had similar habits of mind. To master his vast new brief, Harriot read every text he could find, contemporary and classical, English, Portuguese and Spanish, and spoke to innumerable sea-men on London's thriving quaysides.[11] Like Ralegh, he had to know everything. Within a short time, Ralegh's fleets had the highest level of scientific expertise in the known world; one of his captains, Thomas Cavendish, used Harriot's techniques to make the first planned circumnavigation of the world in 1586.

How much this explosion of imperial activity was an extension of Ralegh's previously declared ambitions and how much a reaction to the renewed pressures of court life is difficult to tell. In itself it represented a kind of independence for him, his own sphere of influence, but also offered an infinite prospect. Elizabeth referred to the Americas as *meta incognita*, the unknown limit: in a sense, that was the attraction for both of them: a place of unrestrained promise, political, personal and financial, an impossibly perfect cure for Ralegh's horror of poverty, for Elizabeth's fear of constraint. It was where their hope of liberty converged. But Ralegh also now had Durham House, and, surrounded by his intellectual coterie of like-minded men, he shaped for himself a place of safety, of respite. Now when he woke after his five hours of sleep he dedicated the new-found time to reading and scientific exploration, not to waiting on Elizabeth's favour in the privy chamber.[12] Was there a danger that in sending him in search of this great unbound gift of empire, she would lose him entirely? Elizabeth seems to have thought so. I quoted earlier a couple of Ralegh's lines encapsulating his dream: 'To seek new worlds, for gold for praise, for glory,/To try desire, to try love severed far'. The poem continues:

When I was gone she sent her memory
More strong than were ten thousand ships of war,
To call me back, to leave great honour's thought,
To leave my friends, my fortune, my attempt,
To leave the purpose I so long had sought.

The lines do not have to be interpreted literally for them to embody the complex dynamic between the two of them. America represented a kind of hope to both of them, but did Elizabeth want Ralegh to have another source of hope beyond her favour? True, she had awarded him the patent, but was she always so certain? And what degree of assurance did she want Ralegh to feel? Perhaps recognizing the implicit pull away that all this activity represented, Elizabeth chose this same month, March, to bolster Ralegh with perhaps her most lucrative gift, a twelve-month licence to export woollen broadcloths, one of England's few staple products for international trade, which was worth over £3,000 each year. Burghley viewed the gift with some dismay, later scrutinizing it closely and concluding that it was too generous to Ralegh, while Walsingham made his position equally clear as early as June by putting his weight behind what must have been the first petition by a group of merchants accused of infringing Ralegh's commercial rights. Elizabeth, needless to say, took Ralegh's part. Despite the wealth that it bestowed on Ralegh, Elizabeth's gift revealed her customarily cautious prodigality, and also paradoxically increased his dependence on her: a man who burned through money like Ralegh could not live without fresh capital, and this new licence was only to be renewed annually. Although Ralegh did have it renewed and extended in three of the next five years, the kind of financial liberation that the licence offered also served to feed his addiction. To continue receiving such largesse he had to please her, year after year.

By now the flow of money in and out of Durham House was extraordinary. Some of it, however, was inadvertent: the Middlesex Session Rolls reveal that on 26 April a gentleman named Hugh Pugh 'stole a jewel worth eighty pounds, a hat band of pearls worth thirty pounds, and five yards of white silk called damask worth three pounds of the goods and chattels of

Walter Rawley esq', a prize haul for what was no doubt an opportunistic crime.[13] The very next day, acting with some alacrity on his patent, Ralegh dispatched two ships to scout locations for what would be the first European colony in north America. The captains were Arthur Barlow and Philip Amadas, the pilot Ralegh's old friend Simon Fernandes. Harriot almost certainly sailed with them.

While Barlow and Amadas were heading for the Carolina outer banks – Fernandes' intended destination with Ralegh in 1578 – events in the Low Countries were isolating England yet further. Elizabeth's last suitor, her Monsieur, died of illness on the last day of May. Elizabeth was devastated; the ravages of time were at her heels after all. Walsingham wrote to Stafford on 2 July that 'We cannot yet shake off our sorrow [. . .] There hath no day passed without tears, for these three weeks past.' Into an already oppressive atmosphere at court, then, came worse news still. Unbeknownst to either Walsingham or Stafford, two days earlier the Spanish had finally succeeded in assassinating the Prince of Orange, his assassin ironically the very man who had first told him of Alençon's death.[14] Monsieur was no loss in military terms – his campaign in the Netherlands had been disastrous for both himself and his putative allies – but Orange's death, and more particularly its manner, was a major blow to English – and Elizabeth's – security. The execution of Francis Throckmorton a few days later on the tenth cannot have brought much, if any, peace of mind: he was the only person the government could find to punish fully for the treasonous plot, and it was said he died stubbornly refusing to ask for Elizabeth's forgiveness.

These events go a long way towards explaining why, at the height of his triumph – basking in Elizabeth's favour, his income exploding, and ships at sea that could find him a private empire – we find Ralegh sounding a note of caution and retreat. On 26 July he wrote to Richard Duke, the owner of Hayes Barton, and offered to pay any price quoted for the old house. 'I will most willingly give you what so ever in your conscience you deem it worth', he wrote – and, perhaps of greater value, offered his services and influence – 'resting ready to counterveil all your courtesies to the uttermost of my power'. Ralegh's tone to Duke, quite uncharacteristically, even edged towards pleading: 'for the natural disposition I have to that place, being born in that house, I had rather seat myself there than anywhere else'.[15] Richard Duke, however, was resolute in his indifference; royal favour had its limits, and Ralegh's broadcloth licence seems to have been particularly unpopular among the merchants in nearby Exeter.

It says something about Ralegh that his childhood home meant so much to him, and it hints at aspects of his personality – sentimentality, insecurity, a kind of diffidence – that have been lost to us behind the quasi-mythic gilded figure he made of himself. Where did he feel that he truly belonged? East Budleigh was not, after all, an address for a man who expected to spend considerable time at court. Nor, given that it did not have significant land attached, did it offer a great deal of scope for the kind of expansive improvements to turn it into the kind of property a man of his stature would be expected to have. But it may have represented a kind of liberty to him, a place apart from the dark tensions of Whitehall. The degree to which Elizabeth acknowledged how much he hankered after a distant family home, however, is open to question.

XIV: *AMORE ET VIRTUTE*

But when she better him beheld, she grew
Full of soft passion and unwonted smart:
The point of pity pierced through her tender heart

EDMUND SPENSER

There is a story told of the great Elizabethan clown, Richard
Tarlton – one of the Queen's Men from 1583 until his death in
1588 – that he once broke out of his jesting before Elizabeth
one evening at court and pointed at Ralegh. 'See how the knave
commands the queen,' Tarlton said, adding – despite the
queen's evident displeasure – that Ralegh's power was intoler-
ably great. Tarlton then turned to Leicester and similarly
assaulted his wealth and influence too, much to the delight of
everyone present.[1]

But if Leicester and Ralegh were popularly perceived as alike
in their corruption, their paths were beginning to diverge quite
significantly. Leicester's transformation into the de facto leader
of the Puritan, anti-Catholic faction – both at court and in the
country – was by now complete. His opposition to Spain was
– as well as being self-aggrandizing – ideological, a moral
crusade. Ralegh, for his part, leaned quite hard on the idea that

he was a no-less-committed enemy to Spain in particular, and international Catholicism in general – he probably had to, given his historical links with Oxford's court Catholic party – but the truth was that Ralegh's war with Spain was primarily political: he believed passionately in England's potential as a global power and Spain was unquestionably the principal obstacle in the fulfilment of that vision. Ralegh resented the encroachments of its empire abroad on his own ambition – never mind England's – and despised the threat that it and its proxies presented at home. But he seems to have been largely indifferent to the ideological content of the struggle.

In this, he and Elizabeth were wholly alike. If the factions at Elizabeth's court were on most issues fluid, here they can be reduced into three: the war party; the peace-at-any-price party; and, between them, the peace-first, war-as-last-resort party. The queen herself was in the latter, by far the smallest group; Ralegh liked to give the impression that he stood alongside Walsingham and Leicester in the first category, but the truth is that his position was far more ambiguous and contradictory: he judged neither people nor nations by their religions but by their politics – and the extent to which they stood in his way. And willingly or otherwise, he seems to have allowed Elizabeth to exploit that, using him to avoid war, hence the earlier dalliance with Arran – and now, in the summer of 1584, an apparent rapprochement with Spain and its agents. They were a faction of two again. In earlier decades, Elizabeth might have used Leicester for such work, someone she trusted without question plausibly being positioned as a friend to Spain; it was another area in which Ralegh usurped the position of his sometime patron, and a mark of the deep and abiding faith she held in him.

On 1 August, a few days after Ralegh had attempted to repurchase his family home, two justices of the peace in Cornwall arrested a man named John Froste and threw him into Saltash Prison. Froste had recently returned from Spain, where Ralegh had sent him, he claimed, to negotiate with an English exile over the purchase of a manor.[2] In some respects of course this is trivial, but less so when you consider that the exile in question was Francis Englefield. As we have already noted, Englefield – also a close friend of Nicholas Sanders – had been a thorn in Elizabeth's flesh since the beginning of her reign and, blind or not, had been complicit in every significant Catholic plot against her. He was, without doubt, an unusual choice of person to do business with. That is particularly so given that, while Englefield still nominally owned his familial lands, the use of them had been appropriated by the queen some twenty years previously.

What, then, was Ralegh doing? If we assume the property transaction to be what it appears to be – that is, something of a red herring – the principal attraction of Englefield had to be his status as one of Philip's most trusted advisers about English affairs, and a direct line into the circle of conspirators in exile, who were by no means a homogenous bunch. Indeed, like many another group of revolutionaries with similar but not identical aims, there were at least two competing factions, in places overlapping but nevertheless distinct, who despised and distrusted each other: the Hispano-papal axis on one side, of which Englefield was a part and which included the Jesuit missionaries, and the party around Morgan and Mary Stuart on the other.

If we cannot at this point find any more information about the dialogue between Ralegh and Englefield, we can certainly see how Ralegh's own propaganda obscured more complex behaviours, and how the autonomy of action that Elizabeth offered him – and which he offered to Elizabeth too in the form of deniability – equipped him to fulfil her wide-ranging needs in ways that no one else at court could. Whatever the tendency of her foreign policy, Elizabeth always liked to keep as many choices on the table as possible, and maintained private lines of communication with those whom someone as ideologically committed as Walsingham certainly regarded as beyond redemption.

It was, however, an inauspicious time to have less-than-perfect credentials in the fight against international Catholicism, even with Elizabeth's consent. August was also the month that saw the appearance in Paris of a masterfully brutal attack on Leicester titled *The Copy of a Letter Written By A Master of Cambridge*, but known almost immediately and ever since as *Leicester's Commonwealth*. The Leicester it reveals is a rapacious libertine, lustful for power: a deceitful, faithless murderer. Evidence of its success as a libel can be found in the fact that it distorted every portrait of Leicester for the following 400 years.

Although published anonymously, *Leicester's Commonwealth* was almost certainly largely the work of Ralegh's erstwhile friend Charles Arundell. It was immensely popular: copies of it probably constituted a large proportion of the 800 books George Emerson smuggled into England in August; the following spring one of Walsingham's Parisian spies heard there were a thousand copies at a print shop in Rouen, another that Arundell's rooms in Paris were filled with a great number of them. But by definition, most copies were brought in beneath the government's radar. It was everywhere: copies were smuggled into prisoners in the Tower; it was read, discreetly but openly, at court.[3]

The pamphlet's virulent animosity towards Leicester could not go unanswered, but although Sidney circulated a weak manuscript rebuttal, the government chose to suppress *Leicester's Commonwealth* as part of the wider Catholic attack on England rather than attempt to refute its charges. This was probably correct: Leicester's unpopularity made a defence difficult and, while the tract's more thoughtful passages make a cogent case for religious toleration, the Protestant authorities were hardly likely to take that at face value. Among the dicta of Henry Howard which Fagot had passed to Walsingham was the proposition that full religious toleration was intended as a smoke screen to enable the murder of England's leading reformed families. Besides, the Catholic exiles did not see the publication as a stand-alone project: Ralegh's correspondent at the Spanish court, Francis Englefield, recommended it be seen as part of a propaganda effort that might be the English Catholics' only real weapon, and argued for similar efforts to be published with *Leicester's Commonwealth*'s 'skittish humour [that] will both stumble and kick'.

If no one was sure who precisely was behind the document, neither Walsingham nor Leicester are likely to have missed its sympathies for the Catholic court party at the turn of the decade, one symptom of which was its obvious goodwill towards Ralegh. Indeed, Arundell calls on Ralegh to bear witness against Leicester much as he did in his depositions against Oxford – an act that in itself suggests Ralegh must have to some degree confirmed the truth of those depositions to the authorities, but which again must have created political difficulties for Ralegh at court. If Ralegh did believe that Leicester had commissioned pirates to sink Simier's ship on its return journey in 1579, he probably had little desire to pronounce publicly on the subject in 1584.

The government's initial efforts to suppress the pamphlet clearly failed, because on 12 October it took the unusual step of issuing a proclamation against 'false, slanderous, wicked, seditious and traitorous books'; *Leicester's Commonwealth* is not specifically named, but it is quite clear what is being targeted. The proclamation was a defensive measure, closing ranks around Leicester and giving no quarter to his enemies: an attack on one of Elizabeth's chief ministers is an attack on her monarchy and a threat to her safety:

> [In] their most shameful, infamous and detestable libels they go about to reproach, dishonour and touch with abominable lies . . . many of her most trusty and faithful councillors . . . greatly touching thereby her Highness' self in her regal and kingly office, as making choice of men of want both of justice, care and other sufficiency to serve her Highness and the commonweal. And further, in the said books and libels they use all the means, drifts, and false persuasions they can devise or imagine to advance such pretended titles as consequently must be most dangerous and prejudicial to the safety of her Highness' person and state.

Slanders against Leicester are wilfully read here as treasons against her; but he is safe, as are they all, beneath the shadow of her wings.

But if the government was focused on steadying itself defensively against assault, then Ralegh's imperial plans offered some kind of antidote, more than a little tinged with escapism, with the ancillary benefit of burnishing his anti-Spanish credentials. Over the summer, he had commissioned from Richard Hakluyt – temporarily returned from Paris where he was now secretary to Elizabeth's ambassador, Edward Stafford – a *Discourse of Western Planting*. The proposal, to be presented to Elizabeth in manuscript, is essentially a vigorously anti-Spanish prospectus for Ralegh's American colonial ambitions, but it reveals how closely interpenetrated Elizabeth and America were for Ralegh, in a way that transcends political necessity and moves towards the conflated sense of the two that had been a feature of Metsys' recent portrait. Hakluyt proposed colonization as a strange consummation of Ralegh and Elizabeth's shared imperial destiny, a proxy relationship in which the surrogacy metaphor barely contained the sexual freight Hakluyt made it bear. He wrote in his dedication to Ralegh how:

> you freely swore that no terrors, no personal losses or misfortunes could or would ever tear you from the embraces of your own Virginia, that fairest of nymphs . . . whom our most generous sovereign has given you to be your bride? If you persevere only a little longer in your constancy, your bride will shortly bring forth new and most abundant offspring, such as will delight you and yours, and cover with disgrace and shame those who have so often dared rashly and impudently to charge her with barrenness. For who has the just title to attach such a stigma to your Elizabeth's Virginia, when no one has yet probed the depths of her hidden resources and wealth, or her beauty hitherto concealed from our sight?[4]

The following month, Amadas and Barlow returned from Chesapeake and the Carolina banks to offer detailed and secretive debriefings at Durham House. Not content with their accounts, Ralegh then took personal charge of the propaganda effort and wove together an eloquent and seductive narrative of their voyage to be circulated in public, despite being published under the names of the two captains:

> we viewed the land about us, being whereas we first landed, very sandy and low towards the waters side, but so full of grapes, as the very beating and surge of the sea overflowed them, of which we found such plenty, as well

there as in all places else, both on the sand and on the green soil on the hills, as in the plains, as well on every little shrub, as also climbing towards the tops of high cedars, that I think in all the world the like abundance is not to be found.[5]

To mark his new-found status as governor of an as-yet unpeopled English colony, Ralegh also had a seal cast. On it he had written a new personal motto, to replace that he had borrowed from Gascoigne. Out went *tam marti quam mercurio*, made for war as much as wisdom; in came *amore et virtute* – love and virtue, virtue connoting valour and courage as well as a cleaving to principle. The latter was of course one of the qualities that he was most conspicuously thought to lack as Elizabeth's favourite, and his appropriation of it is a quintessential Raleghan gesture, challenging his enemies to give him the lie. But one way in which he succeeds in his claim to virtue is by marrying it to love, which in the context of the autumn of 1584 is a means of identifying himself with and through the queen. On one level it is interesting to see the extent to which he was willing to make explicit the basis of his bond with Elizabeth – love being a transcendent claim to friendship, loyalty and favour – idealizing it through its relationship to virtue and yet also demonstrating the cold political reality of it in action. But we might also read virtue to reflect his courage and strength of character, the sheer will power it required to maintain his position at court: for Ralegh, Elizabeth's love was virtue's reward.

Yet Ralegh still seems trapped between hubris and anxiety: the greater the gifts he received, the higher his status, the more exposed he became. His successes were vertiginous and the potential loss of her favour gnawed at him even as he sought to establish other safeties.

* * *

Monday 23 November saw one of the great theatrical events of state, the official opening of Parliament. The Westminster streets were scrubbed clean and carpeted with fresh sand for the long royal procession: lords and gentlemen riding two by two, gold and silver trappings on their mounts; trumpeters; a hundred soldiers; heralds, their blue mantles bearing wings of beaten gold; fifty huntsmen bearing small gilt spears; four men with sceptres; bishops, their red robes lined with white linen, square black caps on their heads; a horse, its golden saddle set with pearls, its golden bridle with precious stones, a diamond on its forehead, pearls on its ears; and then at last Elizabeth, her red velvet mantle lined with white ermine spotted with black, carried on a sedan chair, covered in gold and silver cloth, itself borne by two cream-coloured horses, white plumes fastened to yellow manes and tails. Alongside Elizabeth marched her guard, decked in parliamentary red for the occasion, covered in beaten gold; behind her came twenty-four ladies, followed by two empty carriages, one lined with red velvet, and the other black, gold embroidered.

Somewhere in the procession marched Walter Ralegh, wearing the MPs' customary long red cloth coat lined with white rabbit fur. He was on his way to be sworn in as a member of the House of Commons – one of two knights of the shire for Devon – in the new Parliament, the first elected since 1572. His personal agenda was simple and on Monday 14 December he initiated it by introducing a bill to confirm Elizabeth's grant of patent by act of Parliament: Elizabeth's favour could fade or turn but laws were unwieldy things to revoke.

It is evident he had the support of the administration in this – a mark of how irrepressible he was with Elizabeth's favour to fill his sails. His bill was sent to be discussed in committee, on which sat at least two men who were indifferent to the point of hostility to his rise: Sir Christopher Hatton and Philip

Sidney. And yet it returned to the floor unamended: it was only when debated by his fellow members that things became heated, Ralegh's patent reportedly causing many arguments on the floor of the house. There are no surviving records of the debate but the most plausible point of contention is objection to the privileges being granted to a minor private individual. If Ralegh found such hostility grating, his bill did at least pass the Commons on its third reading; things were different when it reached the House of Lords at the end of the week, however, and the lords and bishops who sat were much harder for Elizabeth to manipulate. After one reading on the nineteenth, Ralegh's bill appears to have been dropped over the Christmas recess, which began the following day. Aside from the fact that Ralegh would not receive the legal assurance he had hoped for, it was a very public rebuff.

As for Elizabeth, she had three objectives in summoning Parliament: addressing the growing sense of alarm over her own personal safety in the wake of the discovery of Throckmorton's plot; combating the Jesuit menace; and eliciting a subsidy. But it was a difficult Parliament to manage: its members trended Puritan, and the overwhelming majority of them had, like Ralegh, never sat as MPs before, two key factors that gave proceedings a restive, skittish uncertainty.[6] Ralegh sat on the subsidy committee and also on a committee that was considering the recruitment of ministers into the Anglican church, the government believing that better recruits would be able to counter Catholic propaganda.[7]

The act for Elizabeth's safety was intended to enshrine the Oath of Association in law – which bound those who took it to avenge Elizabeth's death in the event of her murder and exclude from the succession any intended beneficiary. Fear of assassination was now driving both sides towards pre-emptive strikes. In Spain, a panicked Englefield wrote to both the Pope and Philip II declaring the oath to be the government's first step towards its intended murder of Mary and pleading for action on her behalf; it is a measure of his desperation that he tried to bully Philip into intervention by alleging that he would be seen as conniving at Mary's death to advance his own causes should they fail to rescue her – an accusation which Philip must have found deeply offensive.[8]

But the passage of the safety act was overtaken by events. Or rather, events so fell out as to illustrate vividly why the queen's safety was such a paramount issue. Ralegh was almost certainly in the chamber on 17 December, shortly after his patent bill had returned to the floor from committee; he and his fellow MPs were quietly nodding through the bill against Jesuits with consensual pliancy. That calm was shattered by the MP for Queenborough, a Catholic Welshman named William Parry, who launched into a violent diatribe against the bill, claiming it to be in 'favour of treasons, to be full of blood, danger, despair and terror or dread to the English subjects of this realm, our brethren, uncles and kinsfolks'.[9] Shocked and outraged, the Commons demanded that Parry be brought to the bar of the house, where he further alienated his fellow members by refusing to explain himself to them, declaring that he would only reveal his reasons to Elizabeth in person, a demand that reflected Parry's excessive and misplaced solipsism.

The authorities had reason enough already to be sceptical about Parry. He had been spying intermittently for Burghley on the continent since at least 1577, although it is debatable how much trust Burghley placed in him: the impression one gets is that Parry was more enthusiastic about sending information than Burghley was about receiving it. Smart enough to foment trouble, he fatally lacked the wit and intellectual dexterity to extricate himself afterwards. It is possible, although not certain, that Ralegh knew him, since

Ralegh's friend Edward Stafford was close enough to him to stand joint surety for a bond of £2,000 earlier in the decade – a generous act given Stafford's own heroic levels of personal debt. Reconciling to the Catholic church, Parry insinuated himself into the émigré circles in Paris, and eventually stumbled on the same idea as Gifford to attract Catholic interest: assassination. Thomas Morgan told him he could do some great service for his church. Parry vowed to target Leicester – 'the greatest subject in England, whom I . . . hated', he said – but Morgan had other ideas: 'No no,' he said, 'let him live to his greater fall and ruin of his house: it is the queen I mean.'[10]

Parry had returned to England at the beginning of 1584 and seems to have shared at least some of his intelligence with Elizabeth, who accepted his bona fides at face value, but the truth is that no one could be sure whose side he was really on. Perhaps Parry – a fractious, delusional, disappointed man – was never really sure himself: 'I determined never to do it,' he later said, '[but] I feared to be tempted, and therefore always when I came near her, I left my dagger at home.' He had continued to flirt with the idea of killing Elizabeth in the summer of 1584, disenchanted by what he saw as nugatory reward for his services to the crown.

One plan was to kill her as she walked in her gardens and escape downriver to Parry's constituency at Sheppey and then away. His chosen accomplice, Edmund Neville, a cousin of the exiled Duke of Westmorland and another sometime informant to Walsingham, protested that such a plan would be impossible. 'I wonder at you,' Parry replied, 'for in truth there is not anything more easy: you are no courtier, and therefore know not her customs of walking with small train, and often in the garden very privately, at which time my self may easily have access unto her, and you also when you are known in court.'

Another plan was to approach her while riding in St James's Park, Neville riding one side and Parry the other, and both to shoot her. '[I]f they were an hundred waiting upon her, they were not able to save her, you coming on the one side, and I on the other, and discharging our dags upon her, it were unhappy if we should both miss her.'[11]

If Parry was playing *agent provocateur*, he misjudged the strength of his hand. On 8 February 1585, Neville betrayed him to Walsingham. The unfolding of the plot perfectly illustrates the sealed, hermetic world of the double agent: one agent informing against another about a plot, originally formed to tease out enemy threats, which has already been revealed to its target. It is a game of deadly earnest and consequence but also self-referential and self-fulfilling, a snake swallowing its own tail. No one, not even the actors, knows what is true; intention is everything and that is the one thing always hidden, even – perhaps particularly – at the very moment when it appears to be revealed.

For Elizabeth, however, its meaning was simple. Learning of Parry's plot, she was visibly distraught. Von Wedel, at court as events unravelled, recalled how:

> The queen, when she heard about this doctor, went into the garden, wept aloud, and said she would like to know why so many persons sought her life. She tore open her garment, exposing her breasts, exclaiming that she had no weapon to defend herself, but was only a weak female.[12]

Elizabeth knew of course that Parry had been right, as had Gifford before him. She represented a soft target for assassination, and if the Spanish could get to the Prince of Orange, they could certainly get to her. She could have no security, and certainly not the freedom she so desperately craved, while the succession problem – in the form of Mary Stuart – remained unresolved. It was a paradox: Elizabeth's liberty was constrained by a woman whom she held under increasingly tight house arrest; Mary had been moved south from Sheffield to Wingfield in Derbyshire the previous September, and then again, further south still, to Tutbury in Staffordshire. But the wearying pressure of fear and terror were escalating, and it no doubt seemed to Elizabeth as if her own time, her own luck, may have been ebbing away. Even in Spain, the consensus was that her fear was genuine – although Englefield for one was cynical.

While the Parry crisis was exercising the minds of Elizabeth and her advisers, the wider court was absorbed by the feasts and entertainments of the Christmas season. The festivities built to a climax on 6 January – Epiphany or Twelfth Night – a date Ralegh had particular reason to look forward to that year. He would have made his way to the court at Greenwich from Durham House by boat, as usual, riding with the falling tide downriver, shooting the bridge, coming to rest alongside the red-brick waterfront of the palace, climbing the familiar steps up to the embankment, and then entering through the tall gatehouse tower that spanned the thoroughfare, its feet rising out of the Thames itself.

Once inside, the familiarity of the surroundings would have only served to impress the altered circumstances. Elizabeth had agreed to reward him with a knighthood. The court was packed for Twelfth Night, with the season's theatre being capped this year by the Queen's Men, Tarlton leading the way, in *Five Plays in One*, its title reflecting something of the hectic pace of the courtly pleasures, followed by what was traditionally the greatest of the Yuletide masques, at which Elizabeth herself delighted to dance.[13] Revels accounts carry no details of this year's masque, but other years' accounts give some flavour of the entertainment at a court which placed a premium on display: Venetian Patriarchs in green, with purple head-pieces, and Italian women in white and crimson; Amazons in gilded armour and gowns of crimson cloth of gold, xxsel in silver lace; sages in counterfeit cloth of gold; dancers in mulberry satin and torch-bearers in crimson damask.

There may well have been a point to rewarding Ralegh on one of the most public court occasions of the year, a ringing affirmation of Elizabeth's regard for him, and the press of sometime friends, enemies and rivals, and the merely curious, would have surely afforded Ralegh the outsider no little satisfaction.

When it was time, Ralegh came forward and knelt before her. They were, most likely, in the presence chamber, hung with fine tapestries as always, but no doubt decked for the season in holly and ivy and bay and other green survivals of the winter. She looked down at him, raised the naked blade of her sword and struck his shoulder, saying, '*Soyez chevalier au nom de Dieu.*' He rose, and she continued, '*Advances, bon chevalier.*'[14] He was a mere gentleman no longer.

It was a further assurance, a promise of continued favour as much as a reward for past and present services. If he yearned still for other, greater prizes in her gift he would have known too that knighthood was something she awarded sparingly, and for Ralegh it was a considerable coup. His social status, whatever he pretended otherwise through the studiedly sumptuous extravagance of his dress, weighed him down. There was a reason why Ralegh's friend Spenser made Timias, Ralegh's cipher in the *Faerie Queene*, no more than a squire, capable of heroism without ever being a hero. To transform the child of Hayes Barton into anything greater would have invited ridicule, dragging his epic ambitions down into bathos.

But it must have seemed to some of those looking on that Twelfth Night was a particularly apt occasion for Ralegh to receive such an honour. Traditionally it was the night when households and communities elected a Lord of Misrule from the junior or lesser members to order the entertainment. Henry VIII and Edward VI had both appointed Lords of Misrule who 'received permission to do and say whatever he pleased without ever being called to book for it', according to one disapproving ambassador; Elizabeth had never done so.[15] It is not hard to conceive, with dark glances in Ralegh's direction, a whisper passing round that she had made good that oversight now.

Over in Paris, Mendoza heard that she accompanied the honour with the present of a 180-ton ship with five guns mounted on each side and two 4.5-inch culverins in the bows. Ralegh himself purchased two 120-ton flyboats, and two further 40-ton ships, and had commissioned four more pinnaces.[16] Ralegh was losing no time in capitalizing on her favour: the idea of empire seemed more urgent than ever.

Elizabeth's generosity was not quite what it seemed: the gift was more in the way of a loan. It may have had a certain point to it too: the ship was the *Tiger* and had been one of those under Winter's command in Smerwick Bay, a little over four years earlier. But Ralegh's outlay is extraordinary – even more so when you consider how hard he often had to fight to receive what was, he thought, rightfully his. In February, two days after Neville's shocking revelations, Ralegh was dragged back into an ongoing dispute between the University of Cambridge and his wine licensee in the city, John Keymer. Aggrieved that Ralegh had not consulted it before issuing the licence, the university had deprived Keymer of his trade. Ralegh's first letter to the university's vice-chancellor, Robert Norgate, on 10 February is

a model of deference and civility. Ten days later, when Ralegh
had received no response and Keymer had been gaoled by the
authorities, it was a different matter:

> I cannot a little marvel at your peremptory and proud
> manner of dealing. I was content to use all manner of
> courtesy towards you ... but I perceive that my reason-
> able or rather too submissive dealing hath bred in you a
> proceeding insufferable. You have committed a poor man
> to the prison having done nothing but [that] warranted
> by the Great Seal of England ... I do not know that any
> man, or any men or society, would take so much upon
> themselves before trial [was] made ... having thought
> you would have vouchsafed an answer of my last letters.[17]

Ralegh signs the first letter, 'Your very willing friend'; the
second time Norgate gets the testy, almost threatening, 'Your
friend as you shall give cause'. Precisely because his authority
was not his own, being borrowed or refracted from Elizabeth,
it was a source of considerable vulnerability for him, politically
and emotionally, and he reacted with a contempt that laid clear
his insecurity, in which courtesy becomes synonymous with
submissive humiliation.

Ralegh did get a reply this time. But Norgate knew his man
and goaded him, professing to be shocked at the ungentleman-
ly tone Ralegh had adopted 'being by birth a gentleman; by
education trained up to the knowledge of good letters;
instructed with the liberal disposition of a university, the
fountain and nursery of all humanity: and further, by God's
good blessing, advanced in court, from whence the very name
of courtesy is drawn'.[18] In essence he was calling Ralegh's bluff
– and bluff it was.

Norgate wrote to Burghley – the university's chancellor – the same day, complaining 'how hardly we are used' by Ralegh. Burghley backed Norgate; Ralegh was forced to back down. For all the munificence of his rewards from Elizabeth, her consistent refusal to offer him political authority, the comfort of office, meant his favoured status was in some respects a hollow gift, of as much or as little import as anyone wished to give it. On one reading, Ralegh had England at his feet; but the truth was that England was resisting. His assertion of privilege was met with a kind of contempt and there was nothing he could do about it.

This must have been a particularly debilitating exchange for Ralegh since it also seems to have coincided with an abrupt cooling of Elizabeth's favour for him. Having plied him with rewards in recent months, she evidently felt the need to make humiliatingly clear that she was in no way subject to him – and to underscore the fact that he had no place at court of his own absent her command.

Hatton, once again, was the catalyst. The court was briefly at the Croydon palace of the Archbishop of Canterbury, John Whitgift in the first days of April. Elizabeth complained of Hatton's prolonged absence from court to his friend Heneage, who told her that there were no chambers free for him. Elizabeth sought to discover why this might be the case and was told by a household official that Ralegh had taken Hatton's chambers. Heneage duly had the pleasure of reporting back to Hatton that Elizabeth had told him that she 'had rather see [Ralegh] hanged than equal him with you, or that the world should think she did so'.[19] The whole affair has a slightly stage-managed feel and it may be that Elizabeth thought Ralegh, with the latest securities from her to bolster him, was overplaying his hand.

Ralegh later wrote of Elizabeth, with as much *sangfroid* as he could muster, that 'she gave, she took, she wounded, she appeased', but the experience of such tumultuous reversals and uncertainties must have been, as it was meant to be, psychologically devastating for a man with Ralegh's capacity for doubt. It is little wonder that he sought sanctuary elsewhere; at court he was always battling to keep his head above water, to maintain his status and the fiction of his authority it brought.

Ralegh's vulnerability was apparent to everyone – in itself a further weakness: no one else at Elizabeth's court was as exposed as he was. So obvious was it that Charles Thynne – one of his followers and brother of Maurice Brown's old friend and correspondent – who was in Paris with Hakluyt, was approached by a Jesuit close to Mendoza with a proposition for Thynne's master:

> He has also sounded me about Sir Walter Ralegh, saying that her Majesty's life was not immortal, and that he marvelled that whereas the King of Spain was shortly to take possession of England, Sir Walter Ralegh, whose state then should be most uncertain, doth nevertheless under-take voyages to seek to hinder the Spaniards, and doth daily show himself an enemy to the Catholics; adding thereunto that it was nothing to be favoured of her Majesty, in respect of being favoured of the King of France and especially of the King of Spain; who gives more in one day to his favourites than the queen is worth.[20]

Thynne, having first consulted with Hakluyt, wrote to both Ralegh and Walsingham with this information. His letter to Ralegh hasn't survived, but in Walsingham's he offers, as he puts it, 'to sooth this confessor in his propositions' – that is, to act as a double agent. Not everyone has access to the Spanish ambassador, Thynne notes, so this may be a golden opportunity – although he was astute enough, with Parry's example fresh in the mind, to ask Walsingham for his instructions in writing if he were to befriend an enemy of the state.

Parry was executed on 2 March; with the particular cruelty that seems to have been reserved for those who threatened Elizabeth's life, he was still conscious as he was cut down from the gallows and 'when his bowels were taken out,' an eyewitness reported, 'he gave a great groan'.[21] As a result of Parry's confession, Elizabeth sent the fourth Earl of Derby to Paris to demand that the French government extradite Thomas Morgan, and on 9 March, an English spy named Chute – whom we will meet again – betrayed him to the authorities. He was arrested in his rooms in Paris around ten at night, and all his goods and papers seized.[22] However, although he was imprisoned in the Bastille, the French refused for the moment to deport him back to England. It may not have been precisely the result the English wanted, but it gave them leverage over Morgan.

We don't know how Ralegh responded to Thynne's specific offer, but we do know that he was by now actively engaged in the intelligence effort against Mary, using his connections from his period as part of the Catholic court party to enable access. So Thomas Morgan wrote to Mary from the Bastille on 19 April that he had been approached prior to his arrest by various members of Derby's 250-strong embassy who wished to offer their services to her cause. Key among them was William Langherne, now identified as secretary to Ralegh – 'the queen's dear minion,' Morgan sneers, 'who daily groweth in credit'. We know from his work at All Souls that Langherne had both a taste and a talent for sleight-of-hand and smooth dissembling; and the theatre of deceit around Mary seems tailor-made for his particular gifts.

The said secretary is a good Catholic, and his master and her Majesty's new host Poulet are friends, which moved him the more willingly to take hold of his proffered amity and courtesy, because he thought he might have place to do some office for her Majesty, in order to establish thereby a good intelligence for her.

In particular, Langherne was offering Mary a means of smuggling letters out of Wingfield – something Walsingham and Paulet had put considerable thought and effort into making impossible since the discovery of Throckmorton's treason; 'I cannot imagine how it may be possible for them to convey a piece of paper as big as my finger,' Paulet later boasted at Tutbury.[23] Langherne wasn't working alone, however, and evidence of his brilliant plausibility and charm can be gauged from his chosen associate in the scheme: Dr Edward Atslow.

The Atslow family were clients of Oxford's, which must be the source of his connection to Ralegh's circle.[24] Edward seems to have been the physician of choice for many of the nobility, counting the Earl of Sussex, the Countess of Pembroke and the Earl of Northumberland among his clients. He was said to have saved the latter's life after he had been poisoned.[25] Elizabeth had even sent him with the Bishop of Ross to minister to Mary at Sheffield Castle in December 1570, where he stayed for a month.[26]

This was either a notably generous or unusually short-sighted move on Elizabeth's part because Atslow had already been interrogated in the wake of the Northern Rebellion.[27] He was arrested again in the spring of 1575 as part of the same sweep that forced Morgan to flee the country, 'charged to have written in cipher to a prince who has heretofore disquieted this state by practice' wrote Walsingham to Burghley, arguing that Atslow merited confinement in the Tower. Walsingham got his way: after two interrogations Atslow was imprisoned there until mid-September.[28] He was arrested again in 1579 for seeking international support for Mary, and she went so far as to fake illness in November 1581 as a pretext to summon him.[29]

In sum, Mary can have had fewer men more earnestly devoted to her cause than Atslow; for Langherne to use his undoubted integrity as a cover for projecting against his fellow Catholics was a considerable coup. Nevertheless, we would have to say that, if Mary was his target, he did not succeed in his objectives – or at least left no evidence to that effect. But was she? Ultimately, perhaps, but it is worth emphasizing the rather large coincidence that of the two important recusants with whom we know Langherne to have had contact, Morgan was shortly thereafter arrested and confined to the Bastille, while Atslow was sent to the Tower where Morgan – who regarded Atslow as a close friend – heard, 'Dr Atslow was racked twice almost to the death . . . about the earl of Arundel his matters and intentions to depart England, wherein he was betrayed.'[30]

This, in fact, seems much more like the modus operandi of the Langherne who defrauded the fellows of All Souls, a man who recognized the value of information as a commodity and had no compunction about using it to the detriment of others, for whom using it thus was in fact essentially the point. Unlike Throckmorton, Atslow resisted his torture, and a draft of the government's charges against him shows its case to be correspondingly weak. Among them, however, is that he 'hath practised means to have further intelligence with the fugitives for their relief and conveying letters to them', and he had been specifically questioned about correspondence from Morgan at Walsingham's request. Neither the correspondence nor his interrogation are extant; that too may not be a coincidence, since Walsingham was explicit in his instructions to keep such information restricted. Langherne was never questioned, and his role unremarked upon.[31]

To what extent, then, was Ralegh complicit in these small and cruel betrayals? We do not have direct evidence, but the evidence of what did not happen is compelling. Burghley and Walsingham were monitoring Morgan's correspondence with Mary and undoubtedly read what he had to say about Langherne. Indeed, it is precisely because they had access to his letters that copies of them survive today. What did not happen, at any time, was that Langherne was either arrested or interrogated for making such an offer. If Langherne were acting alone, whether his proposal was sincere or not, there is little doubt that trouble would have quickly found him, but even as an operative in a Raleghan intelligence network, it is doubtful whether Ralegh was powerful enough to protect him. And if, as seems likely, Langherne were working for and with his master in injecting himself into Mary's communications network, Ralegh's reputation was not such that he could float above suspicion. To what extent, then, was he suspect? Or was Elizabeth behind it all?

While Langherne was absent in Paris, Ralegh was continuing to pursue his public imperial agenda, much to the consternation of the Spanish, as Thynne's conversation with Mendoza's confessor revealed, and as Hakluyt went out of his way to mention to Walsingham early in April, possibly from the same source: 'The rumour of Sir Walter Rawley's fleet ... doth so much vex the Spaniard and his factors, as nothing can do more.' Indeed, Mendoza thought it important enough to report to Philip when Ralegh's ships sailed down the Thames on their way to Plymouth towards the end of February.[32]

Seven ships ultimately sailed from Plymouth on 9 April, with the flagship being *The Tiger*, Elizabeth's January gift to

Ralegh, captained by his kinsman Grenville and piloted by his friend Fernandes. It was little more than six months after Barlow and Amadas had returned from their first, exploratory voyage. For such a major undertaking the haste was almost unseemly, speaking to a desperate sense of urgency that was as personal as it was political.

Those seven ships carried some 500 men. Despite the talk of colonization, this would always be an avowedly military operation, a fact Ralegh tacitly acknowledged in his appointments to the venture: he chose Ralph Lane, an English commander with long and ongoing experience of the Irish campaign, as the first governor of Virginia. Indeed, Ralegh had sought Elizabeth out at Greenwich in February and persuaded her to command Sir John Perrot, the father of the man whom Ralegh had fought with in 1580 and now lord deputy of Ireland, to release Lane from his duties to join the enterprise.[33] Lane was, in effect, Ralegh's proxy.

If Ralegh was tempted to undertake the voyage himself, he must have had concerns about such a prolonged absence from Elizabeth; contrariwise, Elizabeth herself seems to have had reservations about requiring him to stay. It was rumoured that she promised to underwrite the costs of the voyage if he did not sail with it. Either the gossip was wrong or Elizabeth thought better of the idea, because Ralegh stayed with her and financed the project himself, but the uncertainty effectively dramatizes the difficulty of the dynamic between the two of them, with Elizabeth's favour allowing Ralegh to pursue enterprises that tended to pull him away from her, thereby weakening his hold on the very thing that empowered him.[34]

Nevertheless, had Ralegh sailed he would have found, as Lane did, that there were tensions – contradictions even – between the military objectives and the practical requirements of establishing a long-term base on a newly discovered continent several thousand miles from home, tensions which were never really addressed in the planning of the voyage, and which therefore proved impossible to resolve on the ground. In many respects, the colony precisely embodied the flaws in Ralegh's thinking which Grey had complained so bitterly to the Privy Council about just three years earlier: the apparent realpolitik candour and intellectual clarity of Ralegh's ideas masked a disjunction from the grinding intractabilities faced by those charged with making them work. The wish was too often father to the thought.

These conflicting loyalties were evident even in something so basic as the choice of the site for the colony. The strategic imperative was for a base close enough to the Spanish sphere of influence to launch attacks on the treasure fleets as they returned to Europe with the riches of central and south America in their holds, but sufficiently far away to deter an all-out assault from the Spanish ships in the Caribbean. There was an economic imperative, too, based on Hakluyt and Ralegh's belief that Virginia could supplant the Mediterranean and the Far East as a supplier of a range of merchandise – wine and sugar, olive oil and iron, salt and figs, citrus fruits and silk, and so on – which the political situation in Europe, combined with the Muslim hegemony over the old eastern overland trade, had made increasingly scarce in the English market. It was an inversion of Gilbert's original intent to seek a North West Passage to the East: Virginia, Ralegh believed, would be England's very own India and Cathay.[35]

It was the specificity of such conflicting demands that ultimately dictated the siting of Ralegh's colony – not that site's utility – a fact that presented Lane and Grenville with a problem since there was no viable harbour anywhere along the relevant length of the eastern seaboard. Hence, attempting to cross the Carolina banks near Wococon Island to reach the chosen harbour at Roanoke, Fernandes grounded the *Tyger* in the shallows. They were lucky not to lose the ship, but a great deal of the party's supplies, intended to last them through their first winter, were in fact destroyed, and the harbour in any case proved insufficient as a naval base.

Another way of looking at this is to say that the need to establish a successful and sustainable commodity-based economy for the colony was at odds with the need for the voyage itself to show a profit. The latter could be – and was – established through privateering, Grenville taking four Spanish ships between his arrival in the Caribbean in May and his return to England in September, but Ralegh had omitted to recruit anyone with relevant agricultural skills and so the hundred-odd colonists whom Grenville left behind on Roanoke were unable to reach self-sufficiency, and seemed unwilling to try. Lane's military discipline could not turn his men into farmers – and in any case there were precious few men in England with experience of the crops Ralegh wanted to plant. Given the choice between easy short-term rewards at sea and hazardous, long-term investment on land, the fighting men who formed the bulk of those on the voyage were always likely to prioritize the former. Again, there are distinct echoes here of Ralegh's own attitude to landed estates such as those awarded him courtesy of All Souls: his preference was to monetize them immediately and invest the capital in privateering and exploration: his vast ambitions were ultimately flawed by the very insecurities those ambitions were intended to resolve.

But if Ralegh was too easily seduced by his own hopes, his motives for doing so were by no means purely selfish. His dreamed-of empire was also designed to be a gift for Elizabeth, an act of reciprocal generosity for her support and nurture: it would be a liberation, offering her freedom from the captivity of fear by weakening Spanish power both in the New World and the old, since it would deprive Spain of the wealth that underwrote its authority and malice in Europe: 'Is it not [Philip] that by his treasure hath hired at sundry times the sons of Belial to bereave the Prince of Orange of his life?' wrote Hakluyt, making explicit the connection between the Americas project and Elizabeth's personal safety. And it would give her too a great empire of her own, from Florida up to the Arctic Circle, which promised unprecedented economic and political dominion, and promoted a vision of Elizabeth that transcended the narrow confines of a small island to command the world and its trade. If the narrative of marriage and its making had dominated the first twenty-five years of her reign, this vision sought to create for her another life, a second act, a kind of rebirth. It must also have been a welcome distraction from the increasing sense of isolation and fear with which Elizabeth, not unreasonably, viewed events as they unfolded across Europe.

In a sense this gives the lie to the customary view of their relationship as functioning wholly *de haut en bas*, with all riches and rewards flowing in the one direction. One anecdote has Elizabeth, tiring of Ralegh's nagging requests for preferment and favour, turning to him and snapping, with sufficient force and clarity for the whole room to hear: 'When will you cease to be a beggar?' Without missing a beat, Ralegh is said to have replied: 'When your Majesty ceases to be a benefactor.'

The truth is more complex: Ralegh spent the vast bulk of his new-found fortune on his imperial projects, which promised to father on Elizabeth a great and powerful empire. Elizabeth enabled him in this, almost certainly consciously so: she allowed him to act for her – but at his own risk. It was not Elizabeth investing her money in the Americas, it was Ralegh: Hakluyt offered an estimate of 100,000 ducats – £25,000 –

spent by 1587. Rarely can one man have devoted so much of his own estate to the pursuit of his country's foreign policy. But was it enough?

XV: THE LESS AFRAID

Desire attain'd is not desire,
But as the cinders of the fire

SIR WALTER RALEGH

By the late spring of 1585, England's political situation in Europe was becoming ever more fraught, the sentiment at court more paranoid and fearful. For Ralegh, perhaps still smarting from Elizabeth's public dismissal of his personal significance to her, the deceptive simplicities of the Virginia experiment must have seemed tantalizingly attractive.

But he may also, on reflection, have considered Elizabeth's *volte face* to be an understandable reaction to the relentless stress and pressure that she had to absorb. News had arrived in April that the Duke of Guise had agreed an alliance with Philip II to exclude the Protestant Prince of Navarre from the French succession and to work together in support of the Catholic cause everywhere. Elizabeth took it as a further sign, if one were needed, that her life and the English throne were being targeted, and her first instinct was to build a collaborative league of her own among the Protestant nations of northern Europe. 'It standeth all such princes upon as profess the gospel to look well to themselves,' she wrote to the King of Denmark. 'That the purpose of the Guise to force the king to deprive the King of Navarre of his succession to the crown of France is a dangerous example, like to be extended to all other princes professing the gospel that be present possessioners of their own dominions.'[1]

And there was much to unsettle Elizabeth domestically too. In mid-April, Philip Howard, Earl of Arundel, whom Von Wedel had seen at court the previous Christmas kneeling before Elizabeth bearing a silver water bowl, was arrested trying to flee the country. It was later said that Atslow had tried to help him escape from the Essex coast during the Parliamentary recess at the turn of the year; more recently Atslow was accused of warning him that he would be next to fall after Parry.[2] He had tried to slip away quietly from Littlehampton, a small harbour on the Sussex coast; twice his captain deferred the crossing, telling Arundel that the winds were against them. When they finally set out under cover of darkness the captain betrayed him, hanging up a light, a pre-arranged signal: the ship was boarded and Arundel seized. It was said that when he was taken, he wore an *agnus dei* containing a letter from the Pope which confirmed him as Duke of Norfolk. A rumour flew around that he had a plan in play to burn Elizabeth's navy, and additional guards were ordered.[3] Arundel joined the Earl of Northumberland, his old friend from Oxford's circle, in the Tower on the twenty-fifth; Atslow was pulled in for interrogation shortly after.

They were therefore both in the Tower in the early hours of 21 June when Northumberland was found dead in his chamber, following reports of a loud explosion: he was lying on his bed with three bullets in his chest within an inch of each other; his heart had been blown apart and his spine, too, was broken. He had bolted his door from the inside and the gun was beside his body: the official verdict was suicide. While such a charge undoubtedly had a considerable stigma, it did mean that Northumberland could keep his estates intact for his family and, more particularly, his heir, also named Henry Percy, whose intellectual interests brought him into Ralegh's circle at Durham House. There were those, however, who wondered about the circumstances of his death. Was he was in fact murdered on the government's orders, as the rumours said, by Sir Christopher Hatton? Camden's half-hearted demurral in his *Annales*, for instance, raises more questions than it answers: 'That the suspicious fugitives muttered of one Bailife that was one of Hatton's men, and was a little before appointed to be the earl's keeper, I omit as being a matter altogether unknown unto me, and I think it not meet to insert any thing upon vain hear-says.'

It is Ralegh who offers the most compelling testimony on the subject. Some fifteen years later, he wrote to Sir Robert Cecil, son of Lord Burghley, on the subject of how the heirs of those who have been executed or murdered do not usually seek to avenge their father's deaths. 'Northumberland that now is thinks not of Hatton's issue,' Ralegh wrote, citing several similar examples. Hatton was nine years dead by then, but from the context this is not an attempt to smear him with responsibility for the murder: indeed Ralegh seems to be confirming something that he believes Cecil will consider an unremarkable fact.[4]

If we take Ralegh's statement at face value – and there seems little reason not to, given that both he and Cecil were in a position to know truths that, being undocumented, are lost to us – it speaks to a disabling sense of fear and panic in the government, desperate and uncertain of the political impact of a treason trial for another leading nobleman, the Percys being one of the great old Anglo-Norman families. Processes were crumbling, corroded by a sense of impending terror. Having imprisoned Northumberland and Arundel, it was uncertain how to proceed: like Mary, the two were too powerful and dangerous to be released. In fact, the case against Northumberland was stronger than that against Arundel, and although Arundel appeared before the Star Chamber and was detained indefinitely at Elizabeth's pleasure, there would be no capital charges against him.

It is also true, however, that the government's unrelenting pressure against the exiles in Paris was bearing fruit: fractures were deepening and judgements were becoming clouded. Charles Arundell, although said to be leading the invading army in the West Country, had fallen out with Paget and Morgan by the summer and was actively briefing against them.[5] Meanwhile, Paulet had taken charge of Mary at Tutbury on 17 April 1585, and Thomas Morgan, still languishing in the Bastille, had been casting around for a new courier who might have access to the house. He took the cavalier and deadly step of accepting the recommendation of Christopher Blount, a Catholic acquaintance but a client of Leicester too. The man Blount recommended was one of Walsingham's best agents, Robert Poley.

It probably seemed to the English that projection against Mary and her Catholic supporters within and without England was at once a long game and a race against time; no one was sure whether they would have time to play it out to its conclusion. In May, an answer to such questions arrived out of the blue when, in an act that one could easily construe as a declaration of war, Philip II seized the many English merchant ships trading in Spanish ports. Surprised, angry and probably somewhat frightened, Elizabeth ordered reprisals; in doing so, she tacitly accepted Ralegh's analysis regarding Spain's strategic vulnerabilities. Sir Francis Drake was to attack Spanish towns in central and south America, while Ralegh himself was charged with taking the Spanish ships operating on the Newfoundland banks and bringing them back to England.[6] Ralegh probably had mixed feelings about the order: he was forced to divert two ships which he had intended to use to supply his new Virginia colony. The future would have to wait.

In May, one of Mendoza's spies reported that Ralegh and Leicester were now on very bad terms, which can hardly have improved Ralegh's equanimity, although he must have hoped that relationship with Elizabeth was secure enough to withstand the earl's malignancy if it were directed his way. When the nineteen-year-old Earl of Essex was introduced at court in September, Leicester's first tentative move against Ralegh, there seem to have been few, if any, ripples.

It had been several years since there is any evidence of Leicester and Ralegh having worked together, fruitfully or otherwise, and Ralegh's attitude to the Spanish threat was closer to Elizabeth's than Leicester's, being less rigidly ideological and more accommodating: there was a reason that Mendoza and others targeted him as a weak link in the English court.[7] But if Elizabeth would have preferred a negotiated peace with her enemy, something Leicester and Walsingham et al thought both unworkable and abhorrent, she had no room for manoeuvre as long as the Catholics thought her life a small price to pay for victory.

Indeed, peace looked a dimmer prospect than ever. The Low Countries had been bereft of leadership since the deaths of Monsieur and the Prince of Orange early the year before; at the end of June, Dutch commissioners offered Elizabeth sovereignty. She refused: although she was increasingly willing to support the Dutch cause publicly, she drew a line at such an overtly aggressive act with a limited upside and potentially bottomless liabilities. Instead, she finally seemed prepared to commit English troops, particularly after Antwerp fell to the Duke of Parma in August.

It is primarily in the context of these apparent preparations for war that Ralegh received three significant appointments from Elizabeth through the summer and autumn of 1585; having asserted her independence from his influence – and reminded the world of his dependence on her – she was free enough, or afraid enough, to begin rewarding him again for his work. In July he became warden of the stannaries – the community of Cornish tin mines which had its own ancient rights and laws expressed through courts and parliaments held on Crockern Tor, high on Dartmoor – followed by lord lieutenant of Cornwall in September and vice admiral of Devon and Cornwall in November. While the posts covered a wide range of duties, what they had in common was responsibility for military and naval matters in the West Country: concentrating so much regional power in one man's hands – and those of a commoner to boot – was, among other things, a considerable statement of trust on Elizabeth's part. Moreover, with broadcloth and now tin, Ralegh had been given authority over a sizeable proportion of England's exports.

On another level, of course, the appointments were a means of formally reconnecting Ralegh with the region that he regarded as home, and that to a significant degree defined his identity. Elizabeth may or may not have known about Ralegh's attempt to buy his childhood home, but she was an acute judge of character – particularly with those who talked as much, and as freely, as Ralegh did – and it is unlikely she was not aware of the region's magnetic pull for him, nor of his need to push away from the court even as he cleaved as closely as possible to her.

Nevertheless, the appointments were not received with wholehearted support. One of Burghley's correspondents wrote to him the following year:

Her Majesty and you have placed Sir Walter Ralegh as Lord Warden of the Stannaries, but . . . no man is more hated than him; none more cursed daily of the poor, of whom infinite numbers are brought to extreme poverty through the gift of the cloths to him; his pride is intolerable, without regard of any, as the world knows; and as for dwelling amongst them, he neither does nor means it, having no place of abode; so that in time of service, this head must either fight without a body, or else the members will cut off such a head.[8]

Insofar as one can tell, these criticisms were not widely shared and are evidently powered by a virulent personal dislike of Ralegh. But the central accusation, that being a creature of Elizabeth and the court meant he would have little time to devote to the problems of the west, was well made. His predecessor in the roles, the Earl of Bedford, had spent some six months of the year in Exeter, replicating on a modest scale the presidency of the north; it was difficult to see how Ralegh could promise the same commitment and retain his favoured place at court. Perhaps Elizabeth was dropping a small hint that things in the future might not be what they had been in the past.

Such concerns aside, what stands out about the tirade is not its opinions per se, but the fact that the – to us – unknown author felt so comfortable writing in such terms about Ralegh to Burghley. It was not about wealth: Ralegh had plenty of that. He had come down to Plymouth towards the end of October to greet Grenville and to discover that, alongside the three Spanish ships captured in the Americas, he had also captured another on the home journey. The *Santa Maria de San Vicente* held some £50,000-worth of ivory, ginger and other commodities. Overall the voyage had made a profit of some £10,000.

But whether he could ever attain sufficient rank to quell the kind of abuse that this correspondent shared with Burghley, to awe his critics into silence, must have seemed to him doubtful.

Leicester had finally led Elizabeth's army to the Low Countries at the beginning of December amid a degree of pomp which Elizabeth, who was paying for it, found offensive and distasteful. He had not forgotten *Leicester's Commonwealth*, however: in January 1586 he was reported to have hired a man to murder Charles Arundell in Paris.[9]

At court, Ralegh took advantage of Leicester's absence to assert himself after their rift of the previous year. Whether he briefed against Leicester specifically is open to question; what is more likely is that he was sceptical of the effort to support the Dutch, which was the great cause of the Puritan movement. He was not alone in this: to neutralize Burghley's scepticism, Walsingham and Leicester went so far as to try to entrap him in a bribery scandal. Ralegh's position was less a strategic political calculation than an economic one: the Dutch's aggressive mercantilism threatened England's – and Ralegh's – commercial interests, and despite Elizabeth's generosity, Ralegh came to believe that they continued to trade with the enemy to such a degree that they rendered such support meaningless. Speaking the following decade, he said:

The nature of the Dutchman is to fly to no man but for his profit, and they will obey no man long ... The Dutchman by his policy hath gotten trading with all the world into his hands, yea he is now entering into the trade of Scarborough fishing, and the fishing of the Newfound-Lands, which is the stay of the West Countries. They are the people that maintain the King of Spain in his greatness. Were it not for them, he were never able to

make out such armies and navies by sea; it cost her
Majesty sixteen thousand pound a year the maintaining
of these countries, and yet for all this they arm her
enemies against her.[10]

It is this kind of thinking, drained of ideology and any degree
of religious solidarity, which complicates portraits of Ralegh as
a Protestant hero against imperial Catholic Spain. Absent
commercial and nationalistic considerations, Ralegh was
remarkably neutral about the Spanish threat. Elizabeth, always
suspicious of excess expenditure in itself, but particularly
where it intersected with militarism, and none too keen on the
Dutch, no doubt delighted in such talk.

It wasn't long before word of such undermining made its way
to Leicester, Davison's studiously non-specific letter to Leicester
being one such example: 'I find that there is some dealing
underhand against your Lordship, which proceedeth from the
younger sort of our courtiers that take it upon them to censure
the greatest causes and persons that are treated in council or serve
her Majesty, a disease that I do not look to see cured in my time.'[11]

Leicester had a specific grievance about Ralegh in any case,
since Ralegh had failed to provide him with promised men
from the Cornish mines, without whose specialist skills the
siege campaigns that characterized military action in the Low
Countries would be rendered largely ineffective. Writing to
Leicester, Ralegh blamed Elizabeth for staying the miners'
commission – although Leicester might well have felt justified
in thinking that Ralegh's persuasive talents were probably not
being put to effective use. As to the other allegations, Ralegh
characteristically addressed them head-on:

I have been of late very pestilent reported in this place to
be rather a drawer back than a fartherer of the action

where you govern. Your lordship doth well understand my affection towards Spain and how I have consumed the best part of my fortune hating the tyrannous prosperity of that estate, and it were now strange and monstrous that I should become an enemy to my country and conscience. But all that I have desired at your Lordship's hand is that you will evermore deal with me in all matters of suspect doubleness, and so ever esteem me as you shall find my deserving good or bad.

In the mean time I humbly beseech you let no poetical scribe work your lordship by any device to doubt that I am a hollow or cold servant to the action, or a mean well-willer and follower of your own.

Clearly Ralegh had been accused – whether to or by Leicester – of acting as a double agent for Spain. With an eye to his associations and the activity of Langherne, which Ralegh evidently countenanced, that was probably not an unreasonable concern. Walsingham certainly seems to have been keeping an open mind on the question of Ralegh's loyalty, having interrogated one of his servants the previous autumn, a scrivener named John Peirson, who had made copies of 'certain books concerning matters of state' which had been given him by William Herle.[12] Peirson testified that he had made copies for Burghley and Philip Sidney as well as Ralegh, a fact that, while it appears to exonerate Ralegh, also highlights Walsingham's suspicion of him. Indeed, when Elizabeth charged Walsingham with defending Ralegh to Leicester, he did so in the least enthusiastic tones he could muster, meticulously distancing himself from the sentiment even as he relayed it to Leicester on 1 April:

[Elizabeth's wish] was that I should signify [unto] your lordship, and to assure you, [upon] her honour, that the gentleman hath done good offices [for you] and that, in the time of her displeasure, he dealt as earnestly for you as any other in this world that professeth most good will towards your lordship. This I write by her majesty's commandment, and therefore I pray your lordship to take knowledge thereof, in such sort as you shall think good.[13]

In defending himself against Leicester it is the wealth of Spain, its tyrannous prosperity, which Ralegh claims to hate, not its religion, or its brutal suppression of Protestant nationhood, or its threat to England and Elizabeth. Ralegh's assurances on the matter are carefully drained of detail and, to be frank, unreassuring, but the suggestion that Leicester should raise any further charges with Ralegh directly implies that, above all else, Ralegh still had supreme confidence in his powers of persuasion.

Whether that confidence was justified is a moot point. Ralegh's postscript to Leicester reads: 'The queen is in very good terms with you and, thank be to God, well pacified and you are again her sweet Robin.'[14] It must have struck a sour note to Leicester to hear Elizabeth's favoured term of endearment from Ralegh's pen, a usage that at best is insensitive on Ralegh's part, and at worst a pointed assertion that he is now the principal intermediary for her affection. Moreover, it would have taken a man with thicker skin than Leicester not to feel patronized at being told by someone as newly risen as Ralegh that he remained on good terms with a woman whom he had known since she was eight.

Leicester would have found it satisfyingly ironic that, over the very weeks these exchanges took place, Ralegh's relationship with Elizabeth seems to have become noticeably tense again. At least, that is what two contemporary sources say, one claiming that 'Raleigh, the "mignon" of her of England, is weary of her or she of him',[15] the other that 'for some days past there has been some anger between them which has much afflicted both of them'.[16] Both give the same reason: Elizabeth's flirtation with Charles Blunt, Lord Mountjoy's brother and a man, as one of the sources puts it, 'young enough to be her grandson'.

Both quotes are from letters to Mary, the first from Thomas Morgan, the second from the secretary to Mauvissière, the French ambassador. The mutuality of interest between the sources, and the similarity of their phrasing, strongly suggests that they derive from the same unknown primary source. That there had been disharmony between Ralegh and Elizabeth was public knowledge; Elizabeth had clearly endeavoured to make it so. It would hardly be surprising therefore, even without any external pressures, if further conflicts had arisen, particularly given the mutual absorption of their relationship over the previous few years. It may be the case then that the report was true, and the evident Catholic interest arose from their perception of Ralegh as a man who could profitably be detached from loyalty to Elizabeth.

But it may also be possible that such public feuding was staged for the benefit of attentive eyes and ears. Following on from the approach to Ralegh from Mendoza's camp and the subsequent activities of Langherne, it was politically useful to project an idea of Ralegh as increasingly discontented at court, a man who might easily go over. It was, after all, a strategy with impeccable Elizabethan pedigree, having worked exceptionally well for many years when Leicester was promoting himself as the Catholic English candidate for Elizabeth's hand.

Certainly in the spring and summer there seems to have been a spike in the intelligence noise about Ralegh, his followers and their suspect loyalties. At the end of March, for example, Walsingham received the first of three letters in quick succession regarding a man named Chute, almost certainly the same man who betrayed Morgan's lodgings to the French authorities. Morgan described him as an English 'spial', but not everyone was so certain. Or, rather, not everyone was sure where his ultimate loyalties lay. Edward Stafford wrote from Paris to warn that Chute had left a few days previously 'to execute somewhat upon her Majesty's person … I am advertised that he carries over certain poisons and drugs to use if he fail of the other'.[17]

Stafford identifies him as one of the Chute family from Appledore in Kent, and he is most likely Edward Chute, the fourth son of Philip Chute, Henry VIII's standard bearer, although it is tempting to note that the elder brother George had a son named Walter who would fight alongside Ralegh at Fayal in 1597.[18] Walsingham knew Chute already: he is probably the Captain Chute whom he had appointed gentleman porter during Mary's incarceration at Wingfield – in charge of the soldiers and responsible for the watch – in November 1584, another man who moved with easy conscience from one side to the other.[19] He was detained as 'a suspect man' in the midst of the Armada crisis; in the early days of James I's reign he is reported to be a speaker of 'seditious words'.[20]

Chute had met in Paris with Catherine de Medici, the Duke of Guise, Arundell and Paget, and had received money from Mendoza. On his return to England he would be carrying letters from Bacqueville, the former French ambassador, 'especially to Mr Rawley', but the letters were really little more than cover so that 'feathered under somebody's wing, he might be able to show his head.' Stafford doesn't explicitly say so, but he seems to imply that such letters were part of a pre-arranged plan.

Bacqueville clearly got wind of this and wrote to Walsingham defending Chute's honesty and honour,[21] but his letter was quickly followed by another from a contact at Rouen reporting that Chute boasted how cunningly he had performed in front of the Privy Council and in a private meeting with Walsingham himself. He was not an English double agent, he boasted, but a mere actor in the Catholic cause.[22]

In some respects Chute cuts rather a forlorn figure, 'a monstrous, long-nosed gentleman' whom the two informers also both derided as transparent, weak, vain and fearful – a man up to the task neither of assassinating Elizabeth nor of persuading others that he might, and therefore putting himself in the way of immense danger, as the Parry case showed. But he nevertheless contributes to the background noise, the static, that makes discerning the true music of sedition almost impossible. The Ralegh connection is one of the few facts we have, but was Chute an English spy projecting against Mary, or a Catholic double agent aiming to turn Ralegh? And then, was Ralegh for turning, as Leicester and Walsingham seemed to worry?

The question has to be asked because Ralegh's name was quite widely used by the members of what has become known as the Babington plot, the last attempt to assassinate Elizabeth and put Mary on the throne in her stead.

The Babington plot began as two separate conspiracies. The first was hatched at Rheims: the year before, an English Catholic by the name of John Savage, returning from the Netherlands where he had fought for the Duke of Parma, fell into conversation there with Dr William Gifford, the exiled brother of George Gifford. Savage had been boasting of his military service; 'a better service than all of this I could tell you', said Gifford. He meant the murder of Elizabeth. It took several weeks for Savage to be persuaded, but ultimately Gifford wore him down and swept aside his scruples, at which point Gifford had some specific suggestions:

as her majesty should go into her chapel to hear divine service, Savage might lurk in the gallery, and stab her with his dagger: or if her majesty should walk into her garden, he might then shoot her through with his dag; or if her majesty did walk abroad to take the air, as she would often do, rather accompanied with women than with men, and those few men but slenderly weaponed, Savage might then assault her with his arming sword.[23]

If Savage were worried about his own safety, Gifford assured him that the killing of such a heretic as Elizabeth would offer him the assurance of a place in heaven. Then, as now, the pieties of martyrdom greased the path to murder.

Savage returned to England and, having failed to prosecute the murder, returned to his studies at Barnards Inn, where with some reluctance he was put in touch with another conspiracy being developed by a Catholic priest by the name of Ballard. Ballard's angle was the putative invasion of England, the rescue of Mary, the organization and raising of the dormant power of the English Catholic gentry. But, as Alva had recognized more than a decade earlier, there could be no successful invasion while Elizabeth lived. To that extent, Ballard was something of a fantasist, a suggestion in no way contradicted by descriptions of his secret persona in England: Captain Fortescue, a dandyish swaggering soldier in velvet hose and satin doublet, a grey cape with gold lace, and a fine hat, silver buttons on its band, the very latest fashion. All Ballard's work would be for nothing if the Elizabeth problem remained unsolved; Savage was his magic bullet.

It was Ballard who drew Babington in. He was a young and wealthy Catholic gentleman from Derbyshire, studying at Lincoln's Inn. He and his friends were disaffected as Catholics were and young men tend to be, rowdy and dissolute, ale-house seditionaries. As one of those luckless friends, Chidiock Tichbourne, said on the scaffold, 'Before this thing chanced, we lived together in most flourishing estate: of whom went report in the Strand, Fleet Street, and elsewhere about London but of Babington and Tichbourne? No threshold was of force to brave our entry. Thus we lived, and wanted nothing we could wish for: and God knows, what less in my head than matters of state?'[24] They sound identical to Ralegh and his peers the decade before.

Their conspiracy was founded in their favourite inns around the Temple and elsewhere in late spring and early summer 1586, and developed in thrillingly clandestine meetings in St Giles Fields. Savage's vow to kill Elizabeth swelled: now six men swore to do it. Babington himself, quite the dashing hero, would rescue Mary. It was their great misfortune that two of their number were Walsingham's agents: Ballard's man, Francis Maude and Babington's new-found friend, Robert Poley. Both did what they could to nurse the plot along until the time was right to reveal it – something requiring the nicest judgement, as Parry's case had all too clearly showed.

But if he and his circle were at heart unserious in their intentions, they were also desperate for fame: needy, vain, boastful, self-mythologizing. 'Do you see yonder gentleman?' Babington said to a friend once, pointing at Tichbourne. 'He is more fit to be a nobleman than a gentleman of mean calling. I doubt not but to see him called unto great honour ere it be long.' In a move startlingly reminiscent of today's martyrdom videos, Babington had the conspirators' portraits painted as a group, with the legend *Hi mihi sunt comites, quos ipsa pericula ducunt* – These men are my companions, whom very dangers draw. Some baulked at the motto and it was changed to the more ambivalent *Quorm haec alio properantibus?* – To what end are these things to men that hasten to another purpose?[25]

Walsingham was interested in the plot for its own sake, but more particularly because he had contrived through Poley in England and another agent in France named Gilbert Gifford – a cousin of George Gifford's – to control Mary's correspondence at Tutbury. Mary believed it was smuggled in and out in ale barrels sealed in a leather pouch. That much was true. But it was also opened, deciphered and resealed by Walsingham's men. Babington wrote to Mary about his plans early in July, going into great detail; 'Six noble gentlemen, all his friends, will undertake the tragical execution of the despatch of the usurper, for the zeal they bear the Catholic cause, and her service,' he said. There is not a little preening along the way: Babington wanted her to admire him for his importance, as much as his courage and zeal. On the seventeenth she responded enthusiastically; it was a fatal mistake.

Who were the six gentlemen? Walsingham at first was desperate to know, even forging a postscript to Mary's letter asking Babington to identify them. Later, with everyone seemingly in custody, and Mary snared, that interest suddenly ebbed. There seemed curiously little enthusiasm in pinning down the names of the men who had agreed to kill Elizabeth, as opposed to those who were merely guilty as accessories to the conspiracy. The fact is so counter-intuitive as to raise more questions than it answers.

Ballard was arrested on 4 August. The others fled on foot to St John's Wood and then on to what they hoped would be a safe house at Uxendon, near Harrow, but after ten days on the run they were taken. There was a wave of associated arrests. Then the interrogations began.

This is the story as the government set it out at the trial of the conspirators in September – although the roles of Poley, Maude and Gilbert Gifford went unmentioned. Nevertheless, it has a satisfying clarity to it: all the ends are tied, all the traitors caught, all found guilty, all to die.

And yet. One man who wasn't mentioned at the trial was George Gifford. Several of the conspirators revealed a knowledge of his vow three years earlier to assassinate Elizabeth, which seems to have come as a surprise to the authorities since Gifford was quickly placed in the Tower. His graffiti is still there in the Beauchamp Tower: *Mala conscientia facit ut tuta timeantur* – A bad conscience makes what is safe seem fearful. Gifford flatly and angrily denied the accusation – a denial we know to be a lie – but Walsingham was oddly content to let the matter rest there.

It was, however, effectively the end of Gifford's career at court. When he died in 1613, it was said that his loss 'would have been less, both for himself and his posterity, if he had gone thirty years ago'.[26] Thirty years earlier was 1583, the year he offered to assassinate Elizabeth. The valediction was either a lucky generalization, or a very precise observation. His own view, looking back on the ruin of his hopes, was that he was 'as deep in disgrace as years', with no aim 'but to make his death show his life's innocence'. Ralegh was one of the few men who stayed loyal to him.

As for Elizabeth, she was evidently closely briefed about the Babington plot as it evolved. She saw one of the conspirators, an Irishman named Robert Barnwell, as he reconnoitred her security arrangements as she walked out one day at Richmond, noting how many were around her and how armed, and her preference for walking alone. In one sense, this is the crux of her reign: her hunger for freedom of movement, for private space, has led her to a place where a man waits, wishing to kill her. But liberty made her stronger: Elizabeth looked him in the eye, and then turned and said loudly to Hatton: 'Am not I fairly guarded, that have not a man in my company with a sword about him?' But she said nothing to reveal him, or, as Hatton said latter, Barnwell would never have made it back to Babington.[27] Why? She knew there was a greater game to play out. How did she know who he was? She had seen the group portrait that Babington had commissioned.

Similarly, mindful of Dr Gifford's exhortation that Savage might kill her on her way to chapel, she showed a very public awareness of precisely that terror: the Spanish ambassador received intelligence at the end of June that 'When the queen was going to chapel the other day, as usual in full magnificence, she was suddenly overcome with a shock of fear, which affected her to such an extent that she at once returned to her apartment, greatly to the wonder of those present.'[28] She found confinement, space pressing in on her, enervating. We don't know what she had seen, but what she was afraid of is readily apparent.

And then there is Ralegh. There is no trace of Ralegh in the trial transcripts. That is not too surprising: treason trials were more propaganda than justice: clarity of message was everything. What is less explicable is the wholesale lack of interest of Walsingham and his interrogators in the series of Raleghan leads provided by the conspirators.

Poley reported that Babington, staying at Poley's chambers in Temple Gardens towards the end of July, had told him 'that one of Sir Walter Ralegh's men had received money and undertaken to kill her majesty within five weeks from that time'.[29] Henry Donne, younger brother of the poet, confessed that around the weekend before his capture, Ballard had lost faith in Babington's bravado and doubted that he did in fact have six men sure to act; he had therefore 'that afternoon sworn unto him two of Sir Walter Ralegh's men to execute the act whensoever he would have them.' It was as if the marginal world of sedition and sour malcontents was trying to reclaim Ralegh for its own.[30]

Donne said Ballard didn't tell him their names; and again the inquisitors' lack of interest is marked, almost a denial of their craft.

Ballard denied Donne's confession when it was put to him, and claimed only to know one of Ralegh's men, by the name of Flyer. Flyer is impossible to identify precisely without further information, but he is almost certainly a member of the Floyer family – variously spelled Flyer, Flower and so on – at least three of whom were certainly in Ralegh's service at different times. William Floyer was Ralegh's agent in Ireland; George Floyer was a captain in the province too. John Floyer was one of Ralegh's sea captains: he had sailed with him in Gilbert's chaotic voyage of 1578.[31]

Denial or not, there was more than enough evidence to pursue these followers of Ralegh: the government had the means to make men talk after all, but with this thread of intelligence they seemed disinclined to do so. Ballard alone of the conspirators was threatened with the rack. And yet, quite possibly, there were two or three of Ralegh's men at liberty who had undertaken to kill Elizabeth. Such hearsay was considered ample to put George Gifford in the Tower.

On Monday 19 September, four days after his trial, Babington tried to contact Ralegh, offering him £1,000 to plead his cause before Elizabeth. Flyer was one of his go-betweens.

Good cousin, speak with Mr Flower, for I wrote to him yesterday. If he received my letter, I know not; but that he keeps me here told me . . . that you had moved Mr Rawley for me, and promised 1000l if he would get my pardon . . . Good cousin, deal for me, or, if you will not, speak with the younger Mr Lovelace, and he will do anything for me. And deliver him this note and bid him tell Mr

Flower that in respect of this service that I can do her
majesty I desire to speak with his master.[32]

The cold sweat, the desperate, sick terror isn't hard to hear.
There was no word from Ralegh, and the next day Babington
and six of his fellow conspirators were led to a scaffold
prepared for them in St Giles Fields, where they had walked
together not many weeks before. Ballard was first to hang; he
was cut down alive and, as the official account records,
'bowelled with great cruelty'. Babington watched coolly, while
the others looked away. He too was pulled from the gallows
while still conscious, crying out as he was cut open, *Parce mihi,
Domine Jesu!* Spare me, Oh Lord Jesus.

It is perfectly true that such bribes were not uncommon, and
Ralegh was a good choice in terms of influence with Elizabeth,
but the apparent implication of several of Ralegh's followers in
the conspiracy itself suggests deeper connections that the
government wished to remain hidden.

Abroad, however, the rumours of Ralegh's involvement
continued to circulate, resonating with his known associations
and apparent detachment from – even hostility to – the
expansive anti-Catholicism of Leicester and Walsingham. On 10
September, before the trial, Mendoza had written to Philip: 'The
whole of the affair that was being planned appears to have been
discovered, some of the leaders having confessed. Of the six men
who had sworn to kill the queen, only two have escaped, namely,
the favourite Ralegh and the brother of Lord Windsor.'[33]

Mendoza does not seem to have known Ralegh personally,
but he knew those that did, like Charles Arundell, and as we
know from Thynne, he had targeted Ralegh previously as a
weak link in Elizabeth's defences. And his information was
good: Edward Windsor, another Oxford alumni, had indeed
fled to the continent. Ralegh of course was serenely in place by

Elizabeth's side, but the use of projecting himself as a willing accomplice to Catholic treasons was quite apparent: it drew out and helped neutralize the genuinely disaffected, albeit at some risk to Ralegh himself. Henry Howard's hatred of Ralegh and his circle at Durham House would, ultimately, cost Ralegh his life.

Even after the executions and the trial of Mary at Fotheringay in October, the exiles continued to hope: Paget was overheard comforting a friend, 'Well, and Sir Walter Ralegh's man scape I care not, he will pay her for all the rest ... By God's blood, there be yet they that will kill her.'[34]

Because there is a thorough paper trail for the Babington conspiracy, we tend to look at it in isolation, but the truth is that the world of the Catholic émigrés in Paris and elsewhere was endlessly compromised, and it is impossible to know now – as indeed it was then – who was loyal to whom. So, for instance, the Spanish thought Charles Arundell was an English double agent – this despite the fact that he facilitated the turning of Edward Stafford, the debt-ridden English ambassador, who received money from both Philip II and the Duke of Guise. There were those on both sides who thought Thomas Morgan, desperate for his liberty, became an English spy in the Bastille – and some thought he had in fact betrayed Mary in the course of the exposure of the Babington plot. Walsingham never really trusted either Poley or Gifford. Both Babington and Ballard tried to betray the conspiracy in the days and hours before they were arrested. We should not judge any of them too harshly; necessity, exile and debt were cruel and tyrannous masters.

In fact, we should probably stop referring to a Babington plot per se; this is not to say that Babington and his fellow recusants were not guilty of conspiring against Elizabeth. But giving it such a name implies a neatness and order which did not in fact exist: there were multiple plots ongoing against Elizabeth, some of which – perhaps most of which – were actually English plots aimed at Mary. Certainly the climate of fear in England, which made the assassination of Elizabeth seem a certainty unless the problem of Mary was addressed, made such projections inevitable.

There is no 'smoking gun' here, but there is ample circumstantial evidence that Ralegh was intimately involved in the intelligence effort against Mary; and one could in any case make a strong *ex post facto* argument for his involvement from the fact that the sole person whom Elizabeth chose to reward with Babington's extensive landholdings – which stretched across Lincolnshire, Derbyshire and Nottinghamshire – was, in fact, Ralegh. And it seems appropriate that, when Ralegh began to sell the property on, as was his wont, the day after Elizabeth's patent granting them to him was issued, William Langherne was there to witness the deeds.[35]

While the Babington plot was winding to its tragic conclusion, Ralegh was deeply involved in his other great enterprises for Elizabeth: Ireland and America. On 21 June, Ralegh had been granted 12,000 acres in county Cork. The quality of it was debatable, in part due to the essential nature of the terrain, but also thanks to the depredations of English military policy. In October, the surveyors found marking out the boundaries of Ralegh's domain exceptionally challenging: 'the lands having been long waste are generally overgrown with deep grass, and in most places with heath, brambles, and furze, whereby and by the extremity of rain and foul weather, that hitherto we have found, we have been greatly hindered in our proceeding.'[36]

At the end of July, on the twenty-seventh, around the time Ballard was signing up Ralegh's men to assassinate Elizabeth,

Drake unexpectedly brought home to Plymouth Ralegh's colony from Roanoke. How much notice Ralegh had of this apparent failure is uncertain: Drake, returning from the rich despoiling of the Spanish Americas, had swept north up the Carolina coast to view the prospective site for a harbour from which to attack Spain. Dismayed by what he had found, and finding the settlers scouring the horizon for their supply ships, agriculture having been long forgotten in favour of scavenging from the native Americans, Drake anchored out in the roads. He offered them supplies of his own, and a ship, the *Francis*, to transport to a better site in Chesapeake Bay. In the midst of loading, a vicious storm had blown the *Francis* out to sea, where the winds meant it had no alternative but to sail for home. With the *Francis* went the resolve of the colonists and they voted to return home en masse. Within days, a supply ship duly arrived from Ralegh; then came another fleet, which Ralegh had sent under Grenville's captaincy: they were both too late.

It could have been catastrophic, but Ralegh had his teeth into the idea and was not letting go. Always a thoughtful man, despite his predilection for glib plausibilities, he assessed the colony's failure honestly and concluded that he could not do it alone. Even with the huge resources that he had invested in it, his expenditure was dwarfed by the scale of the undertaking – and thrown impossibly off balance by the comparative yields of agriculture and trade as against privateering and theft. The kind of young men attracted to the latter were almost entirely unsuited to the former and commensurately impossible to motivate. Ralegh needed a community, committed to the land, which could root itself in North America, perpetuating its existence and with a stake in its profitable life. It was the same model about to be rolled out in Ireland. Ironically it was also the mirror image of Ralegh's personal approach to landowning.

In January 1587, a charter was established for a city of Raleigh in Virginia, under the quiet leadership of John White, with the intention of siting it on Chesapeake Bay, which had a harbour sufficient to meet Ralegh's wider strategic ambitions. White sailed in May. By February, Ralegh's Munster holdings had grown to 42,000 acres, a reversal of government policy from the previous summer when 12,000 acres, Ralegh's allotment, was specified as the maximum allowed. It was among the greatest of Elizabeth's gifts – but again it was a gift that promised reward without actually offering it. Ralegh had to make it work. If he did so, both he and Elizabeth would profit, he financially and she politically, with a secure and settled Ireland drained of its antipathies and treasons. The Munster plantation was a challenge, a small kingdom, if he could fashion it so – perhaps too an anvil on which to trial and fashion a template for the greater empire to the west.

This was, if Ralegh but knew it, the last, long high tide of his influence and power. No doubt if he reflected on the last decade he would have recognized a steady and steep ascent in favour since his crisis of fortune towards the end of the 1570s, but if he acknowledged the scope of his rewards there was still the consuming terror of failure and fall. Even if he were not psychologically disposed to self-doubt, he would have known enough about the vicissitudes of fortune from his experience with the court Catholics to breed a vertiginous and disabling anxiety. Elizabeth was his anchor, but the truth was that, while she still revelled in his company and had need of his services, she was running out of gifts she was prepared to offer him. She had no need of his diligence in the great offices of state – she had other people for that and, in any event, she wished to keep him for herself – and while she could in theory have ennobled him, Elizabeth had clear and traditional ideas about the social order, as Sir Philip Sidney had discovered, and it is hard to imagine she would even have countenanced such an idea. Besides, she may have felt she had given him something like a kingdom in America, if he could make it such. Surely that should suffice?

Nevertheless, at the end of April Elizabeth appointed him to succeed Hatton as captain of her guard. The role itself had little in the way of award attached, save an annual quantity of tawny cloth and black fur from which to cut his uniform, but the reward was in the role: permanent and unfettered access. That lovely Elizabethan construction, 'trusty and well-beloved', used by her of Ralegh in a letter that February, seems a perfect summation of her reading of him.[37] He could not be closer to the heart of the queen's private, interior world, and charged as he was with her security, her very life, he was receiving a rare and intimate affirmation of her belief in his loyalty. But they must both have believed that his future fortune lay across the seas and oceans of the west.

Was Elizabeth not now commissioning him to tame Ireland as he was to subdue America, peopling it with Englishmen and women, bringing it under the civilizing shadow of Elizabeth's wings? He was not simply being charged with building Elizabeth an empire. The very scale of his landholdings, both actual and theoretical, meant that he *was* the empire, and to the extent that his imperial vision was itself an aspiration, more projection than project, a triumph always deferred, so was his authority – real only so far as Elizabeth wished it to be so. As Elizabeth was to him, so was he to England's colonies.

Meanwhile, she had need of his services again. The two strands of Ralegh's public relationship with Elizabeth – the groundwork of empire and the politics of anti-Catholicism – came together in the late summer of 1586, when two pinnaces of his, the *Serpent* and the *Mary Sparke*, arrived at Southamp-

ton, having netted a substantial prize off the Azores. It was
what would in most circumstances be regarded as piracy:

> for that we would not be known of what nation we were,
> we displayed a white silk ensign in our maine top [mast],
> which they seeing, made account that we had been some
> of the king of Spain's Armadas, lying in wait for English
> men of war: but when we came within shot of her, we
> tooke down our white flag, and spread abroad the Cross
> of S. George, which when they saw, it made them to fly
> as fast as they might, but all their haste was in vain, for
> our ships were swifter of sail then they.[38]

The prize was Pedro Sarmiento de Gamboa, whom we have
met in passing already, governor of the Straits of Magellan, and
a conquistador par excellence, at once hard and supple, brutal
and sophisticated. Brought up to London on 14 September, the
day Babington was sentenced to death, Sarmiento was sent on
to meet Ralegh the following day at Windsor, where Elizabeth
had retreated, out of fear it was said, no doubt taking comfort
in the green chequered pastures, the soft wood-crowned hills
that surrounded it, in hawking and hunting. Over the next six
weeks, a small plot emerged, woven together by Ralegh,
Elizabeth and Burghley. Ralegh agreed to waive the ransom
that might have otherwise been due to him with a prisoner of
such stature. There was a simple reason for this: Elizabeth, and
Burghley wanted Sarmiento to take a message back to Philip:
'if old scores were forgotten, and your Majesty would be a good
friend again, the queen would withdraw the English from
Holland and Zeeland'.[39]

As always with Elizabeth, her seriousness in making the offer
was indecipherable; she was back doing what she did best,
attempting to mislead other governments about her intentions.

The Venetian ambassador to Spain had it about right: 'The whole affair is kept a profound secret, and it is not impossible that it may prove to be an artifice of that exceedingly clever woman to throw things out of gear, and to cause the heat of armament to cool.'[40]

As for Ralegh, Sarmiento told him, as Mendoza's confessor had suggested two years previously, that Elizabeth's favour could not last for ever, and that he should consider seeking Philip's. Ralegh acquiesced, offering to prevent English ships sailing to attack Spain or its shipping and to act against Don Antonio, the claimant to the Portuguese crown, then in London. He offered too to sell Philip a large ship of his own, heavily armed, for 5,000 crowns, the transaction to be carried out in Lisbon.

Sarmiento left England at the end of October. Unfortunately his party was attacked while passing through the south of France and Sarmiento ended up a prisoner again, this time in the Navarre province of Béarn in the Pyrenees. Ralegh immediately sent two gentlemen to Navarre to negotiate his release; they carried letters from Elizabeth stressing the urgency of Sarmiento's journey. It was a matter of state, she said, not merely Ralegh's personal affairs.

This, indeed, is one reason why Ralegh and his followers – the notoriously malcontent circle at Durham House – were allowed to dangle in front of the seditious Catholic exiles. Elizabeth believed in the power of deferral as a means of avoiding defeat; her entire foreign policy had been based on it for twenty-five years. But without marriage negotiations to effect her will, she needed others to act on her behalf. Now she wanted peace with Spain, or failing that the deferral of war, and with no resident Spanish ambassador and a large part of her Privy Council hostile, she had to have a proxy with plausibility and contacts: Ralegh had both. But they were not enough to get Sarmiento released.

By February, perhaps sensing Philip's coolness, Ralegh had doubled his offer, suggesting Philip bought two of his ships and promised to persuade Elizabeth against the naval preparations aimed at Spain which would result in Drake's action against Cadiz. The latter help Philip was certainly happy to accept: the cost was nothing compared to the savings. But he was sceptical as to the rest of his offer: 'out of the question' he wrote to Mendoza. He had been burned once already by Hawkins on a similar venture, so now 'we must guard ourselves against the coming of the ships under this pretext being a feint or a trick upon us – which is far from being improbable'.[41]

On such suspicions, and the accident of Sarmiento's kidnapping in Navarre, Elizabeth and Ralegh's attempt to stop the Armada foundered. The war party in both countries had won. Ralegh was left with one thing only for his strenuous efforts towards Sarmiento: a story the conquistador had told him about a great golden city deep in the South America interior, at the head of the Orinoco river. It was called, Sarmiento said, *el dorado*, the golden one. Ralegh thought he had found his – and Elizabeth's – third empire, and a source of treasure that would at last rival that of Philip: a world with no limits. In the dream of an imperial England, he thought he saw a quick and easy way to free England and Elizabeth from the threat of Spain once and for all.

It was similar thinking, both bold and desperate, that informed Ralegh's apparent advice to Elizabeth about the fate of Mary Stuart. Secretary Davison had the impossible task of persuading Elizabeth to sign Mary's death warrant, something she was, as she always had been, violently opposed to doing. On 20 February he approached her as she talked quietly with Ralegh in the privy chamber at Greenwich. Elizabeth called Davison over, Ralegh looking on, and told him how she had dreamed the night before that Mary had been executed, a fact that had, in the dream, made her so mad she couldn't account for her actions.

Davison, mindful of the ill-disguised threat, nevertheless pressed Elizabeth for her decision on the warrant. Elizabeth said yes, she had agreed to sign it, but she resented being asked to assume the whole burden of responsibility for Mary's death. That is the law, Davison said.

'There are wiser men than [you] of other opinion,' Elizabeth replied. She was, I think, referring to Ralegh.[42]

Ultimately, what she wanted was someone to take the burden from her, a man who was willing to assassinate Mary. What good, she asked, were those 'precise fellows . . . who in words would do great things for her surety but indeed perform nothing'? Words meant nothing; action was all. Given that she had just been talking to Ralegh, and that he had advocated just such an approach to Ormond in Ireland – and would again at the turn of the century with regard to Essex – it seems more than likely that this particular policy was being cultivated by the two of them, if no one else. It certainly had Ralegh's stamp as a practical solution to a procedural problem. The other fact that betrays his hand is that the man whom Elizabeth finally recommended to Davison for the task was Wingfield. It stretches credulity to suggest his name occurred to her without any input from Ralegh, a man whom Wingfield had tried to murder in the street at the turn of the decade.

The cold and practical amorality of such ideas contributed greatly to Ralegh's unpopularity. Vast ambition, dizzying insecurity, and a willingness to suspend due process for narrow advantage were alarming characteristics for a man with influence over the queen. But it is a measure of the journey on which Elizabeth had brought him that the diffident young man of ten years before – lascivious, drunken, restless – was capable of recommending the murder of a former queen of France and

Scotland to her cousin. She had taken a man of indifferent loyalty under the shadow of her wings and he had emerged a man willing to articulate thoughts for her that other men discarded or suppressed, and do things that other men would not. He was her creature in a way no other man had been.

It is the supreme paradox of Elizabeth's relationship with Ralegh that it was intensely, relentlessly public and yet so private that little formal record of it survives. One explanation is inherent in the brief scene with Davison: a sense of complicity and trust that surrounds the two of them, a comforting mutuality of interest and thought, exclusive and complete. Another explanation is their self-control: they were remarkably undemonstrative together – or at least, to the extent they were demonstrative it was considered unremarkable – and they contrived to keep their conversations to themselves to an extraordinary degree at a court where absolute privacy for the queen was almost impossible. Those facts in themselves are testament to the strength and depth of the bond between them.

Nevertheless, those who looked on – both at court and anywhere court gossip was relayed – thought they comprehended them immediately. Elizabeth's persona had always been to some degree compromised by her sexuality: that is, her audience was inclined to read into the national melodrama of her marriage proposals, into her flirtatiousness, her lifelong pleasure in the company of men such as Seymour and Leicester, various degrees of indecency. Ralegh's apparently swift ascent to influence seemed to confirm that libidinal narrative: for those that knew of his reputation already, the seductive Ralegh was tailor-made for the role of the queen's favourite. To the more lascivious-minded, their relationship – her favour, his service – seemed instantly understandable; people thought they knew the story, its low and sordid arc. By the time Ralegh arrived centre stage Leicester, long considered the love of her life, had grown tired of waiting for her and married someone else. Two decades of marriage projects had come to nothing: Elizabeth, alone, seemed freer than ever to follow her desires. Ralegh, meanwhile, was little more than a provincial nobody with expensive tastes and expansive ambitions. That they should be lovers was almost a given and every public mark of affection – every touch, every glance, every quiet shared confidence – was read as confirming that fact.

But was it true? Were they lovers as Von Wedel confidently reported? The truth is unknowable, of course – what, after all, would genuine evidence look like, as opposed to the kind of gossip that fathered so many of Leicester's children on Elizabeth? In some respects, the age difference is a red herring. It was not at all uncommon for a young man to marry a wealthy older woman – a typical scenario being an apprentice marrying his master's widow. Against that you have Ralegh's later aphoristic comment, 'They that want means to nourish children will abstain from marriage; or (which is all one) they cast away their bodies upon rich old women'.[43] Ralegh cannot have been unaware of the comments and perceptions that circulated about Elizabeth generally, and his relationship to her in particular, and it is equally unlikely that he would have written such a thing without being aware that it would be read in the context of that relationship. But the vehemence of his discomfort, like Hatton's rebuttal of the accusation quoted earlier, draws so much attention to itself it is difficult to avoid the conclusion that he is protesting too much.

On balance, however, I am inclined to think they weren't lovers. Not that such a thing would have been impossible or even implausible, but because it doesn't accord with what seems to me to be the dominant tone of their relationship. Over the course of the six or seven years to 1587, there seems to be an expressive calm between them, which sits ill with the tempestuous passions that a fully sexual relationship would more likely have aroused. It might be observed that Elizabeth was inconstant in her favour to him, but she did that with everyone – it was how she had learned to govern and she did so highly effectively – and one could make a case that she did it less with Ralegh than anyone. Later, when Ralegh married, there would be pain for both of them, but in these years when their relationship was at its zenith, there is a steady and enduring sense of comfort and ease between them, a care that transcended the fraught and difficult uses to which they were sometimes compelled to put each other. I think we can call that love.

Indeed, the dynamic between them seems more familial than anything else. That does not wholly preclude other factors – they both had intoxicating charm and wit, and if he had youth on his side, she had power – but the Kat Astley connection is surely key. Without pressing too hard on the evidence, it is not difficult to see a maternal solicitousness in Elizabeth's care of Ralegh, a sometimes awkward tender balance between yielding and censure. There is no evidence, meanwhile, that Ralegh shared any of his wealth and status with his own mother; it may be going too far to say that he abandoned her, but when she died in 1594, she did so in modest circumstances.

In the end, what seems most apparent is that Ralegh and Elizabeth shared a clear-sighted understanding of each other's profoundest needs. It is almost literally true, of course, that Ralegh hoped to give her the world, and his failure to do so is a different story. When he first attracted her favour, she was at a transitory point, in search of an identity beyond the redundant threat of marriage and the struggle for independence, in search of freedom from the fear of assassination and invasion. Ralegh was not necessarily the answer to those questions, but he was, I think, at the heart of her adaption to and triumph over those new realities. He recognized the panic and confinement that Elizabeth felt, and he sought – through attempts to cut the burden of Mary Stuart's threat as much as the golden elusive dream of empire – to liberate her from that prison, those limitations.

Meanwhile Elizabeth, in a sense, allowed Ralegh in America and Ireland the liberty that she always longed for – and it may be that she regarded her refusal to give him the chains of office as a gift of the highest order. Instead, she gave him ample opportunity to create his own greater freedom elsewhere.

Yet Ralegh always seems to be looking over his shoulder, uncertain of his place in the world even as he laid claim to a greater share of it. Elizabeth tried to ameliorate that flaw too. Some time in 1587, the summit of Ralegh's favour, he and Elizabeth exchanged verses – the only surviving example of a kind of public private dialogue they excelled in. It captures, I think, the authentic tone of their relationship, or at least the private drama of comfort and gift they played out between themselves, but it also precisely addresses the moment, acknowledging an enthusiasm and feeling its was towards ?????. Ralegh's poem, on his favourite subject of Fortune and how it has stolen his love, is archly melodramatic but in its very self-consciousness and hyperbole revealing of genuine hurt and anxiety. He senses the moment to be one of change and departure, with Elizabeth, his 'true fantasy's mistress', slipping away from him, and recoils from what he fears.

> Then will I leave my love in Fortune's hand;
> Then will I leave my love in worldlings' band,
> And only love the sorrows due to me —
> Sorrow, henceforth, that shall my princess be.

Elizabeth's answer, by way of contrast, is direct, kind and purely affectionate, refusing to take Ralegh's verse at face value, refusing to indulge his rhetoric:

> Mourn not, my Wat, nor be thou so dismayed,
> It passeth fickle Fortune's power and skill
> To force my heart to think thee any ill.
> No Fortune base, thou sayest, shall alter thee?
> And may so blind a witch so conquer me?

Her poem nevertheless moves towards a conclusion that acknowledges the emotional seriousness within the self-dramatizing melancholy, and addresses the bleak insecurity, the troubled self-worth that lay beneath Ralegh's public persona. She offers him a kind of benediction which might stand, I think, for the wider gift of her grace and favour, for a life free from self-doubt:

> Revive again and live without all dread,
> The less afraid, the better thou shalt speed.[44]

It resolves, then, into a valedictory blessing, an assurance of unity but also a farewell, offered from the shore as the tide begins to turn.

END NOTES

Introduction

1. Francis Osborne, 'Historical Memoires of Queen Elizabeth and James I', in Scott, *Secret History of the Court of James I*, pp. 49–50.
2. In Oldys (ed.), *The Works of Sir Walter Ralegh*, vol. I, p. 67.

Chapter I: A Decayed Estate

1. Von Wedel, 'Journey Through England and Scotland', *Transactions of the Royal Historical Society*, vol. VI, pp. 262–5.
2. Cobbett, *State Trials*, vol. II, p. 34.
3. Naunton, *Fragmenta Regalia*; Fuller's *Worthies*, vol. I, p. 419.
4. Brushfield, *Raleghana*, vol. I, pp. 4–5.
5. Latham and Youings (eds.), *The Letters of Sir Walter Ralegh*, pp. 381–7.
6. 1855A ???, Devon Record Office.
7. Marsden, *Select Pleas in the Court of Admiralty*, vol. II, pp. 31–4.
8. Foxe, *Actes and Monuments* (1570); Holinshed, *Chronicles* (1587); Fuller's *Worthies*, vol. I, p. 401.
9. Hooker brings Prest's martyrdom into his additions to Holinshed's *Chronicles* too. See p. 1,309. Her fate also features in Fuller's *Worthies*, vol. I, p. 401.

10. Holinshed (1587), pp. 1,015–1,027; Hooker, *The Life and Times of Sir Peter Carew*, pp. 47–53.

11. Fuller's *Worthies*, vol. I, p. 420.

12. Cresswell (ed.), *Edwardian Inventories for the City and County of Exeter*, pp. 77–8.

13. See Duffy, *The Stripping of the Altars*. Duffy has also noted the anecdote about Ralegh's annexation of church property in the preceding paragraph.

14. Churchyard, *General Rehearsal*.

15. See *DNB* entry for Katherine Astley; Latham and Youings (eds.), *The Letters of Sir Walter Ralegh*, p. 225.

16. Marcus, Miller and Rose (eds.) *Elizabeth I: Collected Works*, p. 34.

17. Giovanni Michiel, Venetian ambassador in England, to the Venetian Senate, 13 May 1557, *CSP Venice*, vol. VI: 1555–8, pp. 1,085–7.

18. *CSP Foreign, Elizabeth*, vol. I: 1558–9, pp. 524–34.

19. Sir Thomas Wriothesley, later first Earl of Southampton, quoted in Johnson, *Elizabeth: A Study in Power and Intellect*, p. 16.

Chapter II: Leagues of Smoke

1. Doran (ed.), *Elizabeth: The Exhibition at the National Maritime Museum*, pp. 12–13.

2. Marcus, Mueller and Rose (eds.), *Elizabeth I: Collected Works*, p. 159.

3. Noailles, 21 February 1554, quoted in Strickland, *Lives of the Queens of England*, vol. IV, p. 76.

4. Simon Renard to Emperor Charles V, 17 February 1554, *CSP Spain*, vol. XII: 1554, pp. 106–9.

5. Simon Renard to Emperor Charles V, 24 February 1554, ibid., p. 125.

6. Marcus, Mueller and Rose, eds, *Elizabeth I: Collected Works*, p. 46.

7. Ibid., p. 41.

8. 24 February 1554, *CSP Spain*, vol. XII: 1554, p. 125.

9. Elizabeth in conversation with the French ambassador Castelnau, in Jenkins, *Elizabeth the Great*, p. 53.

10. Foxe, *Acts and Monuments* (1583 edition), p. 2,094.

11. Marcus, Mueller and Rose (eds.), *Elizabeth I: Collected Works*, p. 159.

12. Bacon, *Apothegms*, p. 404.

13. Foxe, *Acts and Monuments* (1583 edition), p. 2,097.

14. Giovanni Michiel, Venetian Ambassador in England, to the Doge and Senate, 19 October 1556, *CSP Venice*, vol. VI, p. 718.

15. 9 September 1553, *CSP Spain*, vol. XI: 1553, p. 228.

16. *CSP Venice*, vol. VII: 1558–80, p. 330.

17. *Letters and Papers, Foreign and Domestic, Henry VIII*, Volume XII, Part 1: January–May 1537, p. 361.

18. Ridley, *Elizabeth I*, p. 31.

19. *CSP Spain*, vol. X: 1550–2, p. 325.

20. Ibid., p. 493.

21. 24 March 1565, *CSP Spain (Simancas)*, vol. I: 1558–67, p. 409.

22. Leicester to La Forêt, 6 August 1566, quoted in Von Raumer, *Elizabeth and Mary Stuart*, p. 40.

23. ?1559 (but calendared under September 1561), *CSP Venice*, vol. VII: 1558–80, p. 329.

24. Licenciate de Games to the King of the Romans, 12 November 1553, *CSP Spain*, vol. XI: 1553, p. 352; Lord Paget to the Emperor, 14 November 1554, *CSP Spain*, vol. XIII: 1554–8, p. 90.

25. Walsingham to Leicester, quoted in Read, *Lord Burghley and Queen Elizabeth*, p. 200.

26. Jenkins, *Elizabeth the Great*, pp. 71–2; Hayward, *Annals of Elizabeth*, p. 10.

27. Michael Surian, Venetian Ambassador at the court of Philip II, ?1559 (but calendared under September 1561), *CSP Venice*, vol. VII: 1558–80, p. 328.

28. 'Dialogue on the Queen's Marriage', in Strype, *The Life of the Learned Sir Thomas Smith*, p. 249.

29. Letter to Lord Burghley, July 1572, Lettenhove, *Relations Politiques des Pay-Bas et de l'Angleterre*, vol. VI, p. 437.

30. 29 December 1558, *CSP Spain (Simancas)*, vol. I: 1558–67, pp. 20–1.

31. Michiel Surian to the Most Serene Signory, ?1559 (but calendared under September 1561), *CSP Venice*, vol. VII: 1558–80, pp. 327–32.

32. Earl of Bedford to Sir Nicholas Throckmorton, 14 February 1566, quoted in Mumby, *The Fall of Mary Stuart*, p. 56.

33. Ibid.

34. 12 February 1559, *CSP Spain (Simancas)*, vol. I: 1558–67, p. 29.

35. 24 March 1565, ibid., p. 409.

36. Baron Brenner to the Emperor Ferdinand, June 1565, in Klarwill, *Queen Elizabeth and Some Foreigners*, p. 87.

37. 23 June 1568, *CSP Foreign, Elizabeth*, vol. VIII: 1566–8, p. 487.

38. 28 June 1568, ibid., p. 491.

39. Duke of Norfolk to Robert Ridolfi, March 1571, *CSP Vatican*, vol. I: 1558–71, p. 391ff.

40. *CSP Venice*, vol. VII: 1558–80, pp. 448–51.

41. Read, *Lord Burghley and Queen Elizabeth*, pp. 51–2.

42. Ibid., p. 52.

43. Sir Thomas Smith and Henry Killigrew to Elizabeth I, *CSP Foreign, Elizabeth*, vol. X: 1572–4, p. 9.

44. Sir Thomas Smith to Lord Burghley, 10 January 1572, ibid., p. 14.

45. Francis Walsingham to Lord Burghley, 13 July 1572, Digges, *Compleat Ambassador*, p. 220.

46. Dr Valentine Dale to Lord Burghley, 12 December 1573, *CSP Foreign, Elizabeth*, vol. X: 1572–4, p. 446.

47. Read, *Lord Burghley and Queen Elizabeth*, p. 65.

48. Lord Burghley, 'Instruction to earl of Lincoln', 26 May 1572, Digges, *Compleat Ambassador*, p. 211.

49. News from London to Guerau de Spes, 21 August 1572, *CSP Spain (Simancas)*, vol. II: 1568–79, p. 406.

Chapter III: In a Country Strange

1. Ralegh, *History of the World*, Oldys (ed.), *The Works of Sir Walter Ralegh*, vol. VI, p. 238.
2. See, for example: 25 September 1569, *CSP Foreign, Elizabeth*, vol. IX: 1569–71, p. 126.
3. See Williamson, *Hawkins of Plymouth*, pp. 169–70.
4. Quoted in Whiteheads, *Gaspard de Coligny*, pp. 227–8.
5. *CSP Foreign, Elizabeth*, vol. IX: 1569–71, p. 27.
6. Ralegh, *History of the World*, Oldys (ed.), *The Works of Sir Walter Ralegh*, vol. VI, p. 158.
7. Ralegh, *History of the World*, Oldys (ed.), *The Works of Sir Walter Ralegh*, vol. VI, p. 211.
8. Ralegh, *History of the World*, Oldys (ed.), *The Works of Sir Walter Ralegh*, vol. V, p. 344.
9. Quoted in Prouty, *George Gascoigne, Elizabethan Courtier, Soldier and Poet*, p. 54.

Chapter IV: The Deceits of Fortune

1. Harvey, *Marginalia*, p. 171.
2. Latham, *The Poems of Sir Walter Ralegh*, pp. 47–8; Rudick, *The Poems of Sir Walter Ralegh: A Historical Edition*, pp. 28–9.
3. Sturgess (ed.), *Register of Admissions to the Honourable Society of the Middle Temple*, vol. I, 1501–1781, p. 39.
4. Latham and Youings (eds.), *The Letters of Sir Walter Ralegh*, p. 37.
5. Clark, A (ed.), *Register of the University of Oxford*, vol. II, part 3, p. 48; ibid., vol. II, part 3, p. 16.
6. Sturgess, op. cit., p. 39.
7. *Calendar of the Inner Temple Records*, p. 197; *History of the Inns of Court*, pp. 265, 282.
8. Cobbett, *State Trials*, vol. II, p. 16.
9. Williamson, *Hawkins of Plymouth*, pp. 200–1.
10. Churchyard, 'A commendation of Sir H. Gilbert's ventrous journey', reprinted in Quinn, *The Voyages and Colonising Enterprises of Sir Humphrey Gilbert*, pp. 216–19.

11. Whetstone, *Touchstone for the Time.*

12. Stern, *Sir Stephen Powle of Court and Country*, p. 24.

13. Von Wedel, 'Journey Through England and Scotland', *Transactions of the Royal Historical Society*, vol. VI, p. 268.

14. Stow, *Survey of London.*

15. Jeaffreson (ed.), *Middlesex Session Rolls*, vol. I, 1550–1603, p. 111.

16. Ibid., p. 110.

17. Naunton, *Fragmenta Regalia;* Fuller, *Worthies of England*, vol. II, p. 419.

18. 'History of the World', preface, Oldys (ed.), *The Works of Sir Walter Ralegh*, vol. II, p. iii.

19. Nicholl, *The Reckoning*, p. 179.

20. See Louis Montrose, *The Subject of Elizabeth*, pp. 115–17.

21. De Quadra to Philip II, 13 September 1561, *CSP Spain (Simancas)*, vol. I: 1558–67, p. 214.

22. Clapham, *Certain Observations Concerning the Life and Reign of Queen Elizabeth*, p. 89.

23. Mears, *Queenship and Political Discourse in the Elizabethan Realms*, p. 63.

24. Bohun, *The Character of Queen Elizabeth*, pp. 351–2.

25. De Feria to Philip II, 14 December 1558, *CSP Spain (Simancas)*, vol. I: 1558–67, pp. 7–13.

26. Elizabeth I to La Mothe, the French ambassador, 15 June 1572, quoted in Strickland, *Lives of the Queens of England*, p. 361.

27. Bohun, *The Character of Queen Elizabeth*, p. 350.

28. Sir John Harington to Robert Markham, 1606, in *Nugae Antiquae*, vol. I, p. 358.

29. Ibid.

30. Ibid., p. 362.

31. 14 December 1558, *CSP Spain (Simancas)*, vol. I: 1558–67, p. 7.

32. Sir John Harington to Robert Markham, 1606, in *Nugae Antiquae*, vol. I, pp. 357–8.

33. Francis Osborne, 'Historical Memoires of Queen Elizabeth and James I', in Scott, *Secret History of the Court of James I*, p. 45.

34. Letter to Walsingham, 7 August 1578, *CSP Foreign, Elizabeth*, vol. XIII: 1578–9, pp. 121–3.

35. Quoted in Read, *Lord Burghley and Queen Elizabeth*, p. 145; Wright (ed.), *Queen Elizabeth and her Times*, Volume 2, p. 1.

36. Elizabeth to Sir Thomas Smith and Dr Wilson, 15 September 1571, *CSP Scotland*, vol. III: 1569–71, p. 701, quoted in Jenkins, *Elizabeth the Great*, p. 193.

Chapter V: The World's Eye

1. Reed, *Norwich*, Appendix 1.

2. Mears, *Queenship and Political Discourse in The Elizabethan Realms*, pp. 40–6; Adams, *Leicester and the Court*, pp. 116–20.

3. 'A treatise of the office of a councillor and principal secretary to her majesty', quoted in Mears, op. cit., p. 55.

4. 'Discourse of War in General', Oldys (ed.), *The Works of Sir Walter Ralegh*, vol. VIII, p. 257.

5. Bruce (ed.), *Diary of John Manningham*, p. 102; Burton, 1622, *Description of Leicestershire*; Bacon, *Apothegms Old and New*, in *Works*, vol. II, p. 459.

6. History of the World, preface, Oldys (ed.), *The Works of Sir Walter Ralegh*, vol. II, p. vi.

7. Nashe, 'Strange News', in *Works*, vol. I, p. 31.

8. 'Biographical introduction', in Pigman (ed.), Gascoigne, *A hundreth sundrie flowres*, pp. xxxiv–xxxviii; SP 12/86/59; quoted in Prouty, p. 61. The letter is undated, although the editor of *CSP* ascribes it to May 1572.

9. 'The Green Knight's Farewell to Fancy', Gascoigne, *Works*, vol. I, p. 381.

10. 'Discourse of War in General' in Oldys (ed.), *The Works of Sir Walter Ralegh*, vol. VIII, p. 282.

11. Harvey, *Marginalia*, p. 167.

12. McKeen, *A Memory of Honour: the Life of William Brooke, Lord Cobham*, pp. 32–4.

13. Ibid., p. 64; Rowse, *Ralegh and the Throckmortons*, p. 338.

14. McKeen, op. cit., pp. 64–5.
15. The Lords of the Council to Sir Henry Crispe, Mr. William Crispe, Sir Thomas Scotte and Edward Boyes, 21 October 1571, RYE/47/2/18b, East Sussex Records Office; *Acts of the Privy Council*, vol. VIII, 1571–5, 4 April 1574, p. 217; McKeen, *A Memory of Honour: the Life of William Brooke, Lord Cobham*, p. 298; *Acts of the Privy Council*, vol. IX, 1575–7, 31 October 1576, p. 223–4.
16. Sir William Fleetwood to Lord Burghley, 22 October 1578, *Cecil Papers*, vol. II: 1572–82, p. 224.

Chapter VI: The Virgin Queen

1. De Silva to Philip II, 12 March 1565, *CSP Spain (Simancas)*, vol. I: 1558–67, p. 404.
2. Elizabeth I, *Collected Works*, pp. 57–8.
3. Montrose, *The Subject of Elizabeth*, pp. 88–9.
4. 14 December 1558, *CSP Spain (Simancas)*, vol. I: 1558–67, p. 8.
5. Baron Brünner to the Archduke Maximilian, 5 December 1559, in Klarwill, *Queen Elizabeth and Some Foreigners*, p. 159.
6. 'It is still said by the vulgar that one Master Pickering will be her husband.' Il Schifanoya to Ottaviano Vivaldino, Mantuan Ambassador with King Philip at Brussels, 6 February 1559. *CSP Venice*, vol. VII: 1558–80 (1890), p. 27.
7. Captain Thomas Crayer to Lord Grey, 24 March 1554, *CSP Foreign, Mary*: 1553–8, p. 67.
8. *DNB*, 'Sir William Pickering'; de Quadra to the Duke of Alba, 9 September 1559, *CSP Spain (Simancas)*, vol. I: 1558–67, p. 96; de Quadra to de Feria, 29 October 1559, ibid., p. 109.
9. de Feria to Philip II, 10 May 1559, *CSP Spain (Simancas)*, vol. I: 1558–67, p. 67.
10. Dymock's Examination, 6 August 1562, *CSP Foreign, Elizabeth*, vol. V: 1562.
11. Sussex to Sir William Cecil, c. 1560, quoted in Jenkins, *Elizabeth and Leicester*, p. 71.

12. De Quadra to Philip II, 20 June 1652, *CSP Spain (Simancas)*, vol. I: 1558–67, p. 248.

13. Sir Henry Nevell to Sir William Cecil, 11 July 1570, *Cecil Papers*, vol. 1: 1306–1571, p. 474.

14. Cecil in conversation with Foix, the French ambassador, 27 November 1565, in Von Raumer, *Elizabeth and Mary Stuart*, pp. 37–8.

15. Francis Osborne, 'Historical Memoires of Queen Elizabeth and James I', in Scott, *Secret History of the Court of James I*, pp. 84–5.

16. Baron Brünner to Archduke Maximilian, King of Bohemia, 5 December 1559, in Klarwill, *Queen Elizabeth and Some Foreigners*, p. 158.

17. Quoted in Jenkins, *Elizabeth and Leicester*, p. 72.

18. 'A letter from Robert, Earl of Leicester, to a lady' quoted in Jenkins, *Elizabeth and Leicester*, p. 188.

19. Naunton, *Fragmenta Regalia*; St John Brooks, *Sir Christopher Hatton*, pp. 31–2; *DNB*, 'Sir Christopher Hatton'.

20. Christopher Hatton to Elizabeth I, 5 June 1573, in Nicolas, *Memoirs of Sir Christopher Hatton*, pp. 25–6.

21. Edward Dyer to Christopher Hatton, 9 October 1572, ibid., p. 17.

22. Simon Renard to Prince Philip, 19 February 1554, *CSP Spain*, vol. XII: 1554, pp. 119–21.

23. Baron Brünner to the Emperor Ferdinand, 6 August 1559, in Klarwill, op. cit., pp. 113–15.

24. 'The Confession of Wightman, servant to the Lord Admiral', Haynes, *State Papers*, p. 69.

25. 'Examination of Harington', 25 January 1549, *Cecil Papers*, vol. I: 1306–1571, p. 63.

26. 'The Confession of Katharine Ashley', in Haynes, *State Papers*, p. 96.

27. *DNB*, 'Thomas Seymour'.

28. Marcus, Mueller and Rose (eds.), *Elizabeth I: Collected Works*, p. 140

29. Neale, *Elizabeth I*, p. 86; *CSP Domestic, Edward, Mary and Elizabeth*, 1547–80, pp. 157–8; Letter to the Countess of Shrewsbury, Talbot Papers, vol. P, fol. 565, in Lodge (ed.), *Illustrations of British History*, vol. I, pp. 511–16; *CSP Domestic*,

Elizabeth, 1581–90, pp. 9–13; quoted in Chambers, *Elizabethan Stage*, vol. I, p. 107.

30. Francis Osborne, 'Historical Memoires of Queen Elizabeth and James I', in Scott, *Secret History of the Court of James I*, p. 76; Von Wedel, 'Journey Through England and Scotland', *Transactions of the Royal Historical Society*, vol. VI, p. 263.

31. '"News from Heaven and Hell": A Defamatory Narrative of the Earl of Leicester', Peck, DC (ed.), *English Literary Renaissance* 8 (1978), pp. 141–58.

32. Murdin (ed.), *A Collection of State Papers Relating to Affairs in the Reign of Elizabeth from 1571 to 1596*, p. 204.

33. Harington, *A Tract on the Succession to the Crown*, Markham (ed.), p. 40.

34. 29 April 1559, *CSP Spain (Simancas)*, vol. I: 1558–67, p. 63; Brantôme, *Famous Women*; Jenkins, *Elizabeth the Great*, p. 251.

35. 'Conversations with Drummond' in Herford and Simpson (eds.), *Ben Jonson: Works*, vol. I, p. 142.

36. Quoted in Chamberlain, *The Private Character of Queen Elizabeth*, pp. 166.

37. Francis Osborne, 'Historical Memoires of Queen Elizabeth and James I', in Scott, *Secret History of the Court of James I*, p. 75.

38. Rowse, *The Case Books of Simon Forman: Sex and Society in Shakespeare's Age*, p. 31.

39. Gascoigne, *Works*, vol. II, p. 554.

40. Quoted in Montrose, *The Subject of Elizabeth*, p. 193.

41. Elizabeth, Lady Leighton to Sir Thomas Leighton, undated but after 1579, in Nicolas, *Memoirs of Sir Christopher Hatton*, p. 228.

42. Hurault, *A Journal Of All That Was Accomplished by Monsieur de Maisse, Ambassador in England from King Henri IV to Queen Elizabeth Anno Domini 1597* (ed.) and trans. Harrison, pp. 27, 40.

43. De Silva to Philip II, 2 July 1564, *CSP Spain (Simancas)*, vol. I: 1558–67, p. 366.

44. De Silva to Philip II, 22 July 1564, ibid., p. 369.

45. De Silva to Philip II, 5 May 1565, ibid., vol. I: 1558–67, p. 429.

46. Thomas Morgan to Mary Stuart, 20 July 1585, Murdin (ed.), *State Papers*, p. 449.

47. Peck (ed.), *Leicester's Commonwealth*, p. 72.

48. Ibid., p. 95.

49. Bath MSS; Hatton to Leicester, 18 June 1578, from the court at Hampton, quoted in St John Brooks, *Sir Christopher Hatton*, p. 170.

Chapter VII: The Wind of Faction

1. Nelson, *Monstrous Adversary*, p. 191.

2. Ibid., pp. 47–9; Camden, *Annales*, vol. 3, p. 223; *DNB*, 'Rowland Yorke'; 'Gascoigne's Voyage into Holland', Gascoigne, *Works*, vol. I, p. 354ff.

3. Lodge (ed.), *Illustrations of British History*, vol. II, p. 16.

4. Read, *Lord Burghley and Queen Elizabeth*, pp. 128–30.

5. Nelson, *Monstrous Adversary*, p. 167.

6. Bossy, *Giordano Bruno and the Embassy Affair*, p. 213.

7. Arundell interrogation, PRO SP12/151/46, ff. 103–4.

8. BL Cotton Titus C.6, ff. 5–6.

9. Arundell interrogation, op. cit.

10. Howard to Elizabeth I, 29 December 1580, BL Cotton Titus C.6, ff. 7–8.

11. Ibid.; Arundell interrogation, op. cit.

12. Arundell, 'A True Declaration of the Earl of Oxford's Detestable Vices and Unpure life', PRO SP 12/151/45, ff. 100–2.

13. Bossy, 'English Catholics and the French Marriage', *Recusant History*, 5, p. 3.

14. Quinn, *The Voyages and Colonising Enterprises of Sir Humphrey Gilbert*, p. 335.

15. *CSP Spain (Simancas)*, vol. II: 1568–79, p. 583, p. 591, p. 607.

16. Details of the ships are in State Papers Domestic, Elizabeth SP 12/126, printed in Quinn, *The Voyages and Colonising Enterprises of Sir Humphrey Gilbert*, pp. 209–12; for the ownership of the *Falcon* see Quinn, *England and the Discovery of America 1481–1620*, p. 250.

17. Quinn, ibid., p. 329–33.
18. Churchyard's poem is reproduced in Quinn, ibid., pp. 216–19.

Chapter VIII: The Fort of Fame

1. Quinn, *The Voyages and Colonising Enterprises of Sir Humphrey Gilbert*, p. 206.
2. *DNB*, 'Sir Francis Knollys'.
3. Ewen, *The Golden Chalice: A Documented Narrative of an Elizabethan Pirate*; Castelnau to Walsingham, 13 June 1585, *CSP Foreign, Elizabeth*, vol. XIX: August 1584–August 1585, p. 519.
4. 'Observations on the Navy and Sea Service', Oldys (ed.), *The Works of Sir Walter Ralegh*, vol. VIII, p. 347.
5. Taylor (ed.), *The Troublesome Voyage of Captain Fenton 1582–3*, p. xli.
6. *Acts of the Privy Council*, vol. VIII, 1571–5, pp. 342–3.
7. Quinn, *England and the Discovery of America*, p. 249.
8. Taylor (ed.), *The Troublesome Voyage of Captain Fenton 1582–3*, p. 202.
9. Ibid., pp. 196–7.
10. Quinn, *The Voyages and Colonising Enterprises of Sir Humphrey Gilbert*, p. 207.
11. Ibid., pp. 213, 215.
12. 'Observations on the Navy and Sea Service', Oldys (ed.), *The Works of Sir Walter Ralegh*, vol. VIII, p. 345.
13. Quinn, 'A Portuguese Pilot in the English Service', *England and the Discovery of America*, p. 250.
14. Sir John Gilbert to Sir Francis Walsingham, 20 December 1578, SP 12/127 24, in Quinn, *The Voyages and Colonising Enterprises of Sir Humphrey Gilbert*, pp. 215–6.
15. Jilbert v Hawkins, PRO Chancery, C. 24/50.
16. Markham (ed.), *Voyages of Pedro Sarmiento de Gamboa*, pp. 191–4, 195.
17. Taylor (ed.), *The Troublesome Voyage of Captain Fenton 1582–3*, p. 196–7.

18. *Acts of the Privy Council*, vol. XI, 1578–80, p. 108.
19. Quinn, *The Voyages and Colonising Enterprises of Sir Humphrey Gilbert*, p. 222.
20. *Acts of the Privy Council*, 28 May 1579, vol. XI, 1578–80, p. 143.

Chapter IX: Excess of Duty

1. Bossy, 'English Catholics and the French Marriage', *Recusant History*, 5, p. 5; see also Peck, DC, 'Raleigh, Sidney, Oxford, and the Catholics, 1579', *Notes and Queries*, vol. 223, 1978, pp. 427–31.
2. Rowse, *Ralegh and the Throckmortons*, p. 69.
3. Mendoza to Zayas, 15 January 1579, *CSP Spain (Simancas)*, vol. II: 1568–79, p. 627.
4. Mendoza to Zayas, 26 July 1579, ibid., p. 681; Camden, *Annales*.
5. Interrogation of Charles Arundell, PRO SP 12/151/47, ff. 105–6.
6. Peck (ed.), *Leicester's Commonwealth*, p. 92.
7. Read, *Lord Burghley and Queen Elizabeth*, pp. 214–15.
8. Charles Arundell, 'A true declaration of the Earl of Oxford's detestable vices and unpure life,' PRO SP12/151/45, ff. 100–2.
9. Oldys (ed.), *The Works of Sir Walter Ralegh*, vol. VI, p. 479.
10. Deposition of Charles Arundell, PRO SP 12/151/48, ff. 107–8.
11. Charles Arundell, 'A true declaration of the Earl of Oxford's detestable vices and unpure life,' PRO SP12/151/45, ff. 100–2; Henry Howard to Elizabeth I, *c.* 29 December 1580, BL Cotton Titus C.6, ff 7–8.
12. Mendoza to Philip II, 11 November 1579, *CSP Spain (Simancas)*, vol. II: 1568–79, p. 704.
13. Glasgow, 'Elizabethan ships pictured on Smerwick map, 1580, *Mariners Mirror*, vol. 52, 1966, pp. 157–65.
14. Stern, *Sir Stephen Powle of Court and Country*, p. 32.
15. Peck (ed.), *Leicester's Commonwealth*, p. 92.
16. 'Articles whereof Oxford would have accused Leicester', PRO SP 12/151/50, f. 110.
17. Howard to Elizabeth, *c.* 29 December 1580, BL Cotton Titus C.6, ff. 7–8.

18. Ibid.
19. Charles Arundell, PRO SP12/151/46, ff. 103–4; Howard to Elizabeth, *c.* 29 December 1580, BL Cotton Titus C.6, ff. 7–8.
20. Howard to Elizabeth I, undated but early January 1581, BL Cotton Titus C.6 ff. 5–6.

Chapter X: The Right-flourishing Man

1. Leicester to Walsingham, 29 August 1578, *CSP Foreign, Elizabeth*, vol. XIII: 1578–79, p. 159.
2. Nelson, *Monstrous Adversary*, p. 229; Rowse, *Ralegh and the Throckmortons*, p. 78.
3. Cox and Norman (eds.), *Survey of London:* vol. XIII: St Margaret, Westminster, part II: Whitehall I.
4. *Acts of the Privy Council 1578–80*, vol. XI, pp. 384, 388.
5. *DNB*, 'Sir Thomas Perrott'.
6. Quinn, *The Voyages and Colonising Enterprises of Sir Humphrey Gilbert*, pp. 230–1.
7. Quinn and Cheshire, *The New-Found Land of Stephen Parmenius*, p. 43; *DNB*, 'William Borough'.
8. Dunlop, *Palaces and Progresses of Elizabeth I*, pp. 62–5.
9. *Acts of the Privy Council 1578–80*, vol. XI, 1578–80, p. 421.
10. Howard to Elizabeth, *c.* 29 December 1580, BL Cotton Titus C.6, ff. 7–8.
11. Oldys (ed.), *The Works of Sir Walter Ralegh*, vol. VI, p. 466.
12. 11 July 1580, *Acts of the Privy Council 1578–80*, vol. XII, p. 93.
13. 'Information which Don Guerau De Spes obtained in England, and related on his coming to Spain', May 1572, *CSP Spain (Simancas)*, vol. II: 1568–79, p. 388.
14. Ridley, *Elizabeth I*, pp. 220–1.
15. Oldys (ed.), *The Works of Sir Walter Ralegh*, vol. V, pp. 789–90.
16. Mendoza to Philip II, 23 March 1580, *CSP Spain (Simancas)*, vol. III: 1580–86, p. 21.
17. *DNB*, 'Arthur Grey, fourteenth Baron Grey of Wilton'.
18. *CSP Spain (Simancas)*, vol. III: 1580–86, p. 25.

19. Sir Edward Horsey to Lord Burghley, 1 June 1580 from the Isle of Wight, *CSP Domestic, Elizabeth*, vol. 140, 1547–80, p. 658.

20. 15 July 1580, *CSP Domestic: Edward, Mary and Elizabeth*, 1547–80, p. 665.

21. Read, *Lord Burghley and Queen Elizabeth*, p. 246.

22. *Acts of the Privy Council*, vol. XII, 1580–1, p. 100.

23. This and other details of Ralegh's campaign are taken from Hooker's *Chronicles of Ireland*, published in the 1587 edition of Holinshed's *Chronicles*.

24. *DNB*, 'Thomas Butler, tenth Earl of Ormond'.

25. Glasgow, 'Elizabethan ships pictured on Smerwick map, 1580', *Mariners Mirror*, vol. 52, 1966, p. 159.

26. Mendoza to Philip II, 16 October 1580, *CSP Spain (Simancas)*, vol. III: 1580–86, p. 53; Official Report to Walsingham, 11 November 1580, Pope-Hennessey, *Sir Walter Ralegh in Ireland*, p. 209.

27. Spenser, *View of the State of Ireland*, p. 139.

28. O'Rahilly, *Massacre at Smerwick*, p. 5.

29. Thomas Baudewyn to the Earl of Shrewsbury, 22 December 1580, in Lodge (ed.), *Illustrations of British History*, vol. II, p. 186; Steven W. May, *Sir Walter Ralegh*, p. 4.

30. Pope-Hennessey, *Sir Walter Ralegh in Ireland*, pp. 212–14.

31. Thomas Baudewyn to the Earl of Shrewsbury, op. cit.

32. Nelson, *Monstrous Adversary*, p. 249ff.

33. PRO SP15/27A[/46], ff. 81–2; reprinted in *HMC Bath*, vol. 5, pp. 204–5.

34. Mendoza to Philip II, 9 January 1581, *CSP Spain (Simancas)*, vol. III: 1580–86, p. 78.

35. Jilbert v Hawkins, PRO Chancery, C. 24/50.

36. Latham and Youings (eds.), *The Letters of Sir Walter Ralegh*, p. 3.

37. 'A discourse touching a war with Spain', Oldys (ed.), *The Works of Sir Walter Ralegh*, vol. VIII, pp. 304–5.

38. Latham and Youings (eds.), *The Letters of Sir Walter Ralegh*, pp. 6–7.

39. Ibid., pp. 1–2.

40. *DNB*, 'Thomas Butler, tenth Earl of Ormond'.

Chapter XI: The Sacred Anchor

1. Montrose, *The Subject of Elizabeth*, pp. 122–7; Doran, 'Virginity, Divinity and Power: the Portraits of Elizabeth I', in Doran and Freeman (eds.), *The Myth of Elizabeth*, p. 186ff.
2. Fuller, *Worthies*, vol. I, p. 419.
3. Ibid., p. 419–20.
4. *CSP Foreign, Elizabeth*, vol. VII: 1564–65, pp. 326.
5. Dunlop, *Palaces and Progresses of Elizabeth I*, p. 63.
6. Rudick (ed.), *The Poems of Sir Walter Ralegh*, p. 58.
7. Naunton, *Fragmenta Regalia*.
8. Rudick (ed.), *Poems*, p. 110; the poem is often given to Sir Edward Dyer, on the basis of an anonymous attribution from a usually reliable source. However, Powle's status as a friend of Ralegh's – a fact not acknowledged in attribution studies – carries greater weight.
9. Ridley, *Elizabeth I*, p. 240.
10. Mendoza to Philip II, 25 December 1581, *CSP Spain (Simancas)*, vol. III: 1580–6, pp. 245–6.
11. Mendoza to Philip II, 1 March 1582, *CSP Spain (Simancas)*, vol. III: 1580–6, p. 249, p. 299; Read, *Lord Burghley and Queen Elizabeth*, pp. 270–1.
12. *Queen Elizabeth and the Revolt of the Netherlands*, pp. 16–17.
13. BL MS Cotton Galba C VII f. 205r–207v. William Herle to the Earl of Leicester, 20 March 1582, www.livesandletters.ac.uk/herle/letters/029.html
14. *Journal of Sir Francis Walsingham*, p. 93; *CSP Foreign, Elizabeth*, vol. XV, 1581–2, p. 580; Ralegh, 'A Discourse of the Invention of Ships', Oldys (ed.), *The Works of Sir Walter Ralegh*, vol. VIII, p. 381.
15. Pope-Hennessey, *Sir Walter Ralegh in Ireland*, pp. 218–19.
16. *Calendar of the Carew Manuscripts*, vol. II, pp. 325–7.
17. Nicolas, *Memoirs of Sir Christopher Hatton*, p. 272.
18. Ridley, *Elizabeth I*, p. 243.
19. Thomas Doyley to Walsingham, 3 June 1582, *CSP Foreign, Elizabeth*, vol. XVI: May–December 1582, p. 61.

20. Nicolas, *Memoirs of Sir Christopher Hatton*, pp. 277–8.
21. *HMC Rutland*, vol. I, p. 142.
22. St John Brookes, *Sir Christopher Hatton*, p. 303.

Chapter XII: A Durable Fire

1. *CSP Colonial: America and West Indies*, Addenda, 1574–1674, p. 17.
2. Maurice Browne to John Thynne, *c.* 1 May 1583, in Quinn and Cheshire, *The New Found Land of Stephen Parmenius*, p. 207.
3. Thynne Papers, TH/VOL/V 1574–1603, f. 254.
4. Gater and Wheeler (eds.), *Survey of London:* vol. 18: *St Martin-in-the-Fields II: The Strand*, pp. 84–6.
5. Thomas Challoner to Sir William Cecil, 2 September 1559, *CSP Foreign, Elizabeth*, vol. I: 1558–9, p. 536.
6. Quinn and Cheshire, *The New Found Land of Stephen Parmenius*, p. 205.
7. Latham and Youings (eds.), *The Letters of Sir Walter Ralegh*, p. 12.
8. Quinn and Cheshire, op. cit., p. 205.
9. Woolley, *The Queen's Conjuror*, p. 198; Dunlop, *Palaces and Progresses of Elizabeth I*, p. 74 ff.
10. Latham and Youings (eds.), *The Letters of Sir Walter Ralegh*, p. 13.
11. Dunlop, op. cit., p. 83.
12. Brushfield, *Devonshire Association, Reports and Transactions*, vol. XII, pp. 182–3.
13. Bossy, *Giordano Bruno and the Embassy Affair*, pp. 15–16.
14. Loomie, *The Spanish Elizabethans: The English Exiles at the Court of Philip II*, pp. 22–3; *DNB*, 'Thomas Morgan'; Shrewsbury to Burghley, 28 February 1572, *CSP Scotland*, vol. IV: 1571–4, p. 138.
15. Naunton, *Fragmenta Regalia*.
16. Read, *Lord Burghley and Queen Elizabeth*, p. 276.
17. Latham and Youings (eds.), *The Letters of Sir Walter Ralegh*, p. 14.
18. Nicholls, *The Progresses and Public Processions of Queen Elizabeth*, vol. II, p. 403.

19. *HMC Rutland*, vol. I, p. 150.

20. See, for example, Nelson, *Monstrous Adversary*, p. 291.

21. Edward Hayes, in Hakluyt (ed.), *Principal Voyages* –, Volume 3, p. 190.

22. Purchas, *Pilgrimes*, vol. III, p. 808.

23. Quinn and Cheshire, *The New Found Land of Stephen Parmenius*, pp. 58–66.

24. Roger Aston to Leicester, 7 July 1582, *CSP Scotland*, vol. VI: 1581–3, p. 138; *DNB*, 'James Stewart'.

25. Read, *Walsingham*, vol. I, p. 223.

26. Cotton MSS, Caligula C ix, f. 95, quoted in Read, *Walsingham*, vol. I, p. 223.

27. Churchyard, *Churchyard's Chip's Concerning Scotland*, p. 72.

28. James VI to Elizabeth, 29 March 1583, *Cecil*, vol. XIII: Addenda, p. 217; *DNB*, 'Sir William Stewart'.

29. Read, *Walsingham*, vol. I, p. 223.

30. Ibid.

31. Bossy, *Giordano Bruno and the Embassy Affair*, pp. 75–83.

32. Jenkins, *Elizabeth the Great*, p. 275.

33. 'A Discovery of Francis Throckmorton's Treasons', *Harleian Miscellany*, vol. III, p. 189.

34. Sir William Cecil to Elizabeth, 6 October 1569, *CSP Scotland*, vol. II: 1563–9, pp. 683–4.

35. Nicolas, *Memoirs of Sir Christopher Hatton*, pp. 168–9.

36. Bossy, *Giordano Bruno and the Embassy Affair*, p. 207.

Chapter XIII: Hollow Servants

1. Mendoza to Philip II, 26 January 1584, *CSP Spain (Simancas)*, vol. III: 1580–6, pp. 513–15.

2. Strong, *The Cult of Elizabeth*, pp. 206–11.

3. VCH *Hampshire*, vol. IV, pp. 5–14.

4. Durrant Cooper, 'Notices of Anthony Babington of Dethick, and of the Conspiracy of 1586', *The Reliquary*, April 1562, pp. 182–3.

5. Nuncio Castelli to the Cardinal of Como, 2 May 1583, in *Mary Stuart and the Babington Plot*, p. 169.
6. *CSP Domestic* Addenda, 1580–1625, p. 104.
7. Hakluyt, op. cit.
8. Quinn and Cheshire, *The New Found Land of Stephen Parmenius*, p. 271.
9. Gilbert, *Queene Elizabethes Achademy*, pp. 3–4.
10. Ibid., p. 5.
11. Shirley, *Thomas Harriot, A Biography*, p. 85.
12. Lloyd, *State Worthies*, p. 564.
13. Jeaffreson (ed.), *Middlesex Session Rolls*, vol. I, 1550–1603, p. 150.
14. Gilpin to Walsingham, 2 July 1584, *CSP Foreign, Elizabeth*, vol. XVIII: July 1583–July 1584 , p. 580.
15. Latham and Youings (eds.), *The Letters of Sir Walter Ralegh*, pp. 24–5.

Chapter XIV: *Amore et Virtute*

1. Bohun, *Character of Queen Elizabeth*, p. 353.
2. *CSP Domestic, Elizabeth*, 1581–90 (1865), p. 193.
3. Thomas Rogers to Walsingham, 11 August 1585, *CSP Foreign, Elizabeth*, vol. XIX: August 1584–August 1585, p. 716; Peck (ed.), Leicester's Commonwealth, pp. 5–13, to which the following paragraphs are indebted.
4. Taylor (ed.), *The original writings & correspondence of the two Richard Hakluyts*, pp. 367–8.
5. Hakluyt, op. cit.
6. Read, *Lord Burghley and Queen Elizabeth*, p. 299.
7. D'Ewes, *The Journal of Sir Simonds D'Ewes*, op. cit.
8. Relation by Sir Francis Englefield to the Pope and Philip II, 8 January 1586, *CSP Scotland*, vol. 8: 1585–86, No 234, pp. 180–1.
9. D'Ewes, op. cit.
10. Holinshed, op. cit.
11. Ibid.
12. Von Wedel, 'Journey Through England and Scotland' in *Transactions of the Royal Historical Society*, p. 267.

13. Chambers, *The Elizabethan Stage*, vol. I, pp. 155–66.
14. Harrison, *Description of England*, p. 103.
15. Jehan Scheyfve, *CSP Spain*, vol. X: 1550–2, p. 443.
16. Mendoza to Philip II, 22 February 1585, *CSP Spain (Simancas)*, vol. III: 1580–6, p. 532
17. Latham and Youings (eds.), *The Letters of Sir Walter Ralegh*, p. 28.
18. Quoted in Oldys (ed.), *The Works of Sir Walter Ralegh*, vol. I, p. 62
19. St John Brooks, *Sir Christopher Hatton*, p. 304.
20. Charles Thynne to Francis Walsingham, [undated] 1585, *CSP Foreign, Elizabeth*, vol. XX, pp. 260–1.
21. *DNB*, 'William Parry'.
22. Thomas Morgan to Mary Stuart, 9 April 1585, Murdin (ed.), *State Papers*, pp. 439–40.
23. *CSP Scotland*, vol. VIII: 1585–6, p. 182.
24. Munk, *Roll*, vol. I, p. 66; Nelson, *Monstrous Adversary*, pp. 100, 129.
25. Charles Paget to Mary Stuart, 18 July 1585, *CSP Scotland*, vol. VIII: 1585–6, pp. 26–31.
26. Leader, *Mary Queen of Scots in Captivity*, pp. 158–63.
27. Sir Thomas Rowe, Lord Mayor of London, to the Privy Council, 17 October 1569, *Cecil Papers*, vol. I: 1306–1571, p. 436.
28. *CSP Scotland*, vol. V: 1574–81, pp. 127–8, 140; Sir Francis Walsingham to Lord Burghley, 30 April 1575, *CSP Scotland*, vol. 5: 1574–81, p. 134; Dr Edward Atslow to Lord Burghley, 18 August 1575, *CSP Scotland*, vol. V: 1574–81, p. 176; Sir Wm. Fleetwood, Recorder of London, to Lord Burghley, 15 September 1575, *Cecil Papers*, vol. II: 1572–82, p. 110.
29. *DNB*, 'Edward Atslow'; Leader, *Mary Queen of Scots in Captivity*, p. 477.
30. Murdin (ed.), *State Papers*, vol. II, p. 452.
31. Pollen and MacMahon, *The Venerable Philip Howard, Earl of Arundel*, pp. 123, 136.
32. *CSP Domestic, Elizabeth*, Addenda, vol. XXIX, No. 9, 1580–1625, p. 141; 15 March 1585, *CSP Spain (Simancas)*, vol. III: 1580–6, p. 534

33. Queen Elizabeth's Warrant to Sir John Perrot, 8 February 1585, *CSP Colonial, America and West Indies*, vol. IX: 1574–1674, Addenda, p. 27.

34. Mendoza to Philip II, 22 February 1585, *CSP Spain (Simancas)*, vol. III: 1580–6, p. 532.

35. Hakluyt, *Discourse of Western Planting*, pp. 16–27.

Chapter XV: The Less Afraid

1. Instructions for Thomas Bodleigh, sent to the King of Denmark, 17 April 1585, *CSP Foreign, Elizabeth*, vol. XIX: August 1584–August 1585, p. 415.

2. Pollen and MacMahon, *The Venerable Philip Howard, Earl of Arundel*, pp. 123, 143.

3. Mendoza to Philip II, 4 May 1585, *CSP Spain (Simancas)*, vol. III: 1580–86, pp. 536–7; Pedro de Çubiaub to –, 1 May 1585, *CSP Foreign, Elizabeth*, vol. XIX: August 1584–August 1585, p. 454.

4. Latham and Youings (eds.), *The Letters of Sir Walter Ralegh*, p. 186.

5. Thomas Rogers to Walsingham, 11 August 1585, *CSP Foreign, Elizabeth*, vol. XIX, August 1584–August 1585, pp. 715–8.

6. 20 June 1585, *CSP Domestic, Elizabeth*, 1581–90, p. 246.

7. Mendoza to Philip II, 1 June 1585, *CSP Spain (Simancas)*, vol. III: 1580–6, p. 538.

8. A.B. to Burghley, *CSP Domestic*, Addenda, 1580–1625, p. 182.

9. Thomas Morgan to the Queen of Scots, *Cecil Papers*, vol. III: 1583–9 (1889), pp. 128–131.

10. D'Ewes, *The Journal of Sir Simonds D'Ewes*, p. 505.

11. Quoted in Read, *Walsingham*, vol. I, p. 250.

12. *CSP Domestic, Elizabeth*, 1581–90, p. 285.

13. Bruce (ed.), *Correspondence of the Earl of Leicester from the Low Countries*, p. 207.

14. Latham and Youings (eds.), *The Letters of Sir Walter Ralegh*, pp. 32–3.

15. Thomas Morgan to Mary, 21 March 1586, *CSP Scotland*, vol. VIII: 1585–6, p. 275.

16. Cherelles to Mary, 2 April 1586, ibid., p. 299.

17. Stafford to Walsingham, 23 March 1586, *CSP Foreign, Elizabeth,* vol. XX: September 1585–May 1586, pp. 468–9.

18. *Archaeologia Cantia,* p. 60.

19. Sir Francis Walsingham to Sir Ralph Sadler, 15 November 1584, *State Papers of Ralph Sadler,* vol. II, p. 451.

20. Lord Buckhurst to Walsingham, 31 July 1588, *CSP Domestic, Elizabeth,* 1581–90, p. 518; *Archaeologia Cantia,* p. 63.

21. Bacqueville to Walsingham, 29 March 1586, *CSP Foreign, Elizabeth,* vol. XX: September 1585–May 1586, p. 496.

22. Maliverey Catilyn to Walsingham, 22 April 1586, *CSP Foreign, Elizabeth,* vol. XX: September 1585–May 1586, p. 713.

23. Cobbett, *State Trials,* vol. I, pp. 1,130–1.

24. Ibid., p. 1,157.

25. *CSP Scotland,* vol. VIII, 1585–6, p. 687; Camden, *Annales.*

26. John Chamberlain to Sir Dudley Carlton, 10 June 1613, in Chamberlain, *Letters,* vol. I, p. 457.

27. Cobbett, *State Trials,* vol. I, p. 1,139.

28. 30 June, *CSP Spain (Simancas),* vol. III: 1580–6, p. 588.

29. Confession of Robert Poley, *CSP Scotland,* vol. VIII: 1585–6, p. 600.

30. Ibid., p. 683.

31. Quinn, *The Voyages and Colonising Enterprises of Sir Humphrey Gilbert,* p. 212; see also Latham and Youings (eds.), *The Letters of Sir Walter Ralegh,* pp. 60, 74, 222.

32. 'Babington's motion the day afore his death', 19 September, *CSP Scotland,* vol. IX: 1586–88.

33. Mendoza to Philip II, 10 September 1586, *CSP Spain (Simancas),* vol. III: 1580–6, pp. 623–4.

34. Gilbert Gifford to Thomas Phelippes in cipher, December 1586, *CSP Scotland,* vol. IX: 1586–8, pp. 222–3.

35. 157 DD/2P/15/1, 18 March 1587, Nottinghamshire Archives.

36. 5 October 1586, *CSP Ireland,* 1586–8, p. 168.

37. Queen Elizabeth to the Lord Deputy, *CSP Ireland,* 1586–8, p. 271.

38. Hakluyt, *Voyages*, vol. VI, pp. 434–5.

39. *CSP Spain (Simancas)*, vol. IV: 1587–1603, p. 1.

40. Hieronimo Lippomano to the Doge and Senate, *CSP Venetian*, p. 237.

41. Philip II to Mendoza, 31 March 1587, *CSP Spain (Simancas)*, vol. IV: 1587–1603, p. 56.

42. 'A discourse sent by Secretary Davison, being then prisoner in the Tower of London, unto Secretary Walsingham, 20 February 1587, *CSP Scotland*, vol. IX, 1586–88, pp. 287–95.

43. 'Discourse of War in General' in Oldys (ed.), *The Works of Sir Walter Ralegh*, vol. VIII, p. 258.

44. Marcus, Mueller and Rose (eds.), *Elizabeth I: Collected Works*, p. 309.

BIBLIOGRAPHY

Manuscript Collections, Calendars, Reports and Reference Works

Acts of the Privy Council, 1542–1604 JR Dasent (ed.), 32 vols, London, 1890–1907.

British Library, London (BL): Cotton, Harley, Lansdowne, Sloane.

Calendar of State Papers (CSP): Colonial, Domestic, Foreign, Ireland, Scotland, Spain (Simancas), Vatican Archives, Venice.

Dictionary of National Biography (*DNB*).

Historical Manuscripts Commission calendars and reports (HMC): Bath, Carew, Rutland, Salisbury, Talbot.

Letters and Papers, Foreign and Domestic, Henry VIII.

Public Record Office, London (PRO).

Victoria County History (VCH).

Individual titles

Adams, Simon, *Leicester and the Court: Essays on Elizabethan Politics*, Manchester, 2002.

Adams, Simon (ed.), *Household Accounts and Disbursement Books of Robert Dudley, Earl of Leicester, 1558–1561, 1584–1586*, Cambridge, 1995.

Aiken, Lucy, *Memoirs of the Court of Queen Elizabeth* (2 vols), London, 1819.

Andrews, Kenneth R, *Elizabethan Privateering: English Privateering During the Spanish War, 1585–1603*, Cambridge, 1964.

Appelby, John C., *Calendar of Information Relating to Ireland from the High Court of Admiralty Examinations 1536–1641*, Dublin, 1992.

Archer, Jane Elizabeth, Goldring, Elizabeth and Knight, Sarah (eds.), *The Progresses, Pageants and Entertainments of Queen Elizabeth I*, Oxford, 2007.

Ascham, Roger, *The Whole Works* (3 vols), Rev Dr JA Giles (ed.), London, 1865.

Aubrey, John, *Brief Lives*, London, 1949.

Aubrey, John et al, *Letters Written by Eminent Persons* (2 vols), London, 1813.

Austen, Gillian, *George Gascoigne*, Woodbridge, 2008.

Axton, Marie, *The Queen's Two Bodies*, London, 1977.

Bacon, Sir Francis, *The Works of Francis Bacon* (10 vols), London, 1819.

Bagwell, Richard, *Ireland Under the Tudors*, London, 1890.

Batho, G.R. (ed.), *The Household Papers of Henry Percy, Ninth Earl of Northumberland (1564–1632)*, London, 1962.

Beer, Anna, *Bess: the Life of Lady Ralegh*, London, 2005.

Beer, Anna, *Sir Walter Ralegh and his Readers in the Seventeenth Century*, Basingstoke, 1997.

Beer, Barrett L., *Tudor England Observed: the World of John Stow*, Stroud, 1998.

Bernard, G.W., *The Tudor Nobility*, Manchester, 1992.

Berry, Philippa, *Of Chastity and Power: Elizabethan Literature and the Unmarried Queen*, London, 1994.

Besant, Walter, *London North of the Thames*, London, 1911.

Bindoff, S.T., *The Fame of Sir Thomas Gresham*, London, 1973.

Bindoff, S.T., *The House of Commons, 1509–1558* (3 vols), London, 1982.

Birch, Thomas (ed.), *Memoirs of the Reign of Elizabeth From the Year 1581 Till her Death*, London, 1754.

Bohun, Edmund, *The Character of Queen Elizabeth*, London, 1693.

Bonar, James, *Theories of Population from Raleigh to Arthur Young*, London, 1931.

Borman, Tracy, *Elizabeth's Women*, London, 2009.

Bossy, John, 'English Catholics and the French Marriage 1577–81', *Recusant History*, 5, 1959.

Bossy, John, *Giordano Bruno and the Embassy Affair*, London, 1992.

Bowes, Robert, *The Correspondence of Robert Bowes*, London, 1842.

Brady, Ciaran, *The Chief Governors: the Rise and Fall of Reform Government in Tudor Ireland 1536–1588*, Cambridge, 1994.

Brantome, Pierre de Bourdeille, Seigneur de, *Famous Women*, London, 1908.

Browne, William, *Britannia's Pastorals*, London, 1625.

Bruce (ed.), *Correspondence of Robert Dudley, Earl of Leicester During His Government of the Low Countries in the years 1585 and 1586*, London, 1844.

Bruce, John (ed.), *Diary of John Manningham*, Westminster, 1868.

Brushfield, T.N., 'London and Surburban Residences of Sir Walter Ralegh', *Western Antiquary*, IV, 1886.

Brushfield, T.N., *Ralegh Miscellanea* (Reprinted from the Transactions of the Devonshire Association for the Advancement of Science, Literature and Art), 1909.

Brushfield, T.N., *Raleghana* (Reprinted from the Transactions of the Devonshire Association for the Advancement of Science, Literature and Art), 1896.

Brydges, Sir Samuel E and Haslewood, Joseph (eds.), *England's Helicon* (3rd ed.), London, 1812.

Burrows, Montagu, *Worthies of All Souls*, London, 1874.

Burton, William, *Description of Leicestershire* (2 vols), London, 1790.

Buxton, John, *Sir Philip Sidney and the English Renaissance*, London, 1954.

Camden, William, *Britannia*, London, 1610.

Camden, William, *Annales, the True and Royall History of . . . Elizabeth Queene of England*, London, 1625.

Carew, Richard, *The Survey of Cornwall (1602)*, Redruth, 2000.

Cayley, Arthur, *The Life of Sir Walter Ralegh, Knt* (2 vols), London, 1805.

Chamberlain, Frederick, *The Private Character of Queen Elizabeth*, London, 1921.

Chamberlain, John, *Letters* (2 vols ed. N.E. McClure), Philadelphia, 1939.

Chambers, E.K., *The Elizabethan Stage* (4 vols), Oxford, 1923

Chapman, George, *The Works* (2 vols), London, 1875.

Chidsey, Donald Barr, *Sir Humphrey Gilbert: Elizabeth's Racketeer*, New York, 1932.

Churchyard, Thomas, *A Discourse of the Queenes Maiesties entertainement in Suffolk and Norfolk . . . whereunto is adjoyned a commendation of Sir H. Gilberts ventrous journey*, London, 1578.

Churchyard, Thomas, *A Generall Rehearsall of Warres*, London, 1579.

Churchyard, Thomas, *Churchyard's Chip's Concerning Scotland*, London, 1817.

Clapham, John, *Elizabeth of England: An edition of the manuscript entitled 'Certain Observations concerning the life and Reign of Queen Elizabeth'* (ed. E.P. and Conyers Read), Philadelphia, 1951.

Clark, Andrew (ed.), *Register of the University of Oxford 1571–162*, Oxford, 1887.

Clarke, E.G., *Ralegh and Marlowe*, New York, 1965.

Clifford, Arthur (ed.), *The State Papers and Letters of Sir Ralph Sadler* (2 vols), Edinburgh, 1809.

Cobbett, William, *Complete Collection of State Trials*, London, 1816.

Colby, F.T. (ed.), *The Visitation of the County of Devon in the Year 1620*, London, 1872.

Colville, John, *Original Letters of Mr John Colville 1582–1603*, Edinburgh, 1858.

Cooper, Charles Henry, *Annals of Cambridge* (4 vols), Cambridge, 1842.

Coote, Stephen, *A Play of Passion: the Life of Sir Walter Ralegh*, London, 1993.

Cox, M.H. and Forrest, G.T., *Survey of London:* vol. XIII: St Margaret, Westminster, part II: Whitehall I, London, 1930.

Cresswell, Beatrix F. (ed.), *Edwardian Inventories for the City and County of Exeter*, London, 1916.

Dalrymple, David (ed.), *The Secret Correspondence of Sir Robert Cecil*, London, 1766.

Davis, H.H., 'The Military Career of Thomas North', *Huntingdon Library Quarterly*, 12, 1948–9.

Daybell, James (ed.), *Women and Politics in Early Modern England*, Aldershot, 2004.

Dee, John, *The Diaries of John Dee* (ed. Edward Fenton), Charlbury, 1998.

D'Ewes, Sir Simonds, *The Journals of all the Parliaments during the Reign of Queen Elizabeth, both of the House of Lords and House of Commons*, London, 1682.

Digges, Dudley, *The Compleat Ambassador*, London, 1655.

Doran, Susan, *Monarchy and Matrimony: The Courtships of Elizabeth I*, London, 1996.

Doran, Susan and Freeman, Thomas S. (eds.), *The Myth of Elizabeth*, Basingstoke, 2003.

Doran, Susan (ed.), *Elizabeth: The Exhibition at the National Maritime Museum*, Greenwich, 2003.

Dovey, Zillah M., *An Elizabethan Progress*, Stroud, 1996.

Drayton, Michael, *Complete Works* (3 vols), London, 1876.

Duffy, Eamonn, *The Stripping of the Altars* 2nd ed, London, 2005.

Dugdale, Sir William, *History and Antiquity of the Four Inns of Court*, London, 1780.

Duncan-Jones, Katherine, *Sir Philip Sidney*, London, 1991.

Duncan-Jones, Katherine and van Dorsten, Jan (eds.), *Miscellaneous prose of Sir Philip Sidney*, Oxford, 1973.

Dunlop, Ian, *Palaces and Progresses of Elizabeth I*, London, 1962.

Durant, David D., *Bess of Hardwick: Portrait of an Elizabethan Dynast* (revised ed.), London, 1999.

Durrant Cooper, William, 'Notices of Anthony Babington of Dethick, and of the Conspiracy of 1586', *The Reliquary*, April 1562.

Eagleston, Arthur J., *The Channel Islands under Tudor Government 1485–1642*, Cambridge, 1949.

Eccles, Mark, 'Brief Lives: Tudor and Stuart Authors', *Studies in Philology*, 79, No 4, 1982.

Edwards, Edward, *The Life of Sir Walter Ralegh* (2 vols), London, 1868.

Edwards S.J., Francis, *The Marvellous Chance: Thomas Howard, fourth Duke of Norfolk, and the Ridolphi Plot 1570–1572*, London, 1968.

Elizabeth I, *Collected Works* (ed.) Leah Marcuse, Janel Mueller, Mary Beth Rose), Chicago, 2000.

Evans, John, *The Works of Sir Roger Williams*, Oxford, 1972.

Ewen, Cecil, *The Golden Chalice: A Documented Narrative of an Elizabethan Pirate*, Paignton, 1939.

Feuillerat, Albert, *Documents Relating to the Office of the Revels in the Time of Queen Elizabeth*, Louvain, 1908.

Feuillerat, Albert, *The Complete Works of Sir Philip Sidney* (4 vols), Cambridge, 1912.

Foley, Henry (ed.), *Records of the English Province of the Society of Jesus* (7 vols), London, 1875–83.

Foster, Joseph (ed.), *Alumni Oxonienses: The Members of the University of Oxford 1500–1714*, Oxford, 1891.

Foxe, John, *Actes and Monuments* (8 vols), New York, 1985.

Fraser, Antonia, *Mary Queen of Scots*, London, 1969.

Fraser, Antonia, *The Six Wives of Henry VIII*, London, 1992.

Froude, J.A., *History of England from the Fall of Wolsey to the Death of Elizabeth*, London, 1863.

Frye, Susan, *Elizabeth I: The Competition for Representation*, Oxford, 1996.

Fuller, Thomas, *The History of the Worthies of England* (3 vols (ed.) P.A. Nuttall), New York, 1965.

Galloway, David (ed.), *Record of Early English Drama: Norwich 1540–1642*, Toronto, 1984.

Garvin, Kathrine (ed.), *The Great Tudors*, London, 1935.

Gascoigne, George, *A Hundreth Sundrie Flowres* (ed. G.W. Pigman III), Oxford, 2000.

Gascoigne, George, *Complete Works* (2 vols (ed.) J.W. Cunliffe), Cambridge, 1907–10.

Gater, Sir George and Wheeler, E.P. (eds.), *Survey of London:* vol. XVIII: *St Martin-in-the-Fields II: The Strand*, London, 1937.

Gilbert, Sir Humphrey, *Queene Elizabethes Achademy* (ed. F.J. Furnivall), London, 1869.

Glasgow, Tom, 'Elizabethan Ships Pictured on Smerwick Map, 1580', *Mariners Mirror*, 52, 1966.

Greenblatt, Stephen Jay, *Renaissance Self-Fashioning: from More to Shakespeare*, Chicago, 1980.

Greenblatt, Stephen Jay, *Sir Walter Ralegh: The Renaissance Man and his Roles*, New Haven, 1973.

Greer, David, '"Thou Court's Delight": Biographical Notes on Henry Noel', *Lute Society Journal* , XVII, 1975.

Greville, Fulke, *Life of Sir Philip Sidney*, Oxford, 1907.

Guy, John (ed.), *The Reign of Elizabeth I*, Cambridge, 1995.

Haigh, Christopher, *Elizabeth I*, London, 1998.

Haigh, Christopher (ed.), *The Reign of Elizabeth I*, London, 1988.

Hakluyt, Richard, *Discourse of Western Planting* (ed.) David B. Quinn and Alison M. Quinn), London, 1993.

Hakluyt, Richard, *The Principal Navigations Voyages Traffiques & Discoveries of the English Nation*, London, 1903–5.

Halliday, F.E., 'Queen Elizabeth I and Doctor Burcot: An Episode of 1562', *History Today*, August, 1955.

Halliwell, James Orchard, *Tarlton's Jests*, London, 1844.

Hamilton, A.C., *The Structure of Allegory in the Faerie Queene*, Oxford, 1961.

Hardwicke, Philip York, Second Earl of, *Miscellaneous State Papers from 1501 to 1726*, London, 1778.

Harington, Sir John, *A Tract on the Succession to the Crown* (ed. C.R. Markham), London, 1881.

Harington, Sir John, *Nugae Antiquae* (3 vols), London, 1804.

Hariot, Thomas, *A Briefe and True Report of the New Found Land in Virginia*, Amsterdam, 1971.

Harlow, V.T. (ed.), *The Discoverie of the Large and Bewtiful Empire of Guiana*, London, 1928.

Harlow, V.T. (ed.), *Colonising Expeditions to the West Indies and Guiana 1623–1667*, London, 1925.

Harrison, William, *Description of England*, London, 1968.

Harvey, Gabriel, *Letterbook of Gabriel Harvey 1573–1580* (ed. Edward J.L. Scott), London, 1884.

Harvey, Gabriel, *Marginalia* (ed. G.C. Moore Smith), Stratford upon Avon, 1913.

Harvey, Gabriel, *The Works* (3 vols) (ed. Alexander B. Grosart), London, 1884.

Hasler, P.W. (ed.), *The House of Commons* 1558–1603 (2 vols), London, 1981.

Haynes, Alan, *Elizabethan Secret Services*, Stroud, 2001.

Haynes, Samuel, *A Collection of State Papers Relating to Affairs . . . From the Year 1542 to 1570*, London, 1740.

Hayward, Sir John, *Annals of the First Four Years of the Reign of Queen Elizabeth* (ed. John Bruce), London, 1840.

Hayward, Sir John, *The Lives of the III Normans, Kings of England*, London, 1613.

Hicks, Leo, 'The Strange Case of Dr William Parry: The Career of an Agent Provocateur', *Studies: an Irish Quarterly Review of Letters, Philosophy, and Science*, 37, 1948.

Hicks, Leo, *An Elizabethan Problem: Some Aspects of the Careers of Two Exile Adventurers*, London, 1964.

Hill, Christopher, *Intellectual Origins of the English Revolution*, Oxford, 1965.

Holinshed, Raphael, *The Chronicles of England, Scotland and Ireland*, London, 1587.

Hooker, John, *The Life and Times of Sir Peter Carew* (ed. Maclean), London, 1857.

Hurault, André, *A Journal Of All That Was Accomplished by Monsieur de Maisse, Ambassador in England from King Henri IV to Queen Elizabeth Anno Domini 1597* (ed. and trans Harrison), London, 1931.

Hutton, Ronald, *The Rise and Fall of Merry England: the Ritual Year 1400–1700*, Oxford, 1996.

Innes, A.D., *Ten Tudor Statesmen*, London, 1906.

Izard, Thomas C., *George Whetstone: Mid-Elizabethan Gentleman of Letters*, New York, 1942.

Jeaffreson, J.C. (ed.), *Middlesex County Records: Volume 1: 1550–1603*, London, 1886.

Jenkins, Elizabeth, *Elizabeth and Leicester*, London, 1961.

Jenkins, Elizabeth, *Elizabeth the Great*, London, 1972.

Johnson, Paul, *Elizabeth: A Study in Power and Intellect*, London, 1974.

Jonson, Ben, *Works* (11 vols ed. Herford and Simpson), Oxford, 1925–52.

Kenny, R.W., *Elizabeth's Admiral: the Political Career of Charles Howard, Earl of Nottingham, 1536–1624*, London, 1970.

Klarwill, Victor von (ed.), *Queen Elizabeth and Some Foreigners*, London, 1928.

Labanoff, Alexandre (ed.), *Lettres, Instructions et Mémoires de Marie Stuart, Reine d'Écosse* (7 vols), London, 1844.

Laboureur, J. Le (ed.), *Mémoires de Michel de Castelnau* (3 vols), Brussels, 1731.

Lacey, Robert, *Sir Walter Ralegh*, London, 1973.

Lambarde, William, *Eirenarcha, of The Office of Justices of the Peace*, London, 1581.

Latham, Agnes, 'A Birth-date for Sir Walter Ralegh', *Etudes Anglaises*, 9, 1956.

Latham, Agnes (ed.), *The Poems of Sir Walter Ralegh*, London, 1962.

Latham and Youings (eds.), *The Letters of Sir Walter Ralegh*, Exeter, 1999.

Le Febure N., *A Discourse Upon Sir Walter Rawleighs Great Cordial*, London, 1664.

Leader, J.D., *Mary Queen of Scots in Captivity 1569–84*, Sheffield, 1880.

Lee, Sir Sidney, *Great Englishmen of the Sixteenth Century*, London, 1904.

Lefranc, Pierre, *Sir Walter Ralegh: Ecrivain*, Paris, 1968.

Lehmburg, Stanford E., *Sir Walter Mildmay and Tudor Government*, Austin, 1964.

Leimon, Mitchell and Parker, Geoffrey, 'Treason and plot in Elizabethan diplomacy: the "fame of Sir Edward Stafford" reconsidered', *English Historical Review*, CXI, 1996.

Lettenhove, Barkin Kervyn de, *Relations politiques des Pays-Bas et de l'Angleterre sous le règne de Philippe II* (11 vols), Brussels, 1882–1900.

Levin, Carole, *The Heart and Stomach of a King: Elizabeth I and the Politics of Sex and Power*, University of Pennsylvania Press, 1994.

Lewis, G.R., *The Stannaries*, Harvard, 1924.

Lloyd, David, *State Worthies* (3 vols), London, 1766.

Loades, D.M., *The Tudor Navy*, Aldershot, 1992.

Lodge, Edmund (ed.), *Illustrations of British History* (3 vols), London, 1791.

Loftie, W.J., *Inns of Court and Chancery*, London, 1893.

Loomie, Albert, *The Spanish Elizabethans: The English Exiles at the Court of Philip II*, London, 1963.

MacCaffrey, Wallace, *Elizabeth I: War and Politics, 1588–1603*, Princeton, 1992.

MacCaffrey, Wallace, *Queen Elizabeth and the Making of Policy, 1572–1588*, Princeton, 1981.

MacCaffrey, Wallace, *Shaping of the Elizabethan Regime*, Princeton, 1968.

Maclean, Sir John and Heane, W.C. (eds.), *The Visitation of the County of Gloucester Taken in the Year 1623*, London, 1885.

MacQueen, John Fraser, *A Lecture on the Early History and Academic Discipline of the Inns of Court and Chancery*, London, 1851.

McCarthy Morrogh, Michael, *The Munster Plantation*, Oxford, 1986.

McDermott, James, *Martin Frobisher*, London, 2001.

McKeen, David, *A Memory of Honour: the Life of William Brooke, Lord Cobham* (2 vols), Salzburg, 1986.

McManus, Caroline, *Spenser's Faerie Queene and the Reading of Women*, Newark, 2002.

Mancall, Peter C., *Hakluyt's Promise: An Elizabethan's Obsession for an English America*, London, 2007.

Markham, C.E. (ed.), *Voyages of Pedro Sarmiento de Gamboa*, London, 1895.

Marsden, R.G., 'Thomas Cobham and the Capture of the 'St. Katherine.', *English Historical Review*, XXIII, 1908.

Marsden, R.G., *Select Pleas in the Court of Admiralty. vol. II, The High Court of Admiralty* (AD 1547–1602), London, 1897.

Martin, C.T. (ed.), *Journal of Sir Francis Walsingham, from December 1570 to April 1583* (Camden Miscellany, vol. VI), London, 1870.

May, Steven W., *Sir Walter Ralegh*, Boston, 1989.

May, Steven W., *The Elizabethan Courtier Poets*, Missouri, 1991.

Mears, Natalie, *Queenship and Political Discourse in The Elizabethan Realms*, Cambridge, 2005.

Merton, Charlotte, 'The women who served Queen Mary and Queen Elizabeth: ladies, gentlewomen and maids of the privy chamber, 1553–1603', PhD diss., U. Cam., 1992.

Mills, Jerry L., 'Recent Studies in Ralegh', *English Literary Renaissance*, 15, 1985.

Montrose, Louis, *The Subject of Elizabeth*, London, 2006.

Morris, John (ed.), *Letterbooks of Sir Amias Poulet*, London, 1874.

Mumby, Frank A., *Girlhood of Queen Elizabeth*, London, 1909.

Mumby, Frank A., *The Fall of Mary Stuart*, London, 1921.

Munk, William, *The Roll of the Royal College of Physicians of London*, London, 1861.

Murdin, William (ed.), *A Collection of State Papers Relating to Affairs in the Reign of Elizabeth from 1571 to 1596*, London, 1759.

Naipaul, V.S., *A Way in the World*, London, 1994.

Nash, T.R., *Collections for a History of Worcestershire* (2 vols), London, 1781.

Nashe, Thomas, *The Works* (ed. R.B. McKerrow), London, 1904.

Naunton, Sir Robert, *Fragmenta Regalia, or Observations on the late Queen Elizabeth, Her Times and Favorites* (English Reprints, vol. 20, Edward Arber (ed.)), London, 1870.

Neale, J.A. *Elizabeth I*, London, 1967.

Nelson, Alan, *Monstrous Adversary*, Liverpool, 2003.

Nicholl, Charles, *The Creature in the Map*, London, 1995.

Nicholl, Charles, *The Reckoning*, London, 1992.

Nichols, J.G. (ed.), *The Legend of Sir Nicholas Throckmorton*, London, 1874.

Nichols, John, *The Progresses and Public Processions of Queen Elizabeth* (3 vols), London, 1823.

Nicolas, Harris, *Memoirs of Sir Christopher Hatton*, London, 1847.

Nolan, John S., *Sir John Norreys and the Elizabethan Military World*, Exeter, 1998.

O'Rahilly, Alfred, *Massacre at Smerwick*, Dublin, 1938.

Oakeshott, Walter, *Sir Walter Raleigh's Library*, London, 1968.

Oakeshott, Walter, *The Queen and the Poet*, London, 1960.

O'Connell, Michael, *Mirror and Veil: The Historical Dimension of Spenser's Faerie Queene*, Chapel Hill, 1977.

Ogburn, Dorothy, *This Star of England*, New York, 1952.

Ogle, Cornelius (ed.), *Copybook of Sir Amias Poulet's Letters*, London, 1856.

Oman, Charles, *A History of the Art of War in the XVI Century*, London, 1937.

Osborne, Francis, *A Miscellany of Sundry Essayes*, London, 1659.

Osborne, Francis, *Historical Memoires on the Reigns of Queen Elizabeth and King James*, London, 1658.

Park, Thomas (ed.), *Harleian Miscellany* (10 vols), London, 1804–18.

Parker G., *The Grand Strategy of Philip II*, London, 1998.

Parks, G.B., *Richard Hakluyt and the English voyages* (2nd ed.), New York, 1961.

Pearce, Robert, *A History of the Inns of Court and Chancery*, London, 1848.

Peck, Dwight C., 'Raleigh, Sidney, Oxford, and the Catholics, 1579', *Notes and Queries*, 223, 1978.

Peck, Dwight C., '"News from Heaven and Hell": A Defamatory Narrative of the Earl of Leicester', *English Literary Renaissance*, 8, 1978.

Peck, Dwight C. (ed.), *Leicester's Commonwealth*, Ohio, 1985.

Perrott, Sir James, *The History of That Most Eminent Statesman Sir John Perrott*, London, 1728.

Plowden, Alison, *The Elizabethan Secret Service*, London, 1991.

Pole, Sir William, *Collections Towards a Description of the County of Devon*, London, 1791.

Pollen, J.H., 'The Politics of the English Catholics during the Reign of Queen Elizabeth', *The Month*, March–August, 1902.

Pollen, J.H. and Butler E.C., 'Dr William Gifford in 1586', *The Month*, March–April, 1904.

Pollen, John H., *Sources for the History of Roman Catholics in England, Ireland and Scotland, from the Reformation Period to that of Emancipation, 1533 to 1795*, London, 1921.

Pollen, John H., *The English Catholics in the Reign of Queen Elizabeth*, London, 1920.

Pollen, John H. and MacMahon, William, *The Venerable Philip Howard, Earl of Arundel*, London, 1905.

Pollen, John H. (ed.), *Mary Stuart and the Babington Plot*, Edinburgh, 1922.

Pope-Hennessey, John, *Sir Walter Ralegh in Ireland*, London, 1883.

Prouty, Charles T., *George Gascoigne, Elizabethan Courtier, Soldier and Poet*, New York, 1942.

Pulman, Michael, *The Elizabethan Privy Council in the 1570s*, Berkeley, 1971.

Purchas, Samuel, *Hakluytus Posthumus: or, Purchas his Pilgrimes* (20 vols), Glasgow, 1905–7.

Quinn, David B. and Shirley, John W., 'A Contemporary List of Hariot References', *Renaissance Quarterly*, 22, 1969.

Quinn, David B., *England and the Discovery of America 1481–1620*, London, 1974.

Quinn, David B., *Ralegh and the British Empire* (revised ed.), New York, 1962.

Quinn, David B., *Sir Humphrey Gilbert and Newfoundland*, St John's, 1983.

Quinn, David B., *The Lost Colonies and their Probable Fate*, Raleigh, 1984.

Quinn, David B., *The Roanoke Voyages 1584–90* (2 vols), London, 1955.

Quinn, David B., *The Voyages and Colonising Enterprises of Sir Humphrey Gilbert* (2 vols), London, 1940.

Quinn, David B. and Cheshire, Neil M., *The New Found Land of Stephen Parmenius*, Toronto, 1972.

Ralegh, Sir Walter, *The Works of Sir Walter Ralegh* (8 vols) ed. William Oldys, London, 1829.

Rattansi, P.M., 'Alchemy and Natural Magic in Ralegh's History of the World', *Ambix*, XIII, 1966.

Read, Conyers, *Lord Burghley and Queen Elizabeth*, London, 1960.

Read, Conyers, *Mr Secretary Cecil and Queen Elizabeth*, London, 1955.

Read, Conyers, *Mr Secretary Walsingham and the Policy of Queen Elizabeth* (3 vols), Oxford, 1925.

Ridley, Jasper, *Elizabeth I*, London, 1987.

Rosenberg, Eleanor, *Leicester, Patron of Letters*, New York, 1955.

Rowse, A.L., *Ralegh and the Throckmortons*, London, 1962.

Rowse, A.L., *The Case Books of Simon Forman: Sex and Society in Shakespeare's Age*, London, 1976.

Rowse, A.L., *The England of Elizabeth*, London, 1950.

Rudick, Michael (ed.), *The Poems of Sir Walter Ralegh*, Tempe, 1999.

Rukeyser, Muriel, *The Traces of Thomas Hariot*, London, 1972.

Rye, William B., *England as Seen By Foreigners*, London, 1865.

Sanderson, Sir William, *An Answer to a Scurrilous Pamphlet—*, London, 1656.

Sargent, Ralph, *At the Court of Queen Elizabeth: The Life and Lyrics of Sir Edward Dyer*, London, 1935.

Sawyer, Edmund (ed.), *Memorials of Affairs of State in the Reigns of Q. Elizabeth and K. James I*, London, 1725.

Scott, Walter (ed.), *Secret History of the Court of James the First* (2 vols), Edinburgh, 1811.

Sharp, Sir Cuthbert (ed.), *Memorials of the Rebellion of 1569*, London, 1840.

Shirley, John W., 'Scientific Experiments of Sir Walter Ralegh', *Ambix*, IV, 1949–51.

Shirley, John W., *Sir Walter Ralegh and the New World*, Chapel Hill, 1985.

Shirley, John W., *Thomas Harriot: A Biography*, Oxford, 1983.

Shirley, John W. (ed.), *Thomas Harriot: Renaissance Scientist*, Oxford, 1974.

Skyrme, Sir Thomas, *History of the Justices of the Peace*, Chichester, 1991.

Sloan, Kim, *A New World: England's First View of America*, London, 2007.

Smith, Alan Gordon, *The Babington Plot*, London, 1936.

Spenser, Edmund, *A View of the Present State of Ireland* (ed. W.L. Renwick), Oxford, 1970.

Spenser, Edmund, *The Poetical Works of Edmund Spenser* (ed. J.C. Smith and E. de Selicourt), Oxford, 1912.

St John Brooks, Eric, *Sir Christopher Hatton*, London, 1946.

Stanford, Michael, 'The Raleghs take to the Sea', *Mariners Mirror*, 48, 1962.

Stebbing, William, *Sir Walter Ralegh: A Biography*, Oxford, 1891 (reissued 1899).

Steggle, Matthew, 'Charles Chester and Richard Hakluyt', *Studies in English Literature 1500–1900*, 43, 2003.

Stern, Virginia, *Sir Stephen Powle of Court and Country*, London, 1992.

Stimson, Dorothy, *Scientists and Amateurs*, New York, 1948.

Stow, John, *Annales or a General Chronicle of England*, London, 1631.

Stow, John, *Survey of London*, London, 1956.

Strachey, Lytton, *Elizabeth and Essex*, London, 1928.

Strathmann, Ernest A., 'Ralegh and the Catholic Polemists', *Huntingdon Library Quarterly*, 10, 1947.

Strathman, Ernest A., *Sir Walter Ralegh: A Study in Elizabethan Skepticism*, New York, 1951.

Strickland, Agnes, *Lives of the Queens of England* (8 vols), London, 1851–2.

Strong, Roy, *The Cult of Elizabeth*, London, 1977.

Strype, John, *The Life and Acts of John Whitgift* (3 vols), Oxford, 1822.

Strype, John, *The Life of the Learned Sir Thomas Smith*, London, 1698.

Stukeley, Sir Lewis, *The Humble Petition and Information of Sir Lewis Stukeley*, London, 1618.

Sturgess, H.A.C. (ed.), *Register of Admissions to the Honourable Society of the Middle Temple* (3 vols), London, 1949.

Symons, Thomas H.B. (ed.), *Meta Incognita: a Discourse of Discovery*, Quebec, 1999.

Taylor, E.G.R. (ed.), *The Original Writings and Correspondence of the Two Richard Hakluyts* (2 vols), London, 1935.

Taylor, E.G.R. (ed.), *The Troublesome Voyage of Captain Edward Fenton 1582–3*, Cambridge, 1957.

Teulet A. (ed.), *Correspondance diplomatique de Bertrand de Salignac de la Mothe Fénélon* (7 vols), Paris, 1838–40.

Thomas, William, *The Pilgrim: A Dialogue on the Life and Actions of King Henry VIII*, London, 1861.

Thompson, Edward, *Sir Walter Ralegh, the Last of the Elizabethans*, London, 1935.

Thompson, James W., *The Wars of Religion in France 1559–1576*, Chicago, 1909.

Thoreau, H.D., *Sir Walter Raleigh*, Boston, 1905.

Townshend, Heywood, *Historical Collections; or an Exact Account of the Proceedings of the Last Four Parliaments of Q. Elizabeth*, London, 1680.

Trevelyan, Raleigh, *Sir Walter Raleigh*, London, 2002.

Trevor-Roper, Hugh, *Historical Essays*, London, 1957.

Tytler, P.F., *Life of Sir Walter Raleigh*, Edinburgh, 1840.

Udall, John, *A New Discoverie of Old Pontificall Practices*, London, 1643.

Van Heuvel, J.A., *El Dorado*, New York, 1844.

Venn, J.A. (ed.), *Alumni Cantabrigienses: Part I, From the Earliest Times to 1751*, Cambridge, 1922.

Vivian, J.L. and Drake, H.H. (eds.), *The Visitation of the County of Cornwall in the Year 1620*, London, 1874.

Von Raumer, Friedrich Ludwig Georg, *Queen Elizabeth and Mary Queen of Scots*, London, 1836.

Von Wedel, Lupold, 'Journey Through England and Scotland', in *Transactions of the Royal Historical Society*, vol. IX, London, 1895.

Walker, Julie M. (ed.), *Dissing Elizabeth: Negative Representations of Gloriana*, Durham, 1998.

Wallace, Willard M., *Sir Walter Raleigh*, London, 1959.

Ward, Bernard M., *The Seventeenth Earl of Oxford, 1550–1604*, London, 1928.

Waters, David, *The Art of Navigation in Elizabethan and Early Stuart Times* (2nd ed), Greenwich, 1978.

Wernham, R.B., *After the Armada: Elizabethan England and the Struggle for Western Europe, 1588–1595*, Oxford, 1984.

Wernham, R.B., *The Return of the Armadas: The Last Years of the Elizabethan War Against Spain, 1595–1603*, Oxford, 1994.

West, William N., 'Gold on Credit: Martin Frobisher's and Walter Raleigh's Economies of Evidence', *Criticism*, 39, 1997.

Whetstone, George, *The Enemie to Unthryftinesse*, London, 1586.

Whitehead, A.W., *Gaspard de Coligny, Admiral of France*, London, 1904.

Williams, Neville, *A Tudor Tragedy: Thomas Howard, Fourth Duke of Norfolk*, London, 1964.

Williams, Norman Lloyd, *Sir Walter Ralegh*, London, 1962.

Williamson, James A., *Hawkins of Plymouth*, London, 1949.

Wilson, Sir Anthony, *The Court and Character of King James*, London, 1650.

Wilson, Charles, *Queen Elizabeth and the Revolt of the Netherlands*, London, 1970.

Wilson, Derek, *Sir Francis Walsingham: A Courtier in an Age of Terror*, London, 2007.

Wilson, Derek, *Sweet Robin: a Biography of Robert Dudley, Earl of Leicester 1533–1588*, London, 1981.

Winstanley, William, *England's Worthies*, London, 1684.

Winton, John, *Sir Walter Ralegh*, London, 1975.

Woolfson, Jonathan, *Padua and the Tudors*, Cambridge, 1998.

Woolley, Benjamin, *The Queen's Conjuror*, London, 2001.

Wotton, Sir Henry, *Reliquiae Wottonianae*, London, 1651.

Wright, H.G., *The Life and Works of Arthur Hall*, Manchester, 1919.

Wright, Thomas (ed.), *Queen Elizabeth and her Times* (2 vols), London, 1838.

Yates, Frances A., *Astraea: The Imperial Theme in the Sixteenth Century*, London, 1975.

Yates, Frances A., *The Occult Philosophy in the Elizabethan Age*, London, 1979.

Zurcher, Andrew, 'Getting It Back to Front in 1590: Spenser's Dedications, Nashe's Insinuations, and Ralegh's Equivocations', *Studies in the Literary Imagination*, 38, 2005.